CLASSROOMS THAT WORK

THEY CAN *ALL* READ AND WRITE

CLASSROOMS THAT WORK

THEY CAN *ALL* READ AND WRITE

Second Edition

Patricia M. Cunningham
Wake Forest University

Richard L. Allington
The University at Albany—SUNY

An imprint of Addison Wesley Longman, Inc.

New York • Reading, Massachusetts • Menlo Park, California • Harlow, England
Don Mills, Ontario • Sydney • Mexico City • Madrid • Amsterdam

Acquisitions Editor: Virginia L. Blanford
Development Manager: Arlene Bessenoff
Marketing Manager: Renee Ortbals
Project Coordination and Text Design: Electronic Publishing Services, Inc.
Cover Designer: Kay Petronio
Cover Design Manager: Nancy Danahy
Full Service Production Manager: Valerie Zaborski
Electronic Page Makeup: Electronic Publishing Services, Inc.
Printer and Binder: The Maple-Vail Book Manufacturing Group
Cover Printer: Phoenix Color Corp.

For permission to use copyrighted material, grateful acknowledgment is made to the copyright holders on pp. 106-114, which are hereby made part of this copyright page.

Library of Congress Cataloging-in-Publication Data

Cunningham, Patricia Marr.
        Classrooms that work: they can all read and write / Patricia M.
    Cunningham, Richard L. Allington.—2nd ed.
            p.   cm.
        Includes bibliographical references and index.
        ISBN 0-321-01339-5 (pbk.)
        1. Language arts (Elementary)—United States. 2. Reading
    (Elementary)—United States. I. Allington, Richard L.
    LB1576.C855 1998
    372.6'044—dc21   97-52381
                                                                        CIP

Please visit our website at http://longman.awl.com/education/

ISBN 0-321-01339-5

    4 5 6 7 8 9 10—MA—01 00 99

DEDICATION

This book is dedicated to all the teachers who work tirelessly and enthusiastically every day to provide good balanced literacy instruction for ALL the children they teach. In spite of constant criticism and little appreciation, they never give up or give in. These teachers are the strongest link in the educational chain.

Photos were taken by Rosalyn D. Morgan, who graduated from the WFU Elementary Education program in 1992 and is currently teaching first grade in the Atlanta area. Some of the art was drawn by Tracy Seiler, who graduated from Wake Forest in 1994 and is currently teaching second grade in Winston Salem, North Carolina.

Brief Contents

CONTENTS

CHAPTER 4

GUIDING CHILDREN'S WRITING/THINKING   85

CHAPTER 5

DEVELOPING DECODING AND SPELLING FLUENCY (COMMONLY CALLED "PHONICS"!)   121

CHAPTER 6

SCIENCE AND SOCIAL STUDIES MATTER TO STRUGGLING READERS   169

PREFACE

Much has changed in the four years since this book was first published. The pendulum that was still over on the "literature-based, process writing" side has swung all the way over to the "phonics" side without even a pause in the middle. Legislatures and school boards all over the nation are mandating the type and amount of phonics that must be taught—to children they have never seen in classrooms they have never entered. It is frightening (and disheartening) to those of us who lived through the last pendulum swing to see it happen yet again—and even more violently. We want to—and indeed do sometimes—stand up and say, "We have done this before!"

We have watched whole schools teach phonics as the first and only approach allowed and seen some children become very good readers and other children not learn to read at all. We have used materials in which almost all the words were decodable and watched some children turn into "word callers"—wonderful oral readers with little or no comprehension. We have watched children spend their reading time doing phonics worksheets and not ever realizing that reading is about books.

In the late sixties, the Beatles sang, "All you need is love." Today we are bombarded with an "All you need is phonics" message. You do need love—but love is not all you need. Life is just not that simple. Children do need phonics, but phonics is not all they need. Teaching children to read is just not all that simple.

If there is one thing we are sure of it is that there is no simple solution—no quick fix. Children come with their own personalities. Children do not all learn in the same way. Until they start cloning children as they have recently cloned Dolly the sheep, successful teachers of reading will have to provide children with a variety of literacy experiences. The pendulum swings because people keep looking for the one best way to teach children to read and refuse to accept the fact that any parent of two children knows, "You can't do things exactly the same way and get the same results when the two children have very different personalities." The question of the best way to teach reading is the wrong question and you can't ever arrive at the right answer when you keep asking the wrong question!

In this second edition of *Classrooms That Work,* we have tried again to pull together the best of what we currently know works for classroom teachers. We directed the book to classroom teachers because, while we believe special teachers play a role in the literacy development of the children that they teach, classroom teachers have the most number of hours with and the greatest responsibility for all their children. We wanted this book to be a positive resource containing practical ideas, activities, and organizational strategies that would result in teachers saying, "I can do that—I see how that would help and fit in with what I currently do." This book should also be helpful to teacher educators, especially those teaching courses in reading diagnosis and remediation and reading methods.

In spite of our intent to devote almost the whole book to "what works," we also decided to summarize in Chapter One some of the failed solutions of the past. Experienced teachers lived through many of these "cure-alls," but they may need to be reminded of the ones that haven't worked. Beginning teachers need to understand the history of our efforts to promote literacy so they can avoid the disappointment of some of the simple solutions of the past.

Chapters Two through Six discuss the components of a balanced reading program. Chapter Two, "Reading and Writing Real 'Things'" describes what we consider to be the most critical component of high-quality classroom instruction. Children who are going to become literate must be in classrooms in which authentic reading and writing are central activities that pervade the school day and the curriculum. They must experience on a daily basis models, materials, and time for real reading and writing.

Based on this foundation of real reading and writing, Chapters Three and Four describe the most successful strategies we know for supporting and guiding children's reading and writing. All strategies described in these chapters have at their core the development of thinking processes. Children are engaged in meaning-seeking communication activities and guided through a variety of activities that increase their competence and develop a metacognitive awareness of what they are trying to achieve as they read and write independently.

Because word knowledge is essential for fluent reading and writing, Chapter Five describes a variety of activities that teachers can use to increase children's decoding and spelling fluency. The phonics activities in this chapter are all based on what we know about how readers actually go about figuring out how to pronounce and spell words. The activities help children look for patterns in words, use as little jargon as possible and emphasize transfer to reading and writing. Chapter Six focuses on the development of knowledge, vocabulary, reading, and writing as children learn science and social studies. Chapter Seven, new to this edition, describes some "above and beyond" strategies that have proved successful for children for whom learning to read is unusually difficult.

Chapters Eight, Nine, and Ten describe how these critical components might be balanced and integrated across a day or a week in a kindergarten, primary, and intermediate classroom. In these three chapters, we provide one model of how these components might fit together into a coherent whole. There are other approaches to achieving coherence and balance, but we have faith that with a good understanding of the individual pieces and one possible model for their integration, classroom teachers will create their own unique and "almost perfect" mix. The classrooms in which many children beat the odds have these components in common but they all operate differently and reflect the different needs and personalities of their children and teachers.

Chapter Eleven moves beyond the classroom and tackles the larger school and social issues that impinge on literacy for all. (For more information about school-wide literacy issues, see *Schools That Work*, Allington and Cunningham, 1996.) Many of the issues raised here—such as class size and community involvement—are beyond the control of the classroom teacher. In all the other chapters, we limited ourselves to what one concerned, committed, and caring teacher could do after shutting the classroom door. We share the frustration of most teachers with not being able to "fix it all." We believe that this frustration can be minimized if you learn to "change the things you can, ignore the ones you can't, and figure out how to tell the difference." Nevertheless, there are some beyond-the-classroom issues that need attention. So, we include "Things Worth Fighting For" to help inform teachers about beyond-the-classroom involvements that we know make a difference. Perhaps, if each teacher took on one of these goals, advocated and fought for it, we would amaze ourselves with our power!

We greatly appreciate the suggestions of those school administrators, teachers, and university colleagues who reviewed the first edition and commented on chapters of the manuscript:

John G. Barnitz, University of New Orleans
Nancy S. Beasley, Athens State College
Marcie Brown, Adrian (MI) Public Schools
Charles H. Clark, Western Illinois University
Susan I. McMahon, University of Wisconsin-Madison
Marguerite Cogorno Radencich, University of South Florida
Rosemary Radzievich, Bloomsburg University
Lynn Romeo, Monmouth University
Helen Stuetzel, Ballston Spa (NY) Central School District
Kathryn F. Whitmore, The University of Iowa

We were overwhelmed by the enthusiastic response of teachers to the first edition of this book. We have tried hard to preserve the best of that first edition and to add to it what we have learned since writing it. We hope that this book will provide encouragement and support for teachers as they work hard to provide all their children with a good, sensible, balanced literacy diet.

Patricia M. Cunningham

Richard L. Allington

CLASSROOMS THAT WORK

THEY CAN *ALL* READ AND WRITE

1
THE PROBLEM AND SOME FAILED SOLUTIONS

The past few decades have not been good decades for children in the United States. The number of children living in poverty rose from 16 percent in the late 1970s to 25 percent—one out of every four of the children in our schools today! The majority of these poor children are white but a greater proportion of minority children in this country live in poverty. Forecasters suggest that even larger numbers will be living in poverty as we move through the turn of the century. In spite of recent legislation, we can also expect that 40 percent of all children will live on Aid to Dependent Children (ADC) for at least one year before reaching the age of eighteen.

Poverty is not the only factor that determines if a child is at risk for reading difficulties, but it is the most pervasive one. With childhood poverty on the rise, we can project that more of the children who arrive in our classrooms will be at risk for academic failure. Predictably, children who are not academically successful are not motivated to continue with school. Ultimately, they make up the vast majority of our high school dropouts. Unlike the circumstances in previous decades, there are fewer farm and factory jobs to provide a living wage for these high school dropouts. Thus, the cycle of poverty/academic failure, poverty/academic failure continues. With the academic standards for high school graduation rising, the outlook is bleak for too many children unless we create classrooms in which all children learn to read and write alongside their peers.

This cycle must be broken, and schools are the most obvious place to initiate this break. While socioeconomic status is highly correlated with academic success, there is not a pure cause-effect relationship. Every teacher knows children who succeed in spite of their lack of background knowledge or home support. Some children come to school at high risk for failure and manage to succeed. Some schools and teachers have an astonishingly high number of these "unexpected" successes. We recognize that children's home backgrounds can influence failure or success, but we believe that what happens in classrooms minute by minute actually determines how much will be learned. Classroom teachers are the most important factor in the success or failure of at-risk children in our schools. They are responsible for the minute-by-minute instruction; the decisions teachers make and the kind of instruction and support they provide make the difference between success and failure. Even in schools with strong instructional support programs and specialist teachers, children spend most of their instructional time with their classroom teacher. For many children, classroom teachers are their last and best hope for school and life success.

Effects of High and Low Home and School Support

Catherine Snow provides dramatic evidence of the importance of classroom teachers in developing literacy. In her book, *Unfulfilled Expectations* (Harvard University Press, 1991), she reports on a naturalistic study of schools serving children from low-income families. The research team visited the homes of children and rated the family support available for literacy learning as high, moderate, or low. They also visited the classrooms these children attended and rated the classroom literacy instruction as providing high, moderate, or low support. They then examined the effects of different classroom and home environments on children's learning. The table below summarizes the impact of two or more years of consistently high-support classroom instruction, a mixed pattern of support (high support classroom one year, low support classroom the next), and low-support.

Percentage of Children Who Achieve Success with Varying Levels of Home and Classroom Support

	High Home Support	Low Home Support
High Classroom Support	100%	100%
Mixed Classroom Support	100%	25%
Low Classroom Support	60%	0%

The findings illustrate the enormous impact that consistently high-quality classroom instruction can provide. Anything less than consistently high-quality classroom instruction had a dramatically negative impact on the achievement of children from homes in which parents did not provide high levels of home literacy support.

For a combined total of more than 50 years, we, as classroom teachers, remedial reading teachers, college professors, and teacher consultants, have observed, researched, talked about, and worried about children for whom learning to read is a struggle. Over the years we have seen schools and classrooms in which, year after year, children at high risk for failure "beat the odds." They learn to read and write and become successful, contributing adults. At first, we thought that there must be some strange, mysterious, even "mystical" variable that allowed certain teachers to succeed while other hardworking, caring teachers failed. In time, however, it has become clear to us (and research supports these observations) that teachers who achieve success with large numbers of high-risk children share certain traits. There are many commonalities in their day-by-day and minute-by-minute classroom instruction. This book is an attempt to describe and generalize about what happens in classrooms where many children beat the odds. In writing this book we draw from many sources, including our own research and our own experiences. Our most important resources, however, are successful teachers of at-risk children. We have spent many years watching, collecting data, interviewing teachers, and asking ourselves, "What are the critical elements in this teacher's classroom that we also see in other classrooms where many high-risk children succeed at becoming literate?" This book is an attempt to synthesize what real teachers do in real classrooms with real children that results in beating the odds. We offer a framework for providing the sort of exemplary literacy instruction offered by those teachers. We hope this book speeds up the discovery process for the thousands of teachers who are working hard to do their very best for the children they teach.

This book is a positive book. The vast majority of its pages are devoted to describing "what works" and how to *do* what works. There have been, however, some "solutions" that worked much better in theory than they did in practice. Believing that "those who do not learn from history are condemned to repeat it," we begin this book with a short description of solutions that became part of the problem.

WHY PHONICS IS NOT THE SOLUTION . . . BUT NEITHER IS JUST READING

At several points in American educational history, code-emphasis instruction (the phonics approach) has been touted as "the answer" to teaching all children to read. Both of us began our teaching in the 1960s, the last time phonics was offered as the answer. It wasn't the answer then and it isn't today. But once again there are claims being made for the effectiveness of phonics approaches and once again some folks are overstating and exaggerating evidence to support code-oriented materials and methods. There is a convergence of research evidence pointing to the critical role that good decoding skills play in good reading. However, there is no convergence in the research evidence indicating what types of phonics instruction, of what intensity, over what duration will produce the largest numbers of children who read well and willingly (see Cunningham, 1995 for a detailed summary).

But this lack of evidence doesn't seem to matter to many proponents of a pro-phonics agenda. Product advertisements, legislative testimonies, and various other materials have recently contained a set of strikingly similar assertions about phonics teaching and learning—assertions that are simply distortions of the research available even though often couched in terms such as "scientifically rigorous research." Here are some assertions that have appeared repeatedly and that we consider "unscientific"—assertions that cannot be drawn from the available scientific evidence.

Unscientific Assertion #1. No One Teaches Phonics

Two recent large-scale federally funded studies (Baumann, J.F., Hoffman, J.V., Moon, J. & Duffy, A., 1997 and Hoffman, J.V., McCarthy, S.J., Elliott, B., Bayles, D., Price, D., Ferree, A. & Abbott, J., 1998) provide overwhelming evidence that virtually all primary grade teachers teach phonics, usually daily. Smaller, more intensive studies of exemplary teachers point to the same conclusion but also point to an interesting phenomenon—these exemplary teachers rarely report using a commercial phonics curriculum material. Instead, they teach phonics knowledge and strategies to children rather than teaching the pages in a phonics workbook (Pressley, M., Rankin, J., & Yokoi, L., 1996 and Pressley, M., Wharton-McDonald, R., Ranking, J., Mistretta, J., Yokoi, L. & Ettenberger, S., 1996).

Unscientific Assertion #2. There Is a Phonemic Awareness Crisis

Recently, a new wrinkle has been added to the phonics campaign—a crisis in phonemic awareness. Oversimplifying a bit, phonemic awareness is the ability to isolate individual sounds (phonemes) in spoken words. For instance, being able to count three sounds in "cat." The evidence indicates that phonics instruction offers little benefit for children who have not developed phonemic awareness. There is compelling evidence to support the conclusion that phonemic awareness is an important understanding in learning to read an alphabetic language like English. But the evidence also indicates that most (80–85 percent) children acquire phonemic awareness by the middle of first grade. The research also indicates that 2 of those 3 or 4 children in each classroom who don't develop phonemic awareness initially can develop it within a few weeks, if offered some targeted tutorial or small group intervention. (Braunger, J. & Lewis, J.P., 1997). The remaining children may require a more intensive intervention.

We have learned much about the importance of children developing phonemic awareness, but the research still offers no clear basis for advocating particular instructional materials or methods. Phonemic awareness is important and it can and should be developed, but it is not "the root of all reading problems" nor will the implementation of elaborate time-consuming commercially produced phonemic awareness programs solve all our reading problems!

Unscientific Assertion #3. Explicit, Systematic Phonics Is the Only Way to Go

There is suddenly much ado about the need to ensure that "explicit, systematic" phonics instruction is offered. Often "incidental, opportunistic" phonics instruction is contrasted negatively against the "scientific" assertions for "explicit, systematic" phonics. The problem is that the available studies of exemplary teachers portray powerful phonics instruction that is "direct and opportunistic" (and it seems systematic also). It seems obvious that well-planned instruction based on student needs would be more effective than a series of random instructional activities. But exactly what sort of "explicit, systematic," or "explicit, opportunistic" phonics instruction does the research endorse?

Simply said, there is no convergence of research on just what sort of phonics instruction should be offered. Often publishers of commercial materials seem to be suggesting that their material has been developed from some set of "scientific" principles, which suggests that there is research evidence found on just what order letters and sounds should be taught and whether the instruction should focus on synthetic or analytic approaches and so on. But there simply is no convergence of research on such points. There is no "scientifically" determined sequence of instruction and no conclusive evidence on what sorts of phonics lessons, or of what duration would most effectively develop the optimum level of decoding efficiency in children.

Unscientific Assertion #4. Decodable Texts Are Essential

Finally, the most recently touted unscientific assertion has to do with the role of, or need for, "decodable texts." Such texts are described as offering children "only words that they have been taught the phonics skills to sound out." The decodable texts displayed at the recent meeting of the International Reading Association reminded us of the 1960s "Nan can fan Dan" and "Nat the Rat" readers. The key point is that there isn't a single study that supports the exclusive use of decodable texts in beginning reading!

In fact, there is evidence that restricting beginning reading materials to any single text type will likely produce a limited set of reading strategies—though the strategies developed seem to vary by the type of text restrictions in place. There is research support for providing children with "manageable" texts—texts that they can read without too much difficulty. There is also evidence that some of the recently published reading series provide reading material that is quite difficult. But none of this suggests that a return to "Nat the Rat" is the solution.

An Unscientific Assertion from the Last Era—Children Will Acquire Decoding Skills from Just Reading

This is the unscientific assertion most responsible for the current phonics frenzy! Both the research and our experience indicate that children need to be taught effective decoding skills and strategies. Most children don't become skillful at pronouncing unknown words just by reading. Phonics instruction is an essential part of a reading program—but it is not the reading program!

WHY RETENTION IS NOT THE SOLUTION . . . BUT NEITHER IS SOCIAL PROMOTION

Retention is the oldest unsuccessful solution for the unsuccessful reader. Retention as we know it today arrived with the advent of graded schools in the late 1800s and early 1900s. Teachers in one-room schoolhouses kept children in certain levels until they could literally "move" to the next level. Many children didn't move very quickly, and we can all visualize those little red schoolhouses with one older boy sprawled out amongst the little ones. Eventually, this unfortunate "laggard" got big enough to do a man's job and left school for the farm or factory.

As schools became larger and grades were divided into different rooms and classes, educators became concerned that keeping children in the same grade for many years was neither good for the ones being kept nor for the normal-aged children who were often "bullied" by the bigger children. Retention was a hot topic in the thirties and forties. The research pointedly noted the lack of positive effects—either educational, social, or emotional—on retained children. The fifties saw the beginnings of "social promotion," in which educators talked about "teaching the whole child" and respecting "individual differences;" children moved from grade to grade along with their peers regardless of what they had learned.

Accountability became the watchword in the eighties and nineties. With the press for public accountability, retention once again became a common solution to the problem of failing to learn to read along with peers. States passed laws mandating minimum standards and, in some cases, tests were developed to determine who could move to the next grade. In some schools we saw, once again, 9-year-olds in the first grade!

The rise of high-stakes assessment, testing in which the results are publicized and schools are ranked, seems to have fostered an increase in both retention practice, and special education placements, as well as calls from school officials and politicians to promote only children who are doing grade level work. In a recent study (Allington & McGill-Franzen, 1992), it was found that many more primary grade children were being retained and/or placed in special education now than fifteen years ago—before high-stakes testing was popular.

We see from this brief history that retention has been an often-tried solution. It continues to be tried because the public, along with many teachers, feels that it should work long-term because, in fact, it seems to work initially. In other words, retained children seem to do better during the year they are repeating the grade and sometimes in the year following. However, in most cases, retained children's achievement gradually slides backward so that, two or three years following the retention, they are once again among the lowest achieving students. Ultimately, retained children become older underachievers. The combination of overage and low achievement are powerful predictors of dropping out of school. If two children are exactly alike and one is retained while the other is sent on, the retained child is four times more likely than the sent-on child to drop out of high school.

Placement in a transitional-grade classroom (e.g., pre-first class) has the same negative effects as simple retention. The original concept of transitional classes was that, through intensified instruction, low-achieving children could be "caught up" to their peers during the transitional-grade year. The notion was that, with smaller classes and more intensive teaching, learning would be accelerated and children would move from a transitional-first-grade into second grade. In practice, however, this intensive instruction did not occur. Without intensive instruction, learning acceleration did not occur. Instead, transitional-grade classes became much like repeating a grade with a different teacher.

Even if retention and transitional-grade classes were effective (which they are not), they would be expensive options for attempting to meet the needs of low-achieving children. The extra year of schooling adds the full cost of that year to the educational expenses. Currently, this cost ranges from $3,500 to $7,500, depending on the district and the state in which the child attends school. Most remedial programs and summer school programs cost less than $1,000 per child and a semester of one-on-one daily tutorial instruction costs from $1,500 to $2,000. Each of these options is not only less expensive, but also more likely to serve the children well.

Everyone knows someone—a cousin, nephew, neighbor, etc.—who was retained and seemed to do just fine. But even in these cases we do not know if the child would have been similarly successful if promoted. Because retention is less damaging for some children and because everyone knows someone for whom it seemed to be relatively less damaging, retention is often seen as the solution for *all* children having difficulties learning to read. Unfortunately, research and experience demonstrate that most retained children do not catch up and stay caught up. For these children, retention has only confirmed to themselves (and to everyone else) that they are "dumb" and can't succeed in school. Once they begin to believe this, it all too often becomes a self-fulfilling prophecy.

Decades of research on retention were summarized in an *Educational Leadership* article, "Synthesis of Research on Grade Retention" (Shepard and Smith, 1990). The authors point out that retained children perform more poorly when they go to the next grade than they would if they had been promoted without repeating a grade; that children view retention as punishment for being bad or failing to learn; that children who are retained have lower levels of self-esteem than those promoted; and that almost any alternative—including remedial help, summer school, and peer tutoring—is more effective than retention.

But social promotion, while providing more benefits to children having difficulty, offers little real support and socially promoted children often continue to have difficulties. The research indicates that social promotion, coupled with effective instructional interventions that increase opportunities to learn, can help children overcome the difficulties they are experiencing. Social promotion without an effective instructional intervention is not a solution to school learning difficulties.

In making decisions about retention, we must ask ourselves, "Will retention benefit the child more than the school?" We think the evidence is so consistent and powerful that we do not believe retention can be justified as positive for children. The evidence that has been gathered in study after study suggests that the best policy is one that keeps children with their peers. This sensible policy would eliminate retention and transitional-grade classes. Retention is not an appropriate solution for struggling readers, but social promotion policies must also be accompanied by well-designed instructional interventions that effectively address the difficulties some children experience.

WHY TRACKING IS NOT THE SOLUTION . . . BUT NEITHER IS WHOLE-CLASS INSTRUCTION

Tracking is the second oldest solution to the problem of children who do not achieve or move along as fast as average children. Tracking occurs in elementary school when children of similar achievement levels (in reading, most commonly) are assigned to the same teacher for all or part of the day. For instance, all of the lowest achieving readers would be assigned to a single teacher for their instruction and, likewise, so would all of the highest achieving readers. Tracking began in the forties and was prevalent in most elementary schools throughout the sixties. Its popularity waned during the seventies and eighties, but it is currently on the rise in some school systems.

Tracking, like most of the potential solutions, is based on flawed logic. The argument is made that not all children will learn at the same rate and that if the slow learners (or the fast learners) are put together with the same teacher, that teacher can teach them on their level and provide the skills they need in order to progress to higher levels. Furthermore, tracking proponents suggest that the teacher can devote all of his or her time to planning for and directly teaching one group of children without having to provide activities to keep another group busy. The tracked children will spend less time in seatwork activities (which don't contribute much to achievement) and more time in direct instruction on the skills and at the level needed. Finally, tracking proponents argue that by dividing the slow, the average, and the fast children, the average ones will not have to be held back while the slow ones are taught and the fast ones have a chance to excel.

Presented in this logical way, tracking seems like a reasonable solution. In practice, however, children placed in the bottom track achieve less than similar children placed in untracked classes (Gamoran, 1986). Let's consider why tracking is a much better solution in theory than it has turned out to be in practice. To do this we will imagine a school with three fourth-grade teachers and a diverse population of children.

We will place this school in the sixties—a decade in which most schools would have had low, middle, and high fourth-grade classrooms. The children would be assigned to each of these tracks before school started based on test scores, grades, and recommendations from their previous teachers. In some schools, the teachers took turns being the "high," "average," or "low" teacher each year. More commonly, however, the teacher with the most seniority or the teacher who the principal considered to be the best teacher was assigned the high group, the next teacher got the average group, and the last teacher hired (or the worst teacher) got the low group. (This teacher often did not return the following year and sometimes did not even make it through that year. In this case, the low group may have had several new teachers or many days of substitute teachers.) Immediately, we can see that one of the inherent problems with tracking is that the children who needed the best, most experienced teacher often got the worst or the least experienced one!

Once assigned to a track, the children usually remained with the same teacher for instruction in all subjects. For children who were either bright in every subject or slow in every subject, this arrangement worked out better than for those who had a variety of strengths and weaknesses. A poor reader who was an average math student was taught both reading and math at the slower pace. By the end of the year, she had been taught less math than the students assigned to the average track and, thus, was no longer an average student in math. Tracking children for all instruction assumes that children are equally slow or bright, which simply is not true.

Finally, we must think about how children were assigned to the three tracks and realize that some children do not take tests well, some do not work hard enough to get the grades that they could earn, and some have disruptive behaviors that make teachers think they are not capable learners. Not all children put in the low track are destined to be low achievers. Once placed here, however, they usually *become* low achievers. This is further compounded by the issue of numbers. Imagine that there are 81 fourth graders to be assigned to our imaginary three tracks. Each teacher should have 27 children. There are not, however, 27 truly bright or 27 truly slow children, and are many more than 27 truly average children. If we could assess the aptitudes of these children in an accurate and objective way and then place them correctly, we would probably put 8 to 10 children in the top and bottom tracks and 64 in the middle track. The nature of "average" means the place where most people are. The further up or down the scale you go, the fewer people you will find. (Picture the bell curve from your Ed Psych course.)

The research on tracking suggests that it makes no difference for average children, that there are a few advantages and disadvantages for those placed in the top track, and that it is harmful to children placed in the bottom track. When you imagine that the bottom-track children (one-third who are truly low achievers and two-thirds who are closer to average) are being instructed in all subjects at below-grade level by less experienced or less capable teachers, you can understand why this solution is, in reality, part of the problem.

Tracking can take other forms as well. Today, it is far less common to have children assigned to one track for all subjects. If we transport our sixties teachers into the present, we are apt to find them switching classes for math and reading. The most common arrangement is for teachers to have a heterogeneous homeroom group to whom they teach science, social studies, physical education, etc., and then track the children for math and/or reading. In order to solve the problem of the hardest-to-teach children having the least-effective or least-experienced teacher, our three fourth-grade teachers might arrange for the one who had the high reading class to have the low math class.

This switching solves some of the problems of all-day tracking. Low children would not be apt to have the least experienced teacher for everything. While many of the low math children would also be in the low reading group, it is still possible for a low math child to be in the average or even the high reading track with this arrangement. The problems, however, of how to accurately and objectively assign children, the disproportionate number of children who really would belong in each track, and the self-fulfilling prophecy, still remain. Unfortunately, some new problems are also created.

Time is lost when children have to pack up and change classes. It takes them a minimum of ten minutes to pack up to leave one class, get to the next class, unpack, and get ready to start again. If children switch for homeroom subjects, math, and reading, 30 minutes each day is spent in transit. This is 10 percent of the instructional time available in most elementary school days.

Children must adjust to as many as three different teachers while teachers could conceivably teach each of the 81 children every day. It is hard for teachers to maintain a level of commitment and concern for the education of each child if they have 81 children to worry about! It is harder still for teachers to know 81 children well—to know their strengths, weaknesses, and individualities. It is also hard to schedule so many children into so many different sections according to achievement, and to maintain any sort of balanced class size; again, we get classes that are not nearly as homogeneous as first assumed.

Finally, since children have different teachers and are grouped with different children for the skill subjects of reading and math, and the content subjects of science and social studies, their day and their curriculum are fragmented. Test data show that children are much better with isolated skills than with problem solving involving these skills. Children can multiply two-digit numbers when they are given a set-up problem, but don't know how to use this knowledge to solve a real-world problem. Children can find main ideas in their reading books, but fail to use this strategy when reading in social studies or writing during language arts. When children and teachers switch classes, opportunities for integration of instruction across curriculum areas (which occur naturally in elementary classrooms) are lost.

While tracking is not the solution, simply putting a diverse bunch of students in a single classroom and offering whole-class instruction in the grade-level book is hardly the answer. As schools recognized the problems inherent in tracking (and as they recognized that tracking was not solving the problems of lower-achieving students), many shifted to heterogeneous classroom groups and to whole-class lessons with all students using the same book, regardless of the appropriateness of that single book for all students. However, as schools have gained experience with whole-class instruction, it has also become obvious that this, in itself, is not a solution for children experiencing difficulty. Thankfully, many schools are now re-examining whole-class instruction, but some see returning to tracked classes as the solution. It is not.

Between tracked classes and whole-class lessons with a heterogeneous group of children, there is an array of options that need to become part and parcel of school organization. In the remaining chapters of this book, we will describe a variety of arrangements—flexible groupings, cooperative groups, working partners, individual conferences and many others that allow classroom teachers, with a heterogeneous class of children, to move all children forward in literacy and learning. The instruction we will describe is not tracked or carried out in fixed ability groups—but it is not whole-class instruction, either. Read on for lots of practical ways to implement "multilevel" instruction in your classroom.

WHY NO SINGLE INTERVENTION WILL WORK FOR ALL

In the past 30 years, there has been a proliferation of special programs created in an attempt to address the needs of children who find learning difficult. These are the remedial reading and math classes, the resource room classes for the learning disabled, and the migrant and bilingual programs that operate in many schools. A common feature of each of these programs is that they were almost always "pull-out" programs—the children to be served were literally pulled out of their regular classrooms and taken down the hall for special instruction. Unfortunately, there was little evidence that such efforts typically provided substantial benefits to the children served (Johnston & Allington, 1991).

Simply put, too many children who participated in these programs did not show any substantial improvement in their reading. Far too many were "lifers"—children who continued to qualify year after year because of continued low achievement. When the most common practices in these programs were examined, however, it became clear that such an outcome was exactly what one might have reasonably expected. There were several key features of these programs that resulted in a lack of any substantial positive effects.

First, the very presence of such programs undermined the responsibility of the regular education program—to educate all children (McGill-Franzen, 1994). Another way of considering these programs is to note that each child who participated represented the failure of the classroom reading program. As these special programs were added, classroom teachers were led to believe that these children were not their responsibility and, often, that they were insuffi- ~~responsibity~~ ciently expert to teach them. In some schools we have studied, as many as three out of four classroom teachers told us that the reading and language arts instruction for remedial and mainstreamed learning-disabled children was not their responsibility! Even though the children spent between 75 and 90 percent of their day in the regular classroom, the classroom teachers assigned responsibility for literacy learning to the reading teacher or special education teacher.

Even when classroom teachers accepted professional responsibility for the literacy learning of these children, the programs typically scheduled the children to go down the hall during some part of their classroom reading period. Thus, the classroom teacher had less time to teach the children with the difficulties than the ones without them—even though one would think that the former group would benefit from more instruction. In addition, because transitions from the classroom to the reading or resource room (or hallway) take time, children who participated had less time available to learn to read.

The children who went down the hall were more likely to experience curriculum fragmentation than those who remained in the classroom. Again, one might suppose that the ones who left would benefit from the richest, most organized, and most consistent curriculum plan. However, they were the ones who hopped from lesson to lesson all day long. These were the children who found it difficult to keep up with their classwork, but who were given even more dissimilar materials than anyone in the school. These were also the children who were most likely to spend time with the least-trained school personnel—teacher aides. The heavy use of minimally trained paraprofessionals was one reason that children in these special programs had the lowest quality of instruction.

So, when we examined the special programs, we found that they were often not very special (Allington, 1994). If we design special programs that lead classroom teachers to believe that children who participate are not their responsibility, programs that reduce the amount of time available for literacy learning, and programs in which at-risk children are the children most likely to work with minimally-trained paraprofessionals, then we should not be surprised when few children have their reading difficulties resolved through participation in these programs.

Happily, federal program regulations have changed and the exclusive use of the pull-out model is now discouraged (and in some cases banned). Federal Title 1 remedial programs *now require* the classroom teacher and the reading teacher to teach collaboratively planned lessons for low-achieving children. The use of in-class collaborative instruction is emphasized as well as programs that are flexibly designed to better meet the instructional needs of children. Federal special education regulations emphasize the inclusion of children with disabilities in the regular classroom instructional setting (as opposed to a pull-out resource room or self-contained classroom setting). Again, collaborative planning of the goals for the individualized education plan and for daily lessons is recommended as is in-class instructional services.

The federal regulations for both remedial and special education programs now emphasize providing more intensive support on the classroom curriculum and providing classroom teachers with assistance in differentiating instruction effectively.

WHY NO SINGLE APPROACH WILL EVER TEACH ALL CHILDREN

The question of how best to teach children to read and write is one that has been argued, debated, and researched for decades. It is a question to which there is still no definitive answer. Reading instruction began in this country with an alphabetic approach. Children learned the letters and learned to spell and sound out the letters of words. This alphabetic method—which later was called a phonics approach—has gone in and out of fashion but has always had advocates who insist that it is the only sensible approach to beginning reading instruction. There is a variety of instructional materials that rely almost exclusively on phonics instruction to teach reading—including such programs as *Direct Instruction, Reading Mastery, Spaulding,* and *Sing, Spell, Read & Write.*

The most commonly used approach to reading in this country has been the basal reader approach. While there are some basals that use a primarily phonics instruction to teach reading, most begin instruction with a few sight words and some phonics skills that help children recognize unfamiliar words. While basals differ in their emphasis, they have in common the gradually increasing levels of difficulty and the emphasis on teacher-guided reading of short selections.

Throughout the years, many reading experts have advocated a literature or tradebook approach to reading. In the 1960s, Jeanette Veatch (1959) popularized what she called an *individualized reading* approach. The emphasis with this approach is on children selecting real books that they want to read, and on teachers conferencing with them and providing the individual readers whatever help is needed. In the eighties and nineties, the literature approach made a comeback and, today, most teachers incorporate the use of children's literature in their reading program.

A fourth approach, which was widely used in England, Australia, and other countries of the world, also returned to U.S. classrooms in the last decade. This approach, which can be labeled as a language experience/writing approach, is based on the idea that the easiest material for children to read is their own writing and that of their classmates.

Throughout the years, these four major approaches—phonics, basal, literature, and language experience/writing—have been in and out of favor. Generally, one approach has predominated just long enough for people to recognize its shortcomings, then the approach will be abandoned in favor of a different approach with different shortcomings. The question of "which method is best" cannot be answered because it is the wrong question. Each method has undeniable strengths.

Phonics instruction is clearly important because one of the beginning readers' biggest responsibilities is to figure out how our alphabetic language works. Adams (1990) and Cunningham (1995) reviewed decades of research and concluded that, while children can figure out the letter-sound system on their own, directly teaching this system can speed up literacy acquisition. The need for phonics instruction is particularly clear for at-risk children who, lacking much exposure to reading and writing, have had fewer opportunities to figure out how our alphabetic system works.

Basal instruction provides teachers with multiple copies of reading material in which difficulty level is gradually increased, and, which the teacher can use to guide children's skill and strategy development. Because basals contain a wide variety of all types of literature, children are exposed to many genres and topics that they might have missed if all of their reading was self-selected. In addition, basals outline the major goals for each year and provide an organized curricular plan for accomplishing those goals and for ways of evaluating which students are meeting the goals.

The reading of real books is the ultimate aim of reading instruction; however, it has often taken a back seat to phonics and/or basal instruction. Children were expected to "read when they finished their work" or "read at home." Of course, children who came from homes where books were available and where reading was valued were much more likely to engage in real reading than children whose homes lacked these advantages. The literature approach to reading's reemergence has once again reminded us that the purpose of learning to read is to read real books. Children who read real books understand why they are learning to read and what reading really is.

Writing is an approach to reading that allows children to figure out reading "from the inside out." As children write, they spell words that they later see and recognize in their reading. Even when they can't spell a word perfectly, they try to sound it out in order to spell it and actually put to use whatever phonics they have learned. Children who write are more avid and sensitive readers. Reading is a source for writing ideas and information. Reading also provides the writer with models of various writing styles and techniques. Like reading real books, writing is an authentic activity and children who write become more fluent in reading (Tierney & Shanahan, 1991).

In the sixties, the federal government spent hundreds of thousands of dollars trying to find the best approach to beginning reading. Data was collected from first and second grades around the country, which used different approaches to beginning reading. The results of this study were inconclusive. Some approaches did better in certain schools but others did better elsewhere. Virtually every approach had good results in one place and poor results in another. How well a teacher carried out the approach seemed to be the major determinant of how well an approach worked. Some teachers used what the researchers called "combination approaches," such as language experience and basal, phonics and literature, or literature and writing. The study concluded that, in general, combination approaches worked better than any single approach (Bond & Dykstra, 1967). Adams (1990) also concluded that children—especially at-risk children—need a rich variety of reading and writing experiences as well as direct instruction in letter-sound patterns. This finding was confirmed in studies of exemplary primary grade teachers (Wharton-McDonald, et al., 1997).

The question to be asked is not "Which approach?" but rather, "How can we organize classrooms so that we 'have it all'?" The reason the great debate rages on is that there is truth in all of the arguments. To learn to read, children must read real books. Children who write become better writers and better readers. English is an alphabetic language; in order to read and spell the thousands of words necessary for fluent reading and writing, children must be taught how the alphabetic system works and must learn letter-sound relationships. Finally, basal readers provide multiple copies of a variety of literature, which gradually increase in difficulty along with an organized curricular plan that teachers can use to instruct and assess progress.

In addition to the above support for a multi-faceted approach to reading instruction, there is another compelling reason to avoid limiting our instruction to one particular approach. Think about your own family or a family you know well with two or more children. Have you ever noticed or heard others remark on how different the children are? One child needs a clearly-defined routine and set of rules while the other child may need more flexibility because she or he has more self-determination. One child is neat; the other is a slob. (Let's hope they don't have to share the same bedroom!) One child has a restless, creative, problem-solving mind and personality. The other may be as smart (perhaps even smarter on standardized tests), but unimaginative.

Anyone who has ever observed how different children from the same family behave knows that all children do not learn, respond, and think in the same manner. Successful parents recognize the differences in their children and adjust their rules, routines, and interactions accordingly, in order to maximize the potential of each of their children.

Not only do children bring to school huge differences in the amount of reading and writing experiences they have had, but they also come with their own "personalities." The more common term for personalities in educational jargon is *learning styles.* There are commercialized programs based on the idea that you can determine a child's style with a paper and pencil test and then teach according to that style. While it is clear that children do have differences in how productively they learn, these differences are not easily categorized. There is little evidence that such differences can be validly measured—particularly with self-report paper and pencil tests. There is much controversy in education about learning styles and how the concept is used in schools (Johnston & Allington, 1991). To avoid getting into the "styles debate," but still acknowledge the unarguable truth that not all children learn in exactly the same way, we have chosen to talk about the different personalities of children.

Now consider the four approaches to reading that were described earlier, and think about the various personalities of the children you have taught. Some children need and like the structure of basal readers. They know exactly what they are going to read and exactly what to do after they read. Skills are introduced and reviewed in a predictable and logical order. Some children even take pleasure in completing each story and noting the visible signs that they are progressing.

The same order and predictability that allows some neat and tidy children to thrive in basal approaches can be a total turnoff to children with other personalities. "Reading is always the same," they say. "You talk about what you are going to read, learn some new words, read the story, and do two pages in your workbook! Boring!" These adventuresome types like variety in what they read, when they read it, and what they do before and after reading. Put these children in a literature approach based on self-selection and on various ways of sharing, and they are more apt to become readers.

To some children, their own ideas and imaginations are much more interesting than anything a "faraway" author may have written. These children love to "express themselves." They love to talk and tell stories and be the center of attention. These expressive children also love to write; as they write, they use and learn words that they recognize when they read. The children with writing personalities will read, but for them reading is a means, not an end. Reading is one of their sources for ideas about which they can write.

Likewise, some children are better at learning and using letter-sound relationships. They have an ear for sounds—much like the ear some have who become musicians. Other children labor over the letters and sounds and aren't able to blend the sounds they know into words that they know.

One of the major reasons for providing a "comprehensive approach" to literacy is that children bring different personalities into our schools. While it is not possible to clearly determine which children will learn best with what approach, it is clear that when a teacher provides more routes to the goal of literacy, more children will find a route to take them there (Hall, Prevatte, & Cunningham, 1995).

WHY COMPETENCY ISN'T SUFFICIENT BUT BASIC PROFICIENCY IS JUST THE BEGINNING

It wasn't until the 1970s that states began to establish minimum competency levels for reading and began publicizing school achievement information. Also, in the 1970s the federal government initiated the National Assessment of Educational Progress (NAEP) and reported on student reading achievement. After a quarter-century, the expectations are changing. The older minimum competency levels in reading have largely been replaced with a newer, higher standard, known as Basic proficiency on the NAEP.

You may have read in the newspaper that 44 percent of American fourth graders failed to achieve the new Basic proficiency standard on the 1994 administration of the NAEP. You may have concluded (or read) that elementary schools are sliding backwards, that more children are having difficulty learning to read. But that would be an inaccurate interpretation of the NAEP findings because the new Basic proficiency standard represents a higher level of achievement than the old minimum competency levels.

In New York State, for example, the old minimum competency test, which contained short passages and multiple-choice questions required students at the end of third grade to achieve a score of 1.8 (first grade—eighth month). Now that is truly a very minimum competence in reading for a child about to enter fourth grade! But that was the level established and used to judge and rank schools. Most other states also set minimum competency levels at similarly low levels.

The new Basic proficiency level on the NAEP requires students to read short stories, articles, poems, and other longer, complete texts.

> Fourth-grade students performing at the Basic level should demonstrate an understanding of the overall meaning of what they read. When reading text appropriate for fourth graders, they should be able to make relatively obvious connections between the text and their own experiences, and extend the ideas in the text by making simple inferences. (Campbell, Donahue, Reese & Phillips, 1996, p. 42)

In addition to multiple-choice items, many NAEP items require students to compose extended written responses. For instance, after reading a fable about an ant and a turtle, the student is asked:

> "There is a saying, 'Don't get mad, get even.' How does this apply to the story?"

Another asks:

> "Who do you think would make a better friend, Spider or Turtle? Explain why."

A third item offered this task.

> "Think about Spider and Turtle in the story. Pick someone you know, have read about, or have seen in the movies or on television and explain how that person is like either Spider or Turtle."

A final item asked:

> "What do Turtle's actions at Spider's house tell you about Turtle?"

Only 41 percent of fourth graders were able to respond adequately to this question even though only a sentence or two was required. But that item, like the others, requires that the reader go beyond just recalling literal information from the material read. Basic proficiency on the NAEP requires thinking, not just remembering or pronouncing the words correctly.

But basic proficiency, as defined on the NAEP, is the lowest level of acceptable performance—it's just the beginning. At the Proficient and Advanced levels, students are expected to be able to evaluate what they have read against multiple criteria (interestingness, completeness, clarity, etc.). The NAEP results do not suggest that children are not reading as well as they did in the "good old days." What it means to be a competent reader has changed dramatically to reflect what competent readers must actually do. The "bar has been raised" and we must raise the level of our daily literacy instruction.

Michael Knapp (1995) describes classrooms in high-poverty schools that produce a larger number of readers and whose readers attain the new Basic proficiency as classrooms where children engage in huge amounts of reading and writing and where reading and writing are integrated and focused on understanding—discussing, summarizing, evaluating, and comparing the material that has been read. Children spend little time completing low-level worksheets or responding to literal, recall questions. In these schools, from kindergarten on, instruction focuses on thinking and responding to what has been read and written.

CLASSROOMS THAT WORK

From here on, we will leave the negative world of solutions that don't work behind and proceed to describe what does work. We know a great deal about what works, some of which we learned from the methods that didn't work. Describing what works, however, is difficult because you—our reader—have your own particular teaching context. While the principles are the same, effective instruction for kindergartners looks very different from what you might provide to fourth graders. If your classroom has only three or four struggling readers, you are facing a very different situation from the teacher who has nearly a whole class at risk for reading failure.

Another factor that makes it difficult to decide how to structure this book is that, as a reader, you have your own particular learning personality. Some of you are very global in your thinking. You like to "get the big picture" and don't want to be bothered with details until you have a good understanding of where you are headed. Others need to know how things will work step-by-step and can only evaluate the ideas when you have all the details firmly in place. If you are a step-by-step person, you will find that the order of the remaining chapters matches your personality well.

Chapters 2 through 7 will present the "pieces of the puzzle." In Chapter 2, you will learn how teachers create classrooms where reading real books, writing, and sharing what is read and written about are everyday occurrences. Chapter 3 describes the most effective strategies you can use to support and guide children's reading and thinking—either with a basal or with multiple copies of some other reading materials. In Chapter 4, you will learn the most effective strategies for helping students become better writers, and how reading and writing instruction can be combined. Chapter 5 provides strategies for helping children develop a store of words that they can both read and spell, as well as some decoding strategies for figuring out how to read and spell new words. Chapter 6 emphasizes the importance of the knowledge-building subjects of science and social studies and how reading and writing strategies can enhance and be enhanced when used in these subjects. Chapter 7 presents some ways that classroom teachers provide additional instruction and support for children whose literacy levels are way below grade level.

Chapters 8, 9, and 10 put the pieces together. If you are a global learner, you will probably want to skip ahead to those chapters now and then work your way back through the other chapters for the nitty-gritty details. In Chapters 8, 9, and 10, you will see how classrooms at various grade levels provide the most effective literacy instruction possible for a wide range of abilities and personalities found in our schools. These multilevel classroom models are compilations of the most effective instruction we have seen in a variety of classrooms.

Finally, in Chapter 11, we offer ideas that we believe are worth fighting for. The ideas we present involve changes that will improve schools for both children and their teachers.

REFERENCES

Adams, M. J. (1990). *Beginning to read: Thinking and learning about print.* Cambridge, MA: M.I.T. Press.

Allington, R. L. (1994). What's special about special programs for children who find learning to read difficult? *Journal of Reading Behavior, 26,* 1–21.

Allington, R., & McGill-Franzen, A. (1989). School response to reading failure: Chapter 1 and special education students in grades 2, 3, & 8. *Elementary School Journal, 89,* 529–542.

Allington, R., & McGill-Franzen, A. (1992). Unintended effects of educational reform in New York state. *Educational Policy, 6,* 397–414.

Baumann, J. F., Hoffman, J. V., Moon, J., & Duffy, A. (1997). *It's not whole language versus phonics but a matter of balance, eclecticism, and common sense: Results from a survey of U.S. elementary school teachers.* Athens, GA: National Reading Research Center.

Bond, G. L., & Dykstra, R. (1967). The cooperative research program in first-grade reading instruction. *Reading Research Quarterly, 2,* 5–142.

Braunger, J., & Lewis, J. P. (1997). *Building a knowledge base in reading.* Newark, DE: International Research Association.

Cunningham, P. M. (1995). *Phonics they use: Words for reading and writing.* New York: HarperCollins.

Campbell, J. R., Donahue, P., Reese, C., & Phillips, G. (1996). *NAEP 1994 Reading Report Card for the nation and the States.* Office Educational Research and Improvement, U.S. Department of Education.

Gamoran, A. (1986). Instructional and institutional effect of ability grouping. *Sociology of Education, 59,* 185–198.

Hall, D., Prevette, C., & Cunningham, P. (1995). Eliminating ability grouping and failure in the primary grades. In R. L. Allington & S. A. Walmsley (Eds.) *No quick fix: Rethinking literacy programs in America's elementary schools,* Teachers College Press.

Hoffman, J. V., McCarthy, S. J., Elliott, B., Bayles, D., Price, D., Ferree, A., & Abbott, J. (1998). *The literature-based basals in first-grade classrooms: Savior, Satan, or same-old, same-old? Reading Research Quarterly.*

Johnston, P. A., & Allington, R. L. (1991). Remediation. In Barr, R., Kamil, M., Mosenthal, P., & Pearson, P. D. (Eds.), *Handbook of Reading Research, vol. 2,* (pp. 984–1012). New York: Longman.

Knapp, M. (1995). *Teaching for meaning in high-poverty schools.* New York: Teachers' College Press.

McGill-Franzen, A. M. (1994). Is there accountability for learning and belief in children's potential? In E. H. Hiebert & B. M. Taylor (Eds.) *Getting reading right from the start: Effective early literacy interventions.* Boston: Allyn-Bacon.

Pressley, M., Rankin, J., & Yokoi, L. (1996). *A survey of instructional practices of primary grade teachers nominated as effective in promoting literacy. Elementary School Journal, 96,* 363–384. Norwood, MA: Christopher-Gordon.

Pressley, M., Wharton-McDonald, R., Ranking, J., Mistretta, J., Yokoi, L., & Ettenberger, S. (1996). *The nature of outstanding primary grade literacy instruction.* In E. McIntyre & M. Pressley (Eds.) *Balanced instruction: Strategies and skills in whole language,* 251–276.

Shepard, L. A., & Smith, M. L. (1990). Synthesis of research on grade retention. *Educational Leadership, 47,* 84–88.

Tierney, R. J., & Shanahan, T. (1991). Research on the reading-writing relationship: interactions, transactions, and outcomes. In Barr, R., Kamil, M., Mosenthal, P., & Pearson, P. D. (Eds.) *Handbook of Reading Research, vol. 2,* (pp. 246–280). New York: Longman.

Veatch, J. (1959). *Individualizing your reading program.* New York: Putnam.

Wharton-McDonald, R., Pressley, M., Rankin, J., Mistretta, J., Yokoi, L., & Ettenberger, S. (1997). Effective primary-grades literacy instruction-balanced literacy instruction. *Reading Teacher, 50,* 518–521.

2

READING AND WRITING REAL "THINGS"

Walk into a classroom where all of the children are destined to succeed in learning to read and write and what do you see? There will be lots of books and other reading materials, along with evidence that the teacher and the children read and write (Pressley, et al., 1997). Stay in that classroom as the children enter and the day begins and ask yourself, "How much time will the teacher and the children spend reading and writing real things?" Notice that the teacher reads a variety of real things to the children at different points in the day—not just a story after lunch. The teacher may begin the day by showing a cartoon from yesterday's paper or by reading an account of a local football game that many of the students attended. A math lesson may even begin with the teacher reading an advertisement from the newspaper and asking the students, "How much would you really be saving by buying now?"

As the day goes on, several books or parts of books are read or referred to. Some weather poems are read as a springboard into a science unit on weather. Pictures and captions from an art book or magazine are shared as students begin an art lesson. After lunch, the teacher reads from the chapter book currently being read to the class. As the social studies lesson begins, children are reminded of a chapter book that was read aloud earlier in the year and which was set in the historical era about to be studied. Later in the day, after self-selected reading time, the teacher selects several children to share the books they are currently reading. The children simply introduce the book, comment on it and on why they selected it (often, it was recommended by a friend). Each response is brief and is focused on the reader's opinion of the book.

Also notice that the teacher and the children write. The morning begins with the teacher writing a "morning message" on the board. The children watch eagerly to see what interesting event might be planned for the day. Notice also that the walls of the room are literally covered with print. Children's writing is displayed along with posters, maps, timelines, newspaper clippings, and other written material. The teacher creates a bulletin board on which the children may add some of their ideas. Each child has a mailbox into which the teacher or other children may put messages. The teacher also writes in a journal daily, just as the children do. Sometimes, she shares what she has written with the children. Other times, she has written something personal that she may not choose to share.

Now focus on the children. Observe the real things that they read and write. During self-selected reading, everyone reads. During journal time, everyone writes. Notice the other things that children read and write. Notice how some children pick up the newspaper from which the teacher has read and read a different part of it. Also notice how the children work with a partner using encyclopedias and other information sources to find the answers to some "weather expert" questions. Observe the references children make to books they have read when various topics come up. Note that writing takes many forms. Children may come up with some "weather expert" questions to try to stump their classmates, or may compose book reviews and responses to books. They may create summaries of science and social studies materials and caption artwork. Some of the composing activities are brief "quickwrites" before they read just to jot down what they already know about a topic or about what they would really like to learn. Some composing activities involve sustained writing, revision, and publishing activities as children create their own chapter books over a three or four week period.

Children who are successful at becoming literate view reading and writing as authentic activities from which they get information and pleasure, and by which they communicate with others. They know what reading and writing are really for and they want to be successful at it. The literacy-rich classroom communicates the importance of real reading and writing activities by engaging children in a variety of print activities and not relegating reading and writing to a brief period. The teachers know that it is important to take the time to read to children each day. They know it is important to have a time each day in which children read materials that they have selected for themselves. In addition to self-selected reading, the teachers know it is critical that they schedule time each week to engage the children in reading lessons that teach essential reading strategies. The teachers know that writing takes time, so they schedule blocks of time for children to write. They know that sharing reading is important, so they set aside time to allow children to share their books and compositions with each other. In short, these teachers know that if there is no time in the school day for real reading and writing, then children will get a powerful message about the value (or lack of value) of reading and writing. The first and most basic component of classroom instruction is offering children a variety of real reading and writing encounters.

This principle is so logical and makes so much common sense that it is often overlooked in planning instruction. In many classrooms students engage in little reading of real things and have even fewer opportunities to write real things. Oddly, this problem seems to increase as children advance through the grades! Why is it that second-grade teachers typically have students spend more time reading and writing than sixth-grade teachers do? The older students are able to read a wider array of texts and able to write in a greater variety of genres, but, often, older students are given fewer opportunities to read and write than younger students. It is just as important that fifth and sixth graders have lots of opportunities to read and write real things during the school day as it is for first or second graders. In this vein, another oddity is that schools with higher-achieving students usually schedule more opportunities for real reading and writing than schools with many lower-achieving students! All students need these daily opportunities to engage in real reading and writing, regardless of grade level or achievement level.

But not all students have equal access to books in or out of school and limited access to engaging, appropriate books will limit real reading opportunity. Children who attend school in wealthier communities have more books in their classrooms and their school libraries than children from less-advantaged communities. Children from economically more advantaged families have larger numbers of books available in both their homes and their classrooms (Smith, Constantino & Krashen, 1997). Some children come from homes in which books, magazines, newspapers, paper, pencils, pens, markers, typewriters, and computers abound—homes where bedroom libraries of 100 books are common. These are homes where parents and older siblings read and write regularly. Such homes provide children with models of authentic reading and writing experience, materials to read and write with, and time during which reading and writing are the expected activities. These experiences and resources seem to account for some of the achievement advantage so often reported for more advantaged students. While we would love to wave a magic wand and magically transform the homes of all children into literacy-rich environments, this is not within our power. What is within our power is the ability to create literacy-rich environments within our classrooms. In the remainder of this chapter, specific suggestions will be made for providing models, materials, and motivation at the various grade levels.

MODELS, MATERIALS, AND MOTIVATION IN KINDERGARTEN AND FIRST GRADE

Kindergartens have undergone dramatic changes in the last decade and the debate over a socialization/play kindergarten versus an academic kindergarten continues. We would like to suggest a third and different role for kindergarten. We would like kindergartens to simulate what happens in the homes of children in which books and writing tools have been a part of childhood from birth. Children from such homes spend over 1,000 hours actively engaged in some kind of reading and writing before they come to school. That's more hours than most children spend in kindergarten! We can't (and don't want to) spend all of our hours reading and writing, but we must provide as much "quality" time as possible.

A Peek into Literate Homes

Before describing our kindergarten, let us imagine the home environment that we are trying to simulate. If we visited the home of one of the lucky children who have had all those reading and writing encounters, what would we see? What kind of encounters would they be?

The first thing we would probably notice is reading material. The child's bedroom would probably have a shelf of 30–50 books (or more). Among these books would be certain favorites that the child would insist upon having read over and over until the parent (or older brother/sister/grandparent, etc.) could not stand to read again! We would observe the "bedtime story ritual"—a parent reading books aloud after the child is tucked in. During this reading, the parent would ask questions about the pictures ("Can you find the mouse now?"), comment on words and phrases ("Listen, these two words rhyme."), and cue predictions and responses ("What is he going to do now?" "How do you think she feels?"). The parent may read 3–4 books each night before turning out the light. If we could peek into that bedroom when the lights were supposed to be out, we might see the child with one of those often-read books "reading" it to a stuffed animal! We put the word reading in quotes because, in reality, the child knows what to say on each page and has some repetitive parts of the book memorized. The "pretend reading" of a familiar book is one of the most common occurrences when children have had the luxury of books and a captive adult reader.

In addition to the bookshelf of "owned" books, we would probably also see a stack of 4–5 library books. Weekly or biweekly trips to the library to pick out some great new books would be scheduled along with gymnastics lessons and soccer practice. While at the library, the adult who took the child might also pick up some books for pleasure reading along with some functional books such as, *How to Compost, Paying for College,* and *Getting Your Child Ready for Kindergarten.*

In addition to a permanent bedroom library and a changing collection from the lending library, there are many other less obvious sources of reading materials that impact the lives of 3- and 4-year-olds. The newspaper is around and even though the child doesn't read it, someone may read the "funnies" to her or him. In addition, children see adults reading the newspaper and hear them interacting about what they read. "Can you believe they finally caught the guy who broke into the Donahues' house?" "I think we should go car shopping this weekend. The dealers are outdoing themselves with rebates and financing that can't last forever."

There are other things to read, too. Various family members check on their favorite programs in a TV guide. Bills and announcements come in the mail and people react and often read information from them aloud. Birthday cards, letters from Granny, and postcards from friends are sifted out from the junk mail, read, and taped to the refrigerator. Magnetic letters stick to the refrigerator and spell out an older brother's name.

Mealtimes and trips to the grocery store can become literacy events if the child's attention is drawn to the barrage of words available. The child observes that the cook is reading a recipe or directions on the back of a package. An older brother reads the back of the cereal box. The adult shopper reads the ingredients and refuses to buy the cereal because it is all sugar! Trips to and from the grocery store can be opportunities to read as well. There are signs to be read along the way and many 4-year-olds begin their journeys into reading by recognizing words such as K-Mart, McDonald's, and Pizza Hut. In some of these homes, children have access to computers and educational software, including games.

So far, we have been focusing on the omnipresence of reading material, models, and opportunities in the day-to-day life of a preschool child from a literate environment. If we look closely, we will also see writing material. We will see paper—lined and unlined—and we will see young children experimenting with a combination that we call driting (drawing and writing). They will do this in their own inimitable 4-year-old fashion and what they write will be decipherable only to them. They will know what they have written and then will ask some poor adult to read it! (The savvy adult will say, "That's wonderful! I don't have my glasses. Why don't you read it to me!") In other cases, an adult will have provided the caption for an illustration or simply printed the child's name on the artwork.

They will write with real pencils with erasers on the ends, (not those awful fat ones with no erasers that, for no good reason but tradition, they are subjected to once they arrive at school!), with pens, markers, crayons, and chalk. They will write on paper, index cards, checks, envelopes, chalkboards, and (alas) walls! They will write the things they have seen others write—thank-you notes, shopping lists, directions, letters, and memos! Their writing will be posted around the home (the refrigerator does especially heavy duty here). Parents also mail the writing to Grandma and Grandpa who inevitably write back. The children write not just for themselves but for others too. The writing is shared with adults who offer supportive advice about writing when asked.

Take an imaginary journey into the life of a lucky preschooler and you would be overwhelmed by how many reading and writing encounters these young children have. From these encounters, they develop four critical understandings:

1. They know that ideas and words can be written down.
2. They know that when you read or write there is a story or some information that you are trying to understand or communicate.
3. They know that reading and writing are two important things that bigger people do and since they want to be big too, they must learn.
4. They know from overwhelming adult pleasure and approval of their fledgling attempts at pretend reading, of their reading of some signs and labels, and of their writing that they are succeeding at mastering this mysterious code.

When children come to the classroom with an understanding of what reading and writing are, with a strong desire to do it, and with a history of successful beginning attempts, it is no surprise that we can teach almost all of them to read and write. Our literate home simulation kindergartens must provide reading and writing encounters in which all children can develop these four critical concepts.

The Literate Home Simulation Kindergarten

Enter a literate home simulation kindergarten and you will be struck by the amount of things to read. In addition to a substantial classroom library and a comfortable reading area there will be a special place for the books that the class and the teacher have checked out from school or the public library, and that must be read soon before they are taken back. There will be newspapers, magazines, and perhaps a bulletin board on which cartoons, pictures, advertisements, announcements, or something else of interest to kindergartners is added daily. The teacher and the children may cut out and bring in interesting items to add to this board. When the board is full, everything will be taken down and distributed to the children as desired and the process of adding to the newspaper board will begin again.

There will be charts on which language experience stories, favorite poems, and finger plays are recorded. Class books with fascinating titles such as, *The Favorite Foods of Ms. J.'s Big Eaters,* and *Room 112 Goes to the Zoo* record the preferences and adventures of this kindergarten class with photos, drawings, and short sentences. Cereal boxes and other packages will be part of the home and grocery center. Traffic signs will be part of the block's center.

In addition to a multitude of reading materials, our literate home simulation kindergarten will have lots of things with which to write. Paper and pencils (with erasers) will always be available. Each week there will also be some unique writing materials (colored pencils, markers, chalk, finger paint, chocolate pudding, purple stationery, free hotel postcards, wallpaper samples, etc.) that everyone will want to use and that are in the classroom for a "limited engagement." There will also be individual chalkboards and magic slates as well as a couple of old typewriters. (Many people have one to give away as we all switch to computers!) The big chalkboard in the classroom will be divided into thirds and three children each day may "play teacher" and write on the real chalkboard.

Once the materials for reading and writing are available for children to use, we must turn our attention to the models of reading and writing. Of course, the teacher will read—and not just a book after lunch. The teacher will read many types of things—something from the newspaper to be added to the newspaper board, the lunch menu, a simple recipe from a cookbook, a counting book as math begins, a rain poem as it begins to rain, etc.

Often the teacher will draw the children into a story circle in order to read to them and bring them up close to see the book, the artwork, and the print. This is especially necessary when reading from a regular-sized book, but even when reading from big books, proximity matters. The teacher knows that while the story is important and enjoyment is critical, for many children the proximity to the actual text is also critical. It is this proximity that allows the children to see the words as they are read and to notice how the teacher moves from left to right and from top to bottom as the book is read. In addition, the teacher often comments on the artwork, the words, rhymes, and the language as she reads the big books aloud. The teacher's talk sounds much like the bedtime story talk that is found in the homes of the lucky children. The teacher uses her finger or a pointer to track her voice across the print as she reads. Through a variety of strategies, the teacher draws attention to the use of artwork and illustrations, the sound of language, and the details of print. She links the story to the children's life experiences, including the experiences in other books she has read to them.

The teacher will also write down such things as foods that children tell her they like the best to put in the class foods book, a list of questions children want to ask the police captain so they don't forget anything, or a note to the child's parent explaining how the child skinned her knee. The teacher will write on the chalkboard and on chart paper. She will write while the children watch her turn their words or her words into print. She may even use a magnetic letterboard (reminiscent of those letters on the refrigerator that we saw in some homes) to illustrate words, spellings, and how the words are put together. Most of all, the teacher will talk about her own writing as she writes. She will explain what she is writing and how and why she is writing it.

In addition to teacher models of real reading and writing, children need to see that other "big people" read and write. Some savvy teachers get "guest readers" to come in and read something to the children. Some young children actually express amazement when they discover that the custodian, the lunchroom manager, or the secretary can read. If the police captain is coming to talk about safety, he or she might be flattered if asked to read one of his or her favorite books from childhood.

One model available in all schools is the "big kids." Many schools have "buddy" programs in which each fourth or fifth grader is paired with a kindergarten child. Once a week, big buddies come to the kindergarten and read a book (which they have practiced ahead of time) to their little buddy. Big buddies can also write a short note to their little buddy or record something their little buddy dictates to them. Sometimes, these reading sessions are followed by playground or gym time in which the big kids teach a physical skill to the little kids. Schools that have put these buddy systems in place report that they do as much for the self-esteem of the big kids as they do for the literacy development of the little kids!

Finally, there must be time scheduled in each kindergarten day for reading and writing. One kindergarten teacher asks the children to get a large piece of drawing paper as they walk in the door. "Draw and write about something you want to tell us this morning" is the standard way every day begins. Children are encouraged to draw and write (**drite**) in whatever way they can. No words are spelled for them and no corrections are made. The morning then begins with the children sitting in a circle. Each child shows what she or he has dritten and tells the others about it. Since kindergartners always come in the door with things they want to talk about, they are highly motivated to draw and write something each day.

The kindergarten teachers schedule time each day to read to the children and let the children read to themselves or to each other. After reading several books to the children—including rereading some constantly requested favorites—they then help the children select a book to read. When this procedure is followed from the first day of school, kindergartners don't usually object or protest that they can't read. If they do, teachers simply tell them to "tell the story" as they remember it from the pictures, or to "Pretend that you are the teacher and you are reading the book." Children who want to read with a friend are allowed to, as long as they use quiet voices. Kindergarten children are also very motivated to read if they are allowed to pick a stuffed animal or a doll to read to!

In addition to the daily writing or reading time that is scheduled, a print-rich kindergarten classroom provides many opportunities for children to read and write throughout the day. They provide children opportunities to learn the letters of the alphabet and how words are written and read. Our literate home simulation kindergartens are not just for play and socialization. Neither are they "watered-down" first grades. Rather, they try to simulate the "natural" reading and writing activities that occur in the homes of the more fortunate preschoolers and that are critical to success in beginning reading and writing, while providing the sorts of instructional support that lucky children have received at home. Observations made in the homes of children who come to school ready for reading and writing instruction reveal that these children have materials to read and write with, have other people in the home who read and write, and have others who offer support as their reading and writing develop. Literate home simulation kindergartens provide this foundation for all children and help to narrow the gap between the children who arrive with the least and the most advantaged backgrounds.

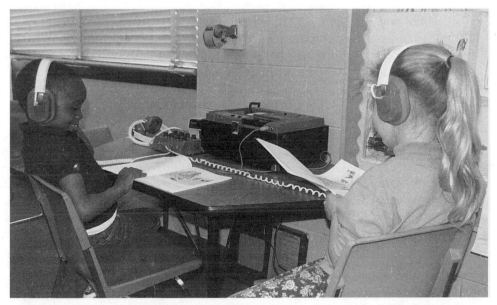

Children love to listen to favorite books again and again. In this class, the teacher has tape recordings of many of the children's favorites. Listening to a favorite book is one of the most popular center activities.

First Grade Classrooms

If you are a first grade teacher whose children have arrived at school from a literate home simulation kindergarten, you will notice that the children all value reading and writing and see themselves as readers and writers. Not all first grade teachers are so fortunate, however. Many first graders lack the understandings developed through a literate home environment or a literate home simulation kindergarten. These unlucky children don't have a clear sense of what reading and writing are for. They haven't gone through the pretend reading and driting stages that develop an "of course I can" attitude. They haven't had lots of "bigger people" models to convince them that reading and writing are two things a person has to learn if he or she wants to be big. They haven't had the kind of support that helped them acquire an understanding of just how our alphabetic writing system works. What do first grade teachers do when faced with this problem?

Well, first they blame the parents, and then they blame the kindergarten teachers, and finally, they decide that if it hasn't been done already, they will have to do it! Once again, real reading and writing materials must be available. Models of "bigger people" reading—the teacher, other adults, and big kids—must be provided along with rich, supportive instruction that occurs throughout the day. Time for self-selected reading and writing must be part of the daily schedule.

Providing the materials, models, and the time in first grade, however, is sometimes "easier said than done." Unlike kindergarten teachers, almost all first grade teachers work under the constraints of a standard curriculum with goals and objectives. There are often skills that must be checked off, books that must be covered, and tests that must be taken. First grade teachers realize the need for developing the foundations described in the kindergarten section, but sometimes feel that they just can't afford the time to do it. The truth is that if children come to you without the critical understandings, you cannot afford to avoid taking the time needed to develop them. Lacking a clear knowledge of what reading and writing are for, and lacking a firm desire to learn how to do them, most children will fail. Once determined to provide materials, models, and time, most first grade teachers discover that adding the "real" reading and writing component is worth the effort. The universal excitement and enthusiasm of first graders renders them eager readers and willing writers, if the teacher accepts their "pretend reading" and driting as valid beginning points.

Children still love to "play teacher" and read to each other or to a stuffed animal. They love to have reading parties on Friday afternoons when they meet in groups of four or five and each child gets to read or tell about a few favorite pages of a book. If you have a mixed class in which some children are reading early in first grade, you can pair these readers with your fledgling readers and let them choose a book to read together. First graders have not yet developed any self-consciousness about not being able to read, and they will gladly accept the teaching of a more proficient child just as they will accept another child's instruction in a new game or song.

Easy Reading Collections

There are an increasing number of easy reading collections available for beginning readers. First grade classrooms should be well-stocked with such materials. Some of these sets are listed below.

Little Celebrations. Scott Foresman/Addison Wesley (Glenview, IL) 75 titles, K-1.

The Sunshine Series: Fiction. The Wright Group (Bothell, WA) 116 titles, K-1 levels, with big books.

The Sunshine Series: Science. The Wright Group (Bothell, WA) 24 titles, K-1 levels, with big books.

Phonics Mini-books. Open Court Publishing, SRA/McGraw-Hill (Mahwah, NJ) 60 titles, K-1, 3 levels.

Look-look-books. Goldencraft (Chicago) 27 titles, 1–2 levels.

Newbridge Early Science books. (Newbridge Educational Publishing) 30 titles, K-2, available in big book and little book sizes.

Literacy 2000. Rigby (Crystal Lake, IL) 55 titles, K-1 levels.

I Can Read Collection. Scott Foresman (Glenview, IL) 31 titles, 1–2 levels.

Step into Reading. Random House (New York) 76 titles, 1–3 levels.

Banners. Scholastic (New York) 120 titles, 1–2 levels, with big books.

Rookie Readers. Children's Press (Chicago) 56 titles.

New Way Readers. Steck-Vaughn-Raintree (Austin, TX) 142 titles, K-2 levels, with tapes.

When writing is coupled with drawing and a "show and tell" sharing session, all first graders can write! When children are at the early scribbling and driting stages, no emphasis should be placed on spelling or handwriting. Children become able to cope with handwriting/spelling/revising demands when they have figured out what writing is and when they have developed some control and proficiency. Think about how you would respond to the first writing efforts of your first graders by imagining how you would respond if your 4-year-old niece proudly presented you with a paper, saying "Look what I wrote!" You would probably try to decipher which direction was "up" and respond, "Wonderful. Why don't you read it to me!" Regardless of age, children who are going to become writers must go through scribbling/driting stages. If they have not done this before first grade, we must allow and encourage their efforts when they get there.

MODELS, MATERIALS, AND MOTIVATION IN SECOND AND THIRD GRADES

If children come to second or third grade and have not been successful in learning to read and write, the task of getting them to engage in real reading and writing becomes more difficult. By second or third grade, good readers are reading ten times as many words each day as poor readers (Allington, 1983). Many teachers of struggling readers acknowledge that children who read nothing but the few pages they are forced to read during a reading group, and who write almost nothing but one-word or one-sentence responses to questions, will never become truly literate. Children who come to second and third grade with a history of failure behind them have lost their, "I can do anything" approach to reading and writing, and have begun to develop avoidance behaviors and the "reading and writing are stupid" attitude. This attitude can be overcome, however, if the second or third grade teacher makes a commitment to models, materials, and time.

Reading to Children

When children come to second or third grade with negative attitudes toward reading, the teacher must make more of an effort to show the children that reading is a source of pleasure and information and that writing is another mode of communication. Teachers should read four types of material to children every day. The first type is something informational. The informational material can come from a newspaper, magazine, encyclopedia, *World Almanac, The Guinness Book of World Records,* or a nonfiction tradebook. Ideally, the teacher should find an opportunity to read from all these sources of information over a month's time. This reading should take place at different times of the day as it fits in with something else that the teacher is doing. Regardless of when the teacher reads this information to the children, the attitude for the teacher to model is one of wonderment:

> "Isn't this fascinating!"
> "Imagine how frightened these people must have been!"
> "Imagine a whale that would fill this whole room!"
> "I was reading this magazine last night and I just couldn't wait to get here this morning and share it with you!"

These informational reading encounters do not have to take very long. In fact, they can lose their effectiveness if they become long, tedious lessons. They should, however, take place frequently—at least once a day—and the source from which the teacher reads should be made available for children to read once their appetites are whetted. Over the school year, the children should hear the teacher use a variety of words and show/read a variety of informational "tidbits," all conveying the message, "I read because there are fascinating things to find out."

Magazines for Children

Classrooms should have magazines as well as books available for children (See *Magazines for Kids and Teens* by Donald Stoll, available from the International Reading Association for magazine reviews and ordering information). Four wonderful informational magazines for second and third grade are:

Ranger Rick. National Wildlife Federation.
3-2-1 Contact. Children's Television Workshop.
Kid City. Children's Television Workshop.
Chickadee. Owl Communications Group.

Second, the teacher should read some of the traditional second and third grade favorites. There are some books that are just part of being seven or eight years old and that no child should miss. Some of these books use sophisticated language and are a little hard for second and third graders to read for themselves, but all children can enjoy listening to them. Teachers should not neglect to include easier books in their read alouds as well. The reading of these books—often a chapter or two each day—should take place at a regular time so that children can look forward to daily escape into literary worlds (much the same way that adult readers read a chapter or two of some escape fiction before turning out the light each night).

Most Loved Second and Third Grade Read-Aloud Books

While it is impossible to list all of the most loved second and third grade read-aloud books, here are a few to get you started.

- *Momo's Kitten*, Taro Yashima and Mitsu
- *Flossie and the Fox*, Patricia McKissack
- *Julian's Glorious Summer*, Anne Cameron
- *Amelia Bedelia*, Peggy Parrish
- *Ramona*, Beverly Cleary
- *Pippi Longstocking*, Astrid Lindgren
- *Tikki Tikki Tembo*, Arlene Mosel
- *Nate the Great*, Marjorie Sharmat
- *Aunt Flossie's Hats*, Patricia Fitzgerald Howard
- *Knots on a Counting Rope*, Bill Martin & John Archambault
- *Charlotte's Web*, E. B. White
- *Owl Moon*, Jane Yolen
- *The Polar Express*, Chris Van Allsburg
- *How the Grinch Stole Christmas*, Dr. Seuss
- *The Beast in Mrs. Rooney's Room*, Pat Reilly Giff
- *James and the Giant Peach*, Roald Dahl
- *Skinny Bones*, Barbara Park

The preceding list contains some books that feature children of various ethnic backgrounds as main characters. There is a treasure trove of good multicultural children's literature. The best source for finding these books is Violet Harris's, *Teaching Multicultural Literature in Grades K-8* (1992). Specific chapters are devoted to detailing the history, well-known authors, and recommended books of African-American, Asian-Pacific American, Native American, Puerto Rican American, Mexican American, and Caribbean children's literature.

Poetry is the third daily must! The poetry available to children today is wonderful and varied. Much of it is funny and the language, rhyme, and rhythm are delightful. Keep a poetry book handy and read one or two of the poems to the children if you have a few empty minutes. When appropriate, reread the poem and have the children chime in on the rhyme or refrain. For the poems that really interest your children, write them on a piece of chart paper and let the children read them with you when you have time. In almost every culture, childhood is a time for chants and songs. Poetry appeals to children's affinity for rhyme and rhythm. Some children, who don't care about information and who are bored by stories, will find that poetry is a real reason for reading.

Finally, many struggling readers haven't experienced the pleasure of reading at home or in first and second grade. This is one good reason that there should be a time each day for the teacher to read some "easy books" to the children and a time for the children to read easy books themselves. In order to help you understand the need for this activity and to commit yourself to this goal, imagine yourself peeking into the room of a fortunate second or third grader as she or he is going to bed. Even though the child is now a reader, an adult probably reads aloud a chapter or two of a book that is a little beyond the child's level. The child is then allowed to read to himself or herself for 15 minutes before turning out the lights. The child may read a recently acquired book but is also likely to pick up from the shelf an old favorite such as, *Are You My Mother?*, *Goldilocks and The Three Bears,* or *Caps for Sale* and read it just for fun! A large classroom supply of easy books is absolutely critical though, if we want second and third graders, who are experiencing difficulty, to pick up books and read.

Favorite Series Books

Series books, such as those listed below, are wonderful materials to use with struggling readers. Series books are easier than a variety of books because the reader builds up a store of information about the characters and the author's style that makes the books predictable. Kids often devour series books—not just because they are easier, but because they like them!

- Norman Bridwell's, Clifford, *the Big Red Dog series.*
- H. A. Rey's, *Curious George.*
- Mercer Mayer's, *Little Critters.*
- Pat Reilly Giff's, *The Polk Street School Kids.*
- Judy Delton's, *Pee Wee Scouts.*
- Else Minarik's, *Little Bear books.*
- Cynthia Rylant's, *Henry and Mudge books.*
- James Marshall's, *George and Martha books.*

Classrooms that can turn reluctant second and third graders into readers are classrooms in which there are many and varied things to read. A few of these things—most importantly the easy-to-read books—are permanent fixtures in the classroom. The other materials—newspapers, magazines, informational books, chapter books, poetry books, etc.—come and go as teachers and children bring them in and return them. Teachers read some whole books along with lots of little "snippets" of things to children. From the wealth and

variety of materials as well as the teacher's modeling of the pleasure and information to be gained, children develop (or redevelop, if they have tried and
failed) the desire to learn to read.

Linda Gambrell of the National Reading Research Center has argued that
teachers should "bless" some books every day. "Blessing" a book simply means
highlighting it by showing it to children and briefly commenting (2–3 sentences) about it. Teachers might quickly show some of the illustrations or read
a paragraph aloud from the book but the goal is to "bless" 5–10 books each day.
Sometimes the blessed books might be clustered by topic, or genre, or author
but the goal is to advertise the good books available in the classroom.

Teachers should encourage children to reread books several times if they
are interested. Many children who find learning to read easy will engage in
repeated readings of books until they have virtually memorized them. The
teacher can model by rereading one or more of the books to the class, particularly the books with wonderful descriptions, powerful words, or repetitive
phrases. Encourage the class to read along (or repeat along as they remember
the lines). During guided reading, teachers should also have children engage in
repeated readings. Have them read silently the first several times. Model fluent
reading and reading with expression. Tell the students that this is their goal.
Perhaps lead them in a choral reading of the story until they get the hang of it.
Remember that fluent reading is useful practice for children who have been
having difficulty, but that it doesn't come easily at first.

Self-Selected Reading

Once the models and materials are in place, children must be allowed time to
spend in self-selected reading. The notion that children should be provided
with time to read was first popularized by Hunt (1970), who referred to this
time as USSR (Uninterrupted Sustained Silent Reading). In the 20 years since
then, the practice has been called a variety of names including, DEAR (Drop
Everything And Read), RSVP (Reading Silently, Very Pleasurable), and SQUIRT
(Sustained QUIet Reading Time). In many classrooms, the time is referred to
simply as, "Choose Your Own Book Time" or "Book Baskets."

Most classroom teachers have tried some version of USSR and many have
given up on the practice. Some teachers feel that it is too artificial and con-
straining to set aside 20 to 30 minutes to read and would prefer to have children
read at various times throughout the day, whenever reading is appropriate.
Other teachers claim that children get bored and just won't sit and read for
even a few minutes. In our experience with hundreds of classrooms, children
will read (and will like it) if the teacher provides lots of books and time to talk
about these books. Struggling readers, particularly, need an available supply of
books that they want to read and can read. Secondly, struggling readers need
to share what they read with others. When adult readers read good books, they
talk to people about those books. When provided with the same opportunity,
children flourish as readers.

In deciding when to have children read, and whether or not a structured
activity such as USSR is needed, teachers should have a specific goal in mind
and then observe to see if that goal is being met. All second or third graders

should spend at least 20–30 minutes each day engaged in the materials they have chosen to read. If you know that all children—including the ones who don't read very well—are engaging in that 20–30 minutes of self-selected reading, then a formal time and structure such as USSR would be redundant in your classroom.

If you know that some children are avoiding voluntary reading, however, you probably need to set aside time in which self-selected reading is the only activity. This time should not include the time spent looking for a book. In fact, some teachers have children choose two or three pieces of reading material before the time begins and do not allow children to get up and change material until the time ends. In other classrooms, a basket of books is placed on each table and the children choose from that basket. The book baskets rotate so that each table gets a different basket the next day. Although this may sound unnecessarily restrictive and unnatural, it is often necessitated by the behavior of the poorest readers who, when observed carefully, are found to spend ten or more minutes "looking for a book" and too little time actually reading the book.

Some teachers use a timer to signal the beginning and end of the self-selected reading time. A timer also keeps the teacher from shrinking the time to 5–10 minutes of reading when the teacher is behind and "the tests" are to be given in a few days! When we engage in activities regularly, we establish some natural time rhythms. Using a timer to monitor the self-selected reading time helps children establish these rhythms. When the timer sounds at the end of the session, the teacher should probably say something like, "Take another minute if you need to get to a stopping point."

Some teachers take a few minutes after self-selected reading to let children share something they have read. Other teachers schedule a weekly time to put the children in small groups to share comments. Many classrooms have "TGIF" celebrations late Friday afternoon that include having some goodies to munch on and time for everyone to read or tell about the best thing they read all week. Teachers find out that the time invested in this weekly activity is more than paid back as they observe children reading what certain children had bragged about the Friday before. (Many teachers invite parents to these celebrations and the parents come because their children all have starring roles!)

Self-Selected Writing

Getting second and third graders to write is sometimes easier than getting them to read. In fact, observational data suggest that children do more writing in second grade than at any other grade level. Most second and third graders have developed some ability to spell and write, and they have lots of things they want to write about. Teachers at the second and third grade level are usually willing to accept whatever writing children are able to produce and focus on their ideas rather than on their mechanics. Many teachers find that it helps for each child to have a writing notebook—preferably, spiral-bound and reserved exclusively for writing. Providing time each day for children to write about "anything they choose," accepting and encouraging their beginning efforts, and providing some time for children to read what they have written, is usually all the motivation that children need. One of the biggest problems faced by teachers whose classrooms are involved with writing something daily is that everyone wants to read what they have written; there is seldom time for this to happen. One teacher solved this problem by designating a fifth of the class as Monday children, a fifth as Tuesday children, etc. (The teacher was a Wednesday person so she read something she had written every Wednesday.) Just before lunch every day, the children whose day it was would get to sit in the "author's chair" and read something they had written or that they were in the process of writing. Other children commented on what they liked or on questions that they had. This sharing only took a few minutes each day, but it motivated the children to write and assured that everyone got a fair chance to be "in the spotlight."

Even though some children come to second and third grade without having experienced the pleasures of reading and writing, almost all of them can still be lured into literacy. They enjoy stories—listening to them, telling them, reading, and writing them. Their early-childhood curiosity is still intact and they want to know how things work and what really happens. They are fascinated by all there is to know about this vast world that we live in. Teachers who make the effort to provide models, materials, and time for daily self-selected reading and writing are usually rewarded by seeing all of their children become readers and writers.

MODELS, MATERIALS, AND MOTIVATION IN FOURTH, FIFTH, AND SIXTH GRADES

If you have children who have been reading and writing for years and who are successful at these activities, the intermediate grades will be the "reaping" years. You reap the rewards of the seeds sown in all those previous years. Your children know that books are sources of pleasure and information and they are developing some control and fluency in their writing. If you make time and materials available and continue to model positive attitudes, you can turn them loose on many student-initiated reading and writing projects. If, however, your children come to you with poor reading and writing abilities and even worse reading and writing attitudes, these will not be the reaping years, but rather, the "weeping" years.

The greatest difference in the instructional program provided for good and poor readers becomes evident in grades four, five, and six. Children who are successful at these grade levels spend more and more time engaged in real reading and writing. On the other hand, children who have been unsuccessful with reading for five to seven years will be discouraged, and so we should not be too surprised when they spend almost no time engaged in reading activities either in or out of school (and often their science and social studies books are simply too difficult for them).

The difficult challenge faced by the intermediate teacher of struggling readers is not only to develop positive attitudes toward reading and writing, but also to transform the negative and often hostile attitudes that these children bring along with them. This is not an easy task and can require a great deal of determination and stamina. Even with a concerted effort, the attitudes of all children may not be turned around. But many can! The knowledge that some children—even after four or five years of failure—can become readers and writers is what must fuel your fire of determination.

In this section, we are going to envision a class with a lot of "resistant" readers and writers. They aren't good at it, don't do it except when forced, and don't want to do it because they think it is "sissy, dumb, and stupid!" (If this does not describe your struggling readers, count your blessings and go on to the next chapter!) Just as in earlier grades, models, materials, and time are the keys to success. All three will need some different twists, however, if they are to succeed with intermediate-aged children who have a history of failure.

Reading to Children

The teacher as a reading and writing model is even more critical at these grades than at the lower grade levels. Intermediate teachers must continue the practice of reading chapter books aloud to the class, and books must be chosen with the highest possible appeal for children of this age. For instance, the following books are among the ones most often selected by upper-grade students. These books represent several different genres and many can easily be linked to science or social studies topics and themes.

Mississippi Bridge. Mildred Taylor
Going Home. Nicholasa Mohr
Zeely. Virginia Hamilton
Stone Fox. John Gardiner
Dear Mr. Henshaw. Beverly Cleary
The Indian in the Cupboard. Lynn Reid Banks
Sign of the Beaver. Elizabeth Speare
Bridge to Terabithia. Katherine Paterson
Tales of a Fourth Grade Nothing. Judy Blume
Class Clown. Johanna Hurwitz
Tell Me a Story, Mama. Angela Johnson
Anastasia Krupnik. Lois Lowry
The Black Stallion. Walter Farley
Streams to the River, Return to the Sea. Scott O'Dell
The Lion, the Witch, and the Wardrobe. C. S. Lewis
A Wrinkle in Time. Madeline L'Engle
Johnny Tremain. Esther Forbes
Across Five Aprils. Irene Hunt

Teachers must make an extra effort to bring real-world reading materials such as newspapers and magazines into the classroom, and to read tidbits from these with an "I was reading this last night and I just couldn't wait to get here and share it with you" attitude. The teacher should also keep a book of poetry handy and read one or two poems whenever appropriate. No intermediate-aged student can resist the appeal of Jack Prelutsky's or Judith Viorst's poems. In addition to poetry, you need your own personal copy of *The Guinness Book of World Records* and a collection of joke and riddle books.

Imagine that you are reading daily from a "grabber" chapter book and that four or five times throughout the day, you read a short article from a newspaper, magazine, or informational book, or share a little poem, joke, riddle, or phenomenal fact with your students. Multiply those five or six reading encounters times 180 school days and you have demonstrated over 1,000 times for your resistant readers that reading is a source of information, pleasure, humor, and wonderment!

Big Reader Buddies

Even with the saturation suggested above, the teacher as model may not be enough to convince some intermediate-aged students. It is still true that most elementary teachers are women and that most poor readers are boys. A lot of poor readers believe that, "Real men don't read books!" Many schools have reported an increased motivation to read when they were able to find some "real men" to read books to their classes. Finding these real men and getting them to come to school regularly is not easy, but if you are on the lookout for them, they can often be found. Service organizations such as the JAYCEES and Big Brother groups are a place to begin your search. City workers, including policemen and

Here are just a few of the many easy-to-read joke, riddle, and "do something" books that even intermediate-aged resistant readers can't resist!

firemen, may be willing to help. Would the person who delivers something to your school each week be flattered to be asked to come and read to your class? If you have some construction being done in your neighborhood, the construction company may feel that it is good PR to allow its workers to volunteer to come into your classroom for a half hour each week and read to your class.

In the kindergarten section of this chapter, we suggested "buddy" programs in which big kids are paired with kindergarten children. Once a week, the big buddies come to the kindergarten and read a book (which they have practiced ahead of time) to their little buddy. Arranging such a partnership allows your older poor readers to become reading models. The buddy system also serves another critical function in that it legitimizes the reading and rereading of very easy books. Once you have a buddy system set up, you can have the kindergarten teacher send up a basket of books from which each of your "big readers" can choose. Tell them that "professional" readers always practice reading a book several times before reading it to an audience. Then, let them practice reading the book—first to themselves, then to a partner in the classroom, and finally to a tape recorder.

Football Players as Reading Models

Cindy Visser, a reading specialist in Washington reports how her school formed a partnership with the local high school football team (*The Reading Teacher, 44*, May, 1991). Football players volunteered to come once a month and read to elementary classes. Appropriate read-aloud books were chosen by the elementary teachers and sent to the high school ahead of time. Interested athletes chose a book and took it home to "polish their delivery." Then, on the last Friday of the month, the athletes donned their football jerseys and rode the team bus to the elementary school. The arrival of the bus was greeted by cheering elementary students and the players were escorted to their classes where they read to the children and answered questions about reading, life and, of course, the big game. This partnership, which was initiated by an elementary school in search of male reading models, turned out to be as profitable for the athletes as it was for the elementary students. The coach reported a waiting list of athletes who wanted to participate and a boost in the self-esteem of the ones who did.

Repeated readings of easy material has long been demonstrated to improve the reading ability of poor readers. Finding easy material that appeals to big kids is very difficult, however. Convincing poor readers to read "baby books" over and over is, under normal circumstances, almost impossible. By setting up a buddy-reader partnership with a kindergarten teacher, you solve the problem of finding easy books by borrowing them from the kindergarten or the library. Once you have a "big reader" program set up, you have transformed the reading and rereading of simple books into a purposeful, self-esteem building activity.

Materials

In addition to newspapers, magazines, poetry, joke and riddle books, and the easy books your students are preparing to read to their buddies, there are other relatively easy but appealing materials you might try to add to your classroom collection. The best list currently available can be found in Marianne Lanino Pilla's *The Best High/Low Books for Reluctant Readers* (1990). In this book, she describes 374 books that she has found to be accessible and appealing to reluctant readers. Of course, new books are being published at a phenomenal rate, so you should constantly be on the lookout for books that appeal to your children.

Collecting appealing books that are easy for reluctant preteens requires determination, cleverness, and an eye for bargains. In addition to obvious sources such as getting free books from book clubs when your students order books, asking parents to donate, begging for books from your friends and relatives whose children have outgrown them, and haunting yard sales and thrift shops, there are some less obvious sources as well. Libraries often sell or donate used books and magazines on a regular basis. Some bookstores will give you a good deal on closeouts and may even set up a "donation basket" where they will collect used books for you. (Take some pictures of your eager readers and have your children write letters telling what kind of books they like to read for the store to display above the donation basket.) In some schools, collections of the high/low books are stored in the remedial reading room and can be borrowed on a rotating basis for use in the classroom.

Books Even Struggling Readers Can't Resist!

There are just a few books that seem so right for upper-elementary-grade reluctant readers that we have to mention a couple of our favorites.

How to Eat Fried Worms. Thomas Rockwell
My Teacher Is an Alien. Bruce Coville
The Chewing Gum Book. Robert Young
Beetles Lightly Toasted. Phyllis R. Naylor

Self-Selected Reading

Now that you have models and materials, you must make sure that each child has time in every day when self-selected reading is the only activity engaged in. Teachers provide this time by setting aside at least 20–30 minutes each day for reading. If this voluntary reading time is new to your students, you might give them a little pep talk so that they realize the importance of the time they spend reading.

The Rotating Book Crates Solution

The goal of every fourth, fifth, and sixth grade teacher of struggling readers should be to have a variety of appealing reading materials constantly and readily available to the children. In one school, four intermediate teachers became convinced of the futility of trying to teach resistant children to read with almost no appealing materials in the classroom. The teachers appealed to the administration and the parent group for money and were told that it would be put in the budget "for next year"! Not willing to "write off" the children they were teaching this year, each teacher cleaned out her or his closets (school and home), rummaged through the book room, and used other means to round up all the easy and appealing books they could find. Then they put these materials into four big crates, making sure that each crate had as much variety as possible. Mysteries, sports, biographies, science fiction, informational books, cartoon books, etc. were divided up equally.

Since they did this over the Christmas holidays, they decided that each classroom would keep a crate for five weeks. At the end of each five-week period, students carried the crate of books that had been in their room to another room. In this way, the four teachers provided many more appealing books than they could have if each teacher kept the books for a single classroom.

The four-crate solution was one of those "necessity is the mother of invention" solutions to try to get through the year without many books; fortunately, it had serendipitous results. When the first crate left each classroom at the end of the five-week period, several children complained that they hadn't gotten to read certain books, or that they wanted to read some again. The teacher sympathized but explained that there were not enough "great" books to go around and that their crate had to go to the next room. The teacher then made a "countdown" calendar to be attached to the second crate. Each day, a child tore a number off so they would realize that they had only 10, 9, 8, 7, etc. days to read or reread anything they wanted from this second crate. Reading enthusiasm picked up when the students knew that they had limited time with these books.

When the third crate arrived, students dug in immediately. A racelike atmosphere developed as children tried to read as many books as possible before the books moved on. When the fourth (and final) crate arrived, children already knew about some of the books that were in it. Comments such as, "My friend read a great mystery in that crate and I am going to read it too," let the teachers know that the children were talking to their friends in other classes about the books in the crates!

While the enthusiasm generated by the moving crates of books had not been anticipated by the teachers, they realized in retrospect that it could have been. We all like something new and different and "limited time only" offers are a common selling device. The following year, even with many more books available, the teachers divided their books up into seven crates and moved them every five weeks so that the children would always have new, fresh material.

Use an analogy to help your children understand that becoming good at reading is just like becoming good at anything else. Compare learning to read with learning to play the piano, tennis, or baseball. Explain that in order to become good at anything, a person needs three things: (1) instruction, (2) practice on the skills, and (3) practice on the whole thing. To become a good tennis player, a person needs to: (1) take tennis lessons, (2) practice the skills (backhand, serve, etc.), and (3) play tennis. To become a good reader, a person also needs instruction, practice on the important skills, and needs to read! Point out that sometimes we get so busy that we may forget to take the important time each day to read and, therefore, we must schedule it just like anything else we do. However, until we make time to read in school, we have no reason to expect children to make time to read out of school.

Have the children select at least two books and explain that they will not be able to look for books once the reading time starts; movement and noise is distracting to some people when they read. Make sure the children understand that during this time they will have no work to do, no questions, and no reports. The only requirement is to read and to talk occasionally with you, their teacher, about the books they are reading.

Once the self-selected reading block gets up and running and children know where they are to be and how they are to read during this time, teachers can spend time holding individual conferences with children. Most teachers designate the children as Monday, Tuesday, Wednesday, etc. and then conference with them on their day, spending three or four minutes with each child. Children know that on their day, they should bring one book that they have selected to share with the teacher. They read a few pages to the teacher and discuss the book and why they chose it. Thus, each child gets a short but dependable conference time with the teacher each week to share what they like about books. The teacher remains familiar with children's independent reading and gains added information about them as readers and children.

Sharing and Responding

Children who read also enjoy talking to their classmates about what they have read. In fact, Manning and Manning (1984) found that providing time for children to interact with one another about reading material enhanced the effects of sustained silent reading on both reading achievement and attitudes. One device sure to spark conversation about books is to create a classroom bookboard. Cover a bulletin board with white paper and use yarn to divide it into 40 or 50 spaces. Select 40 to 50 titles from the classroom library and write each title in one of the spaces. Next, make some small construction paper rectangles in three colors or use three colors of small sticky notes. Designate a color to stand for various reactions to the books.

- red stood for "super—one of the all-time best books I've ever read,"
- blue indicated that a book was "OK—not the best I've ever read but still enjoyable," and
- yellow stood for "yucky, boring—a waste of time!"

Children were encouraged to read as many of the bookboard books as possible and to put their "autograph" on a red, blue, or yellow rectangle and attach it to the appropriate title. Once a week, the teacher led the class in a lively discussion of the reasons for their book evaluations. Some books were universally declared "reds," "blues," or "yellows," but other books collected evaluations in all three colors. As the weeks went on, everyone wanted to read the red books and some would choose the yellow books to see if they were "really that bad." When most children had read these books, a new bookboard was begun. This time each child selected a book title or two to put on the bookboard and labeled/decorated the spot for that book.

In some classrooms the self-selected block ends with a "reader's chair" in which one or two children each day get to do a book talk. They show a favorite book and read or tell a little about the book, and then try to "sell this book to the rest of the class." Their selling techniques appear to be quite effective since these books are usually quickly seen in the hands of many of their classmates.

Other teachers have "reading parties" one afternoon every two or three weeks. Children's names are pulled from a jar and they form a group of three or four in which everyone gets to share their favorite book. Reading parties, like other parties, often include refreshments such as popcorn or cookies. Children develop all kinds of tasty associations with books and sharing books! Still other teachers arrange outings for their children to read to younger children in the school. Each child selects a favorite book and then reads it to a younger reading buddy.

Finding time for children to talk about books is not easy in today's crowded curriculum. There is, however, a part of each day that is not well used in most elementary classrooms—the last 15 minutes of the day. Many teachers have found that they can successfully schedule weekly reading sharing time if they utilize the last 15 minutes. Here is how this sharing time works in one fifth grade classroom.

Every Thursday afternoon, the teacher gets the children completely ready to be dismissed 15 minutes before the final bell rings. Notes to go home are distributed. Bookbags are packed. Chairs are placed on top of the desks. The teacher then uses index cards and writes down each child's name on a card. The index cards are shuffled and the first five names—which will form the first group—are called. These children go to a corner of the room that will always be the meeting place for the first group. The next five names that come out will form the second group and will go to whichever place is designated for the second group. The process continues until all five or six groups are formed and the children are in their places. Now, each child has two minutes to read, tell, show, act out, or otherwise share something from what they have been reading this week. The children share in the order that their names were called. The first person called for each group is the leader. Each person has exactly two minutes and is timed by a timer. When the timer sounds, the next person gets two minutes. If a few minutes remain after all the children have had their allotted two minutes, the leader of each group selects something to share with the whole class.

Teachers who have used such a procedure on a regular basis to ensure that children have a chance to talk with others about what they read find that the children are more enthusiastic about reading. Comments such as "I'm going to stump them with these riddles when I get my two minutes," or "Wait 'til I read the scary part to everyone," are proof that sharing helps motivate reading. The popularity of the books shared with other children is further proof. Having discussions each week on a specified afternoon puts this procedure on the schedule and guarantees that it will get done. Using the cards to form the groups is quick and easy and helps ensure that children will interact with many other children over the course of the year.

The procedure just described, however, worries some teachers because it sounds terribly regimented. What if children don't want to share on Thursday? What if a child wants to share for ten minutes rather than two minutes? What if they don't want to share with the people who end up in their group? These and other questions are valid concerns and must be considered, but we must also consider the alternative. In the best of all possible worlds, reading and sharing would take place daily in a less formal and regimented way. In the real world of many classrooms, however, reading and sharing get pushed aside for the more formal, scheduled activities. It should be the goal of every elementary teacher to be able to say at the end of each week, "All my children took time to read simply for the pleasure of it, had a chance to talk with others about what they were reading, and to hear what their classmates were reading." This goal can be achieved in informal and less-structured ways, and can be achieved with an organized activity such as the one described here. What matters is that reading and talking about what was read play a large role in all children's reading experience.

Contests and Book Reports—Yuck!

Before leaving the subject of voluntary reading in the intermediate grades, we must consider the value of two common practices—reading incentive programs and book reports. Many schools set up reading incentive programs in an attempt to get children to read real books. These programs take many different forms. Children are given T-shirts that proclaim, "I have read 100 books!" or whole classes are rewarded with pizza parties if they can read "the most" books. These reward systems are set up with the best intentions and may even motivate some children to begin reading. Unfortunately, there is another message that can be communicated to children who are exposed to such incentive programs. The message goes something like, "Reading is one of those things I must do in order to get something that I want." Reading thus becomes the means to the end, rather than the end in itself. Many teachers (and parents) report that children only read "short dumb" books so that they can achieve the "longest list."

Book reports are another device used to motivate reading and can often have the opposite effect of what they were intended to have. When adults are asked what they remember about elementary school that made them like or dislike reading, they report that having their teachers read books aloud to the class, being allowed to select their own books, and having time to read them turned the adults on to reading. Book reports are the most commonly mentioned "turnoff." Likewise, few children enjoy doing book reports; their dislike is often transferred to the act of reading. Some children report on the same books year after year and others even admit lying about reading a book.

Children who are going to become readers must begin to view reading as its own reward. This intrinsic motivation can be nurtured only as children find books that they "just couldn't put down" and subsequently seek out other books. Incentive programs and book reports must be evaluated on the basis of how well they develop this intrinsic motivation.

Self-Selected Writing

Perhaps the biggest change that has occurred in the last decade in intermediate classrooms is the prevalence of daily writing. Sometimes called journal writing or personal writing, teachers are providing models, materials, and time for students to write. Many children, even children having difficulties, are more willing and able to write than they were a decade ago.

To establish daily writing time in your class, you would follow many of the same principles described in the reading section. Children need to see writing as something adults do. Teachers also need to write both functional things such as notes, lists, and reports as well as personal expression items such as songs, stories, and poems.

Children need to understand that writing—like reading, tennis, and piano—can be improved by instruction, by practicing specific writing strategies, and just by writing. In classrooms where children understand that reading is one of the most important ways to become a good reader, teachers will find it easy to help children understand the parallels between how reading helps a person become a better reader and how writing will help improve both reading and writing. In Chapter 4, you will find strategies to use for improving the specific writing skills of students. It is also important, however, that children take time each day "just to write," the same way that they take time each day just to read.

Some older children will not write because they have a long history of receiving red marks and unacceptable grades for writing. These children will only begin to write again if you assure them that just doing it is what counts. The daily writing is not graded but the teacher does check to see that something is written. (In some classrooms teachers give children a point each day for writing. These points are then added as bonus points to the final language grade. This should only be used if they "won't do it if it doesn't count for a grade.") Once again, since children do like to share what they have written, setting aside the last 15 minutes of a designated afternoon and using the index cards to put them in groups to share something they have written can be beneficial.

While many teachers use writing folders for daily writing, we have found that it is much easier to keep up with the children's writing and to see their progress if daily writing is done in a spiral-bound notebook that is used exclusively for this purpose. Many teachers find that this notebook, if kept in the children's desks, might become a convenient source of paper for the children; a 60-sheet notebook—that should last half the year—is quickly used up if paper is torn out and used for other purposes. So, teachers often store the notebooks on a shelf for children to pick up each morning and then replace them when they are finished. Most teachers tell children to write about one page. (This is not as much as it sounds because we have children write on every other line so there is space to write additional information or to make corrections if they choose to revise some of these first drafts.) This one-page limit should not be enforced too strictly. Children should understand that they might write a little less one day and a little more another, but that over the course of the week they should average about one page each day.

The biggest problem we have encountered with daily writing is the "what to write about" problem. Just as we let them read about whatever they choose to read about, we want them to write about whatever they choose to write about. In some classrooms, however, many children were "written out" after the first month of school.

From time to time, it is helpful to sit down with children and brainstorm a list of things that the class thinks would be worth writing about. In some classrooms, the children use the first page of their notebooks to record possible topics as they occur to them. Some teachers find it helpful to offer a possible topic for children who couldn't think of anything.

As with the reading, there are elements of structure here that are worrisome. There are some days when children are just not in the mood to write. Should they have to write even when they don't want to? Should everyone write about a page each day? Once a week for 15 minutes is not really enough sharing time. Real writers find their own topics, so children should find their own topics too. Giving students varied springboards to writing and recording such as a two-minute brainstormed list of words, however, has definitely stimulated children who would not write otherwise. Having children review their earlier drafts may foster revision and rewriting on that same topic. Each teacher, looking at a class of intermediate-aged children who have not become writers, must decide how much structure is needed to achieve the goal of having every child write something every day.

SUMMARY

To create powerful classroom environments in which all children learn to read and write, teachers need to be concerned with models, materials, and motivation. Whether the children are 5–6 years old or 11–12 years old, all need to see reading and writing demonstrated and need to be continuously engaged in real reading and writing. This takes time; classroom teachers might begin by deciding about how much time children will spend reading and writing each day. How much time will be set aside for reading to children? How much time will be set aside for teacher-directed instructional activities?

The next question that will need to be answered is where do the books, magazines, and newspapers come from? Throughout this chapter we have suggested a variety of strategies for acquiring these materials, but ideally, classrooms would be well-stocked (as would school libraries) with classroom libraries containing 500–1,000 paperback titles and several magazines for children to read.

In the remaining chapters of the book, we will describe activities that explicitly teach students the strategies they need to develop the self-improving systems that all good readers and writers have. Daily encounters with reading and writing real things are the foundation that supports this strategy instruction.

References

Allington, R. L. (1983). The reading instruction provided readers of differing reading ability. *Elementary School Journal, 83,* 549–559.

Harris, V. J. (Ed.) (1992). *Teaching multicultural literature in grades K-8.* Norwood, MA: Christopher-Gordon.

Hodgkinson, H. (1991). Reform versus reality. *Phi Delta Kappan, 73,* 9–16.

Hunt, L. C., Jr. (1970). The effects of self-selection, interest, and motivation upon independent, instructional, and frustration levels. *Reading Teacher, 24,* 146–151, 158.

Manning, G. L., & Manning, M. (1984). What models of recreational reading make a difference? *Reading World,* 375–380.

Pilla, M. L. (1990). The best high/low books for reluctant readers. Englewood, CO: Libraries Unlimited.

Pressley, M., Wharton-McDonald, R., Ranking, J., Mistretta, J., Yokoi, L., & Ettenberger, S. (1996). The nature of outstanding primary grade literacy instruction. In E. McIntyre & M. Pressley (Eds.) *Balanced instruction: Strategies and skills in whole language* (pp. 251–276). Norwood, MA: Christopher-Gordon.

Shepard, L., & Smith, M. L. (1989). *Flunking Grades.* Philadelphia: Falmer.

Smith, C., Constantino, R., & Krashen, S. (1997). Differences in print environment: Children in Beverly Hills, Compton and Watts. *Emergency Librarian, 24,* 8–9.

Stahl, S. A., & Hayes, D. (Eds.) (1997). *Instructional models in reading.* Mahwah, NJ: Lawrence Erlbaum.

3
GUIDING CHILDREN'S READING/THINKING

In Chapter 2, you were reminded that the real reason we work so hard teaching children to read is so that they will read! You also learned that lots of reading of self-selected materials is critical to the development of good readers. Children do not become readers unless they have time, materials, models, and motivation. For some lucky children, their homes provide all of these essentials. For *all* children to become literate, however, schools must not leave this responsibility to the homes. The first priority in all classrooms that contain struggling readers should be to set up an effective program of daily self-selected reading and writing.

Making sure that children are reading and writing is necessary for their growth. For many children, this essential component, while necessary, is not sufficient. Research (Dole, Duffy, Roehler, & Pearson, 1991; Johnston & Allington, 1991) clearly demonstrates that struggling readers make more rapid progress when given explicit instruction in how to read and write. In Chapters 8, 9, and 10, you will read descriptions of classrooms that provide children with opportunities to read and write and with direct, explicit guidance in how to read and write. In this chapter, and the next four chapters, we will describe the most effective strategies for carrying out that instruction.

Comprehension is the focus of this chapter. Specifically, it will describe how teachers carry out lessons and how they structure activities that teach children how to "think as they read." The focus on thinking is inevitable because that's what reading really is—thinking stimulated by words on a page.

There is a myth about children who have difficulty with reading comprehension, which is that they "just can't think!" In reality, everybody thinks all the time and some struggling readers, who must take care of themselves (and often younger brothers and sisters), are especially good thinkers and problem solvers. If children can "predict" that the ballgame will be canceled when they see the sky darkening up and can "conclude" that the coach is mad about something when he walks in with a scowl on his face, then they can and do engage in "higher-level" thinking processes. The real problem is not that they can't think, but that they don't think while they read. Why don't they think while they read?

Some children don't think while they read because they don't really know that they should! Imagine an extreme case of a child who had never been read to and had never heard people talking about what they read. Imagine that this child goes to a school in which beginning reading is taught in a "learn the letters and sounds" and "read the words aloud perfectly" way. When the child read, he would read words just like you would read this nonsensical sentence:

- He bocked the piffle with a gid daft.

You can read all of the "words" correctly, and you can even read with expression, but you get no meaning. In your case, of course, you get no meaning because there is no meaning there to get. For children who have limited literacy experience and who are taught to read in a rigid phonics-first method with texts that make little sense (*Nan can fan a man*), there is a very real danger that they will not know that "thinking" is the goal. The goal, to them, is sounding out all the words, which is what they try to do. Ask them what reading is and they are apt to look at you as if you are a complete fool and tell you that, "Reading is saying all the words right!"

The ability to decode is critical but when we overemphasize accurate word pronunciation and only provide beginning reading materials in which all the words are "decodable," we can create readers who not only misread the purpose of reading, but who also don't comprehend the story. Children who are trained to concentrate their energies on word pronunciation exhibit word-by-word reading, a low self-correction rate, and a general lack of fluency. In short, their reading just doesn't sound good. It isn't just their comprehension that is affected by an overemphasis on word pronunciation, but also the very act of reading is shaped such that comprehension is virtually impossible.

In Chapter 1, you were reminded that no single-minded approach is going to succeed in increasing literacy for at-risk children. Phonics instruction has a very important place in helping children become literate. English is an alphabetic language and once a reader gets past the most common words, there is a great deal of predictability in the letter-sound relationships. Children should be taught how to recognize common patterns and what to do when they come to an unknown word. This component of a balanced program is the subject of Chapter 5. But, children must begin their reading instruction in a way that puts the focus first on meaning. Only when they know irrevocably that they should be thinking as they read should their attention be drawn to the letter/sound patterns.

Not only are some struggling readers unaware that they should be thinking while they are reading, but many also have inadequate background knowledge for understanding the books and curriculum materials in their schools. Read the next two sentences and think about the implications for your teaching.

Current models do not allow expectancy-based processing to influence feature extraction from words. Indeed, most current models largely restrict expectancy-based processing and hypothesis-testing mechanisms to the postlexical level. (Stanovich, 1991, p. 419).

A Simple Fluency Rating Scale

Oral reading fluency is important so teachers may want to keep track of how fluency develops in children, especially those who arrive with a word-by-word reading style. As children read, listen to them and decide which of the descriptions below best describes their general fluency during this reading. Simply chart fluency each time a child reads. In the process, you may want to take notes about what seems to influence their reading performance.

LEVEL:

Poor—Word-by-word reading primarily.

Fair—Reads primarily in phrases, little intonation, ignores some punctuation.

Good—Reads fluently with expression.

You are probably wondering why we would waste book space (and your time) with these two nonsensical sentences. In reality, these sentences are not nonsensical. They actually have meaning and if you are a research psychologist, you can think and talk intelligently about them! For most of us, however, we can say these words, but we can't really read them because we are unable to think as we say them. Background knowledge, which includes topically-related vocabulary, is one of the major determinants of reading comprehension. In fact, research (Pearson & Fielding, 1991) tells us that the amount of prior knowledge a reader has about a topic is the best determinant of how much will be understood and remembered as it is read. In addition to specific knowledge about the topic, knowledge about the type of text about to be read is called up as well. When a reader begins to read a story or a novel, a whole set of expectations based on other stories that have been heard or read are called up. The reader does not know who the characters will be, but does expect to find characters. The reader also knows that the story will be set in a particular time and place (setting) and that there will be some goals to be achieved or some problems to be resolved. In short, the reader has a story structure in her or his head that allows her or him to fit what is read into an overall organization.

Imagine that you are going to read a *Consumer Guide* article on the new model year cars. Again, you don't know what specific information you will learn, but you do have expectations about the type of information and how it will be related. You expect to see charts comparing the cars on different features and expect to find judgments made about which cars appear to be the best buys.

Now imagine that you are about to read a travel magazine article about North Carolina. You have never been there and don't know anyone who has, so you don't know too many specifics. However, you do have expectations about what you will learn and about how that information will be organized. You expect to learn some facts about the history of North Carolina, along with some descriptions of historical regions and locations in the state. You also expect to find information about places tourists like to visit, such as the coast and the mountains. You would not be surprised to find a summary of the cultural and sporting events that are unique to North Carolina. Information about the climate and the best times to visit different parts of the state, as well as some information on how to get there and places to stay would also be expected. As you begin to read, you may create a mental outline or web, which helps you understand and organize topic/subtopic information.

We refer to the different ways in which various reading materials are organized as text structures and genres. In order to comprehend what we are reading, we must be familiar with the way in which the information will be organized. The fact that most children can understand and remember stories much better than informational text is probably because they have listened to and have read many more stories and, thus, know what to expect and how to organize the story information. If we want to create readers who think about what they read, we must help them become familiar with a variety of ways that authors organize ideas in their writing.

Even with a clear understanding that reading is primarily thinking, sufficient background knowledge, and a familiarity with the kind of text structure being read, you cannot think about what you read unless you can identify a majority of the words. Try to make sense of this next sentence in which all the words of three of more syllables have been replaced by blanks:

> The _____ _____ fresh ideas for action and
> _____ new _____ that will help the _____
> _____ and the _____ meet the challenge of _____ adult
> and _____ _____ worldwide.

Now, read the same sentence but put the words *conference, provided, generated, partnerships, literacy, community, association, promoting, adolescent,* and *literacy* in the blanks.

In order to think while you read, you must:

1. have a mindset that reading is thinking and a determination to make sense of what you are reading,
2. have sufficient background knowledge that you call up and try to connect to the new information,
3. be familiar with the type of text and be able to see how the author has organized the ideas, and
4. be able to identify almost all the words.

Knowing that these four conditions must be in place in order for reading/thinking to take place, we can now consider what kind of lessons and activities we might engage children in that will ensure that they will learn to think while they read.

SHARED READING

Shared reading is a term used to describe the process in which the teacher and the children read together. Shared reading has been used mainly in the primary grades. Typically, a book is read and reread many times. On the first several readings, the teacher does most of the reading. As the children become more familiar with the book, they join in and "share" the reading.

The best kind of books to use with shared reading are predictable books. Predictable books are those in which repeated patterns, refrains, pictures, and rhymes allow children to "pretend read" a book that has been read to them several times. Pretend reading is a stage most children go through with a favorite book that some patient adult has read and reread to them. Perhaps you remember pretend reading with such popular predictable books as *Goodnight Moon, Are You My Mother?*, or *Brown Bear, Brown Bear.* Shared reading of predictable books allows all children to experience pretend reading. From this pretend reading, they learn what reading is and develop confidence in their ability to do it.

Some children come to school with a wealth of shared reading experiences either from home or preschool. Others come to school with virtually no such experiences. A major challenge facing our primary grade programs is in adapting instructional organization in ways that allow those children with limited experiences to fully participate in early literacy lessons. Shared reading is just about the most powerful opportunity possible.

When children are read to "lap style" they have the opportunity to observe the print and the eyes of the person reading. They notice that the reader always reads the top print first, then the bottom print. They notice the eyes moving from left to right and then making the return sweep at the end of the line. Children who can see the words of a favorite book as that book is being read notice that some words occur again and again and eventually come to recognize some of these words. As they learn words, they notice recurring letter-sound relationships.

To simulate lap reading, many teachers use big books. Big books are those in which the pictures and the print is enlarged. Not all big books are predictable, however. They do not all have good story lines and wonderful artwork. If you want to get the maximum benefits from shared reading with big books, you should select your books carefully.

Selecting Big Books

In choosing a book for shared readings in a kindergarten or first grade class, you should consider four criteria. First, the book must be very predictable. The most important goal for shared reading is that even children who have little experience with books and stories will be able to pretend read after several readings, and will develop the confidence that goes along with this accomplishment. Thus, you want a book without too much print, one in which the sentence patterns are very repetitive, and one that contains pictures that support those sentence patterns. Second, you want a book that will be very appealing to the children. Since the whole class of children will work with the same big book and since the book will be read and reread, you should try to choose one that many children will fall in love with. Third, conceptually, the book should take you someplace. Many teachers will choose big books to fit their units or will build units around the books. Finally, the print in the book must be large enough for all children to see, so that they can indeed share the reading with you.

Wonderful Predictable Big Books

There are many wonderful predictable big books from which to choose. Any list will be out-of-date before it is published, but this list includes some of our favorites. All of these books meet our very predictable and lovable criteria.

Brown Bear, Brown Bear, What Do You See? (Bill Martin, Jr., Holt, Rinehart and Winston).
Hattie and the Fox (Mem Fox, Bradbury).
Mrs. Wishy Washy (Joy Cowley, The Wright Group).
The Carrot Seed (Ruth Kraus, Scholastic).
Zoo Looking (Mem Fox, Mondo).
Greedy Cat (Joy Cowley, Katonah, NY: Richard C. Owen).
Joshua James Likes Trucks (Catherine Petrie, Children's Press).

Sharing a Big Book

In doing shared reading with big, predictable books, we try to simulate what happens in the home when a child insists upon having a favorite book read again and again. First, we focus on the book itself, enjoying it, rereading it, and finally, acting it out. As we do this, we develop concepts and oral language. When most of the children can "pretend read" the book, we focus their attention on the print. We do writing activities related to the book and help children learn print conventions/jargon and concrete words. When children know some concrete words, we use these words to begin to build some letter/sound knowledge.

In addition to books, many teachers write favorite poems, chants, songs, and finger plays on long sheets of paper. These become some of the first things children can actually read. Most teachers teach the poem, chant, song, or finger play to the children first. Once the children have learned to say, chant, or sing it, then they are shown what the words look like. The progression to reading is a natural one and children soon develop the critical, "Of course I can read" self-confidence. Once children can read the piece, many teachers duplicate it and send it home for the child to read to parents and to other family members. Parents of struggling readers are especially pleased when they see their children succeeding in school. Parental support and comfort level with the school develops as their children experience success.

Big Books—Not Just for Reading!

Shared reading of big books is where we begin to teach children about the conventions of print (left to right, top to bottom, front to back, spaces between words, and so on). Below are several activities for developing an awareness of these conventions and the language of books, reading, and writing.

1. Identify the author's name on the cover and the title page (illustrator too).
2. Use the language of books, "I'm going to turn to the *first page* of the story . . ." (which usually isn't the first page of the book). "Let's look at the picture at the *top of the page* . . . the page number at the *bottom of the page* . . ."
3. Point to words as you read the story. Show children where your voice is. The idea isn't to point and say each word, but to indicate that those little squiggles are what you are paying attention to. We have worried too much about fingerpointing (especially with young children). Actually, fingerpointing helps children see the match between the voice and the print.

In shared reading, the usual procedure is for children to read something only after they have heard it read many times. During shared reading, children develop five critical understandings:

1. Of course I can read!
2. I read to learn and enjoy. (Saying the words is the *means* to that end.)
3. The sentences I read are made up of words.
4. The words are what I read and words are made up of letters.
5. I look at the words in a specific way (top—bottom, left—right, etc.).

Once children have developed these critical understandings, they are ready to do some reading in which they, not the teacher, do the initial reading. Some teachers and parents fear that children will not learn to read if they are always "just memorizing it." Shared reading is a critical beginning, but once children have developed the confidence that they can read and have a basic understanding of what reading is and how they must look at the page, the sentences, and the words, then they should be given reading instruction during which they do the initial reading. We refer to this instruction, in which the teacher helps and supports but the children do the initial reading, as guided reading.

GUIDED READING

When most of us think of guided reading, we picture a teacher with a teacher's manual in her or his hand and a small group of children sitting around the teacher clutching their basal readers. Guided reading is the part of reading instruction that is familiar to most of us and that we associate with basal readers and reading groups. Guided reading can be done with

This girl is trying to read a predictable big book for herself that the class has read together in a shared reading format. Being able to read is such a source of pleasure and accomplishment for young children that they will choose to read these predictable books again and again.

basals and with small groups, but to think of it this narrowly is to limit ourselves unnecessarily!

The essentials of guided reading are that the teacher explains and/or demonstrates for children the important things to be done while we read. The teacher follows the lead of the students, allowing them to do all the work that they can, and stepping in to support the reader when help is needed. Guided reading is needed when children are reading texts that present new difficulties and require the use of new strategies. In reality, much of what teachers do is to support "thinking." When students think while they read, they ask themselves what strategies they can use to solve the problems they encounter. Because thinking is complex and happens inside your mind, there is little agreement on exactly what or on how many strategies there are. Many teachers use a local or

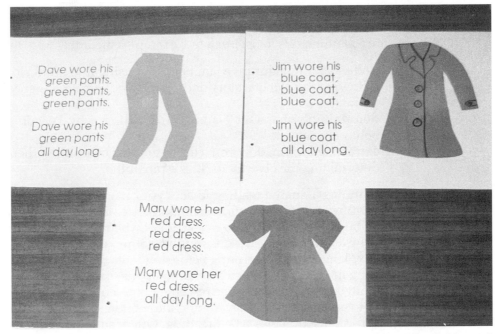

Dave wore his
green pants,
green pants,
green pants.

Dave wore his
green pants
all day long.

Jim wore his
blue coat,
blue coat,
blue coat.

Jim wore his
blue coat
all day long.

Mary wore her
red dress,
red dress,
red dress.

Mary wore her
red dress
all day long.

Here are pages from a teacher-made big book based on the song "Mary Wore Her Red Dress." The laminated construction paper pages are held together with rings and thus can be taken apart and distributed for various activities. This popular song fits into units on colors and clothing.

state curriculum guide to determine which strategies are deemed critical in their school/grade level. Teacher's manuals also provide teachers with lists and suggestions for teaching important strategies.

In considering which strategies to focus on during a guided reading lesson, the teacher considers both the demands of the text that children are about to read and the needs and abilities of the children. There are some strategies that readers need to use on almost all texts. These include:

- calling up relevant background knowledge
- predicting what will be learned and what will happen
- making mental pictures or "seeing it in your mind"
- self-monitoring and self-correction
- using fix-up strategies such as rereading, pictures, and asking for help when you can't make sense of what you read
- determining the most important ideas and events and seeing how they are related
- drawing conclusions and inferences based on what is read
- deciding "what you think"—Did you like it? Did you agree? Was it funny? Could it really happen?
- comparing and contrasting what you read to what you already know
- figuring out unknown words
- summarizing what has been read

In addition to these "generic" strategies that we use regardless of what we are reading, there are some other strategies that particular texts require. These are too numerous to list but a few examples include:

- understanding figurative language and using it to build clear images
- following the plot of a story and figuring out what happened to whom and why
- determining character traits and deciding why certain characters behave as they do
- extracting information from charts, graphs, maps and other visuals
- determining the objectivity/bias of an author

In planning a guided reading lesson, your major task is to decide which thinking strategies will help students make sense of the text they are reading today and be better—more strategic—readers when they are reading on their own. Most guided reading lessons involve some kind of modeling/demonstrating/explaining/brainstorming before students read with some follow-up after reading. If the text is particularly difficult, the teacher may give additional support both before and during the reading. Remember that the goal of guided reading is to assist readers in developing independent control in selecting and using appropriate strategies when reading. Often, support can be in the form of questions—*"What else could you try?" "Have you reread the sentence?"* or brief reminders to employ strategies—*"Don't forget what we do before we read a new story. Remember that making feature lists of the characteristics of frogs and toads helps organize the information."* or even in the form of simple praise for a strategy implemented appropriately—*"Good! You went back and reread the sentence to see if it made sense."* Across the years, teachers have developed many "formats" for guided reading. In the remainder of this chapter, we will describe some formats that have been particularly successful with struggling readers. These formats are designed to foster thoughtful reading and to create readers who independently employ powerful sets of strategies whenever they read.

KWL

One of the most flexible and popular ways of guiding students' thinking is KWL (Ogle, 1986; Carr and Ogle, 1987). The letters stand for what we *Know*, what we *Want* to find out, and what we have *Learned*. This strategy works especially well with informational text. Imagine that the class is about to read about Washington, D.C. The teacher might begin the lesson by finding Washington, D.C., on a map and asking which students have been there. A chart such as the following would then be started:

Washington, D.C.		
What we know	**What we want to find out**	**What we learned**

The students brainstorm what they know about Washington, D.C., and the teacher writes their responses in the first column. When the children have brainstormed all their prior knowledge, the chart might look like this:

Washington, D.C.		
What we know	**What we want to find out**	**What we learned**
capital White House president lives there lots of drugs azaleas in spring cold in winter near Virginia near Maryland		

Next, the teacher would direct the students' attention to the second column and ask them what they would like to find out about Washington, D.C. Their questions would be listed in the second column:

Washington, D.C.		
What we know	**What we want to find out**	**What we learned**

capital
White House
president lives there
lots of drugs
azaleas in spring
cold in winter
near Virginia
near Maryland
	How old is it?
	How big is the White House?
	What else is in D.C.?
	Where is the FBI?
	What kind of government
	   does D.C. have?
	Why do so many people
	   visit D.C.?
	How many people live there?
	What do the people do who
	   aren't in the government?	

Once the questions are listed, students read in order to see which of their questions were answered and to find other interesting "tidbits" that they think are important.

After reading, the teacher begins by seeing which of the questions were answered and then leads the students to add other interesting facts. This information is recorded in the third column. All members of the class are encouraged to contribute to this group task and no one looks back at the book until all initial responses are shared. Disputed or unclear information is marked with question marks.

When all the initial recalls are recorded, children go back to the text to clarify, prove, or fill in gaps. The teacher encourages the children to read the relevant part aloud and helps them explain their thinking. When the information on the chart is complete and accurate, the teacher points out how much was learned and how efficiently the chart helped to record it. Inevitably, there are questions that were not answered in the reading. A natural follow-up to this lesson is to help the children use additional resources to locate the answers to these questions.

Graphic Organizers

Another popular format for a guided reading lesson involves having the students construct or fill in a graphic organizer. The webs are the most commonly used graphic organizer at the elementary level. They are wonderful ways of helping readers organize information when their reading gives lots of topic/subtopic information. Imagine that your class is going to read an informational selection about birds. Here is a web that you might begin to help them organize the information they will be learning:

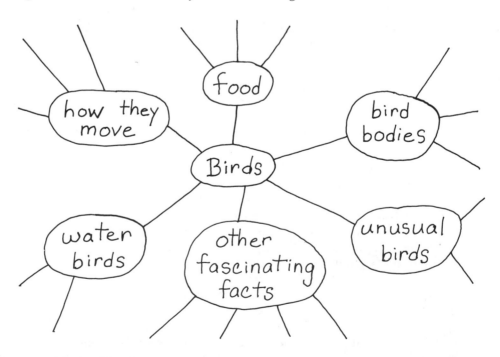

As you set up each spoke of the web, you can discuss with the children what they might expect to find out: "What are some ways you already know that birds move? What do you already know that birds eat? What body parts do birds have? etc." Children then read to find out more about birds. After reading, the children reconvene and complete the web.

Webs can also be used to help children focus on specific aspects of stories they are reading. Imagine that the children are going to read a story about a girl named Amanda and you want them to think about the kind of person Amanda was. You might get them started thinking about character traits by setting up a web such as this:

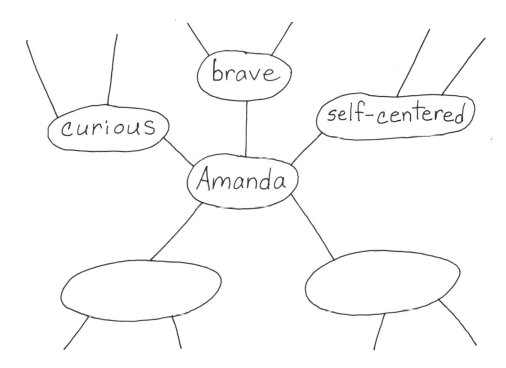

Talk with the children about the meaning of the three adjectives—brave, curious, and self-centered—that you have chosen to describe Amanda, and explain that they will help you add details about Amanda and about things she did in order to support the choice of the adjectives. Then, show the children the blank circles and explain that you want them to add more adjectives describing Amanda. Tell the children that you want each of them to come up with one more adjective that describes Amanda and some specific details to support that adjective.

Webs are an efficient graphic organizer for topic/subtopic information but there are many other ways to show types of relationships. A feature matrix helps children organize information about several members of a category when they are reading. Imagine that the children are reading a selection that compares and contrasts many different types of birds. This information would be better organized in a feature matrix than in a web. Here is what that feature matrix skeleton might look like:

Birds						
	fly	swim	build nests	lay eggs	have feathers	molt
robins						
whippoorwills						
penguins						
ostriches						

Before reading, the teacher and the children talk about the birds listed and about the categories. Children make predictions based on what they know about which birds fly, swim, build nests, etc. The teacher then points out the four blank lines and tells the children that in addition to robins, whippoorwills, penguins, and ostriches, four other birds will be described. The children read in order to decide which features are true of the four birds listed on the matrix and of the four other birds that they will add after reading. Once the children have read the selection, the teacher leads them to fill in a yes/no or a +/- for each feature.

Feature matrices are infinitely adaptable. *Semantic Feature Analysis: Classroom Applications* (Pittelman, Heinlich, Berglund, & French, 1991) is full of wonderful variations. One suggestion from this book that we particularly like includes having kindergartners classify fruit using happy and sad faces, like this:

Fruits (Adapted, p. 40)								
	round	has peel	bumpy peel	orange	red	eat peel	smooth peel	eat seeds
orange	☺	☺	☺	☺	☹			
apple								
banana								

We also like their suggestion that some things do not break down into neat yes/no classifications. They suggest that feature matrices can become much more useful if you consider using an A/S/N (Always/Sometimes/Never) classification scheme.

Data charts are another way of helping children organize information that compares and contrasts members of the same category. Rather than indicate whether or not something has a feature, children fill in particular facts. Here is a data chart used in a science classroom:

Planets in our Solar System			
Name	Size (1 = biggest)	Distance from sun	Earth days in year
Earth	6	92,960,000 mi.	365
Mars			
	1		
		3,660,000,000 mi.	
			60,188

To begin this chart, you might partially fill in the chart for the students, talking as you write about what is needed in each column.

Earth is the sixth largest planet. Its mean distance from the sun is 92,960,000 miles. The year is the number of days it takes a planet to orbit the sun, and the earth year is 365 days.

Now, you point to the second row and have students explain what they will try to put in each column about Mars. For the third row, help them notice that since you put a *1* in the "size" column, this planet has to be the biggest planet. The fourth row must be completed for the planet that is 3,660,000,000 miles from the sun. The planet that takes 60,188 earth days to orbit the sun goes in the fifth row. The remaining four rows are filled in with the remaining four planets.

Webs, feature matrices, and data charts are the most popular graphic organizers used in elementary classrooms, but they are not the only possibilities. Here are two other types of graphic organizers:

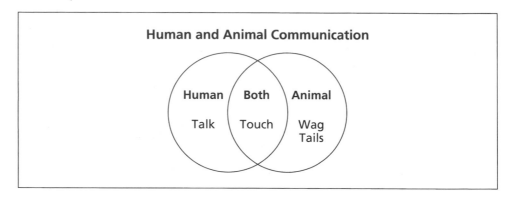

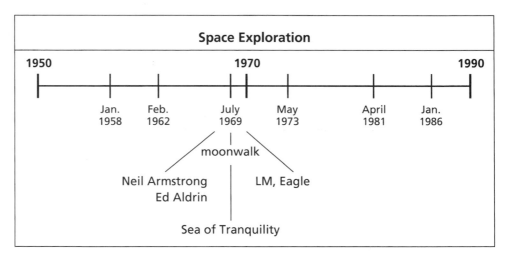

If the relationships depicted by these graphic organizers were obvious to you, it demonstrates how clearly graphic organizers communicate and how well they help students see important relationships in the information they are reading. In the Venn diagram—which we and children like to call a "double bubble," children compare and contrast how animals and humans communicate. The timeline is an excellent device to use when order or sequence is important for instance, in history, historical fiction, and biography. Here, students fill in the important space exploration events that occurred on each date and a few details about each. A variation is to give students a timeline of events and have them fill in the dates.

In one fifth grade classroom that we visited, the teacher had created a permanent timeline that ran across the whole front of the room. The dates on the timeline ranged from 1000 B.C. to 2000 A.D. Several important historical dates were recorded on the timeline at the beginning of the year when the students arrived. Then the era of students' births was marked. Across the year, dates that arose in novels, textbooks, and discussions were placed on the timeline.

Of course, this is just a sampling of graphic organizers and is just to get you thinking about how you can help students see important relationships by considering how you would graphically depict those relationships. When you determine that what you want students to think about as they read is how text is organized, or to show topic/subtopic, compare/contrast, or time/order relationships, a graphic organizer is often the most efficient format for supporting their reading strategy use.

Story Maps

Story maps are a popular and effective device to guide students' thinking when they are about to read a story. There are many different ways of creating story maps, but all help children follow the story by drawing their attention to the elements that all good stories share. Stories have characters and happen in a particular place and time, which we call the setting. In most stories, the characters have some goal they want to achieve or some problem that they need to resolve. The events in the story lead to some kind of solution or resolution. Sometimes, stories have implicit morals or themes from which we hope children will learn.

Here is a story map based on a model created by Isabel Beck (Macon, Bewell & Vogt, 1991).

Story Map
Main Characters:
Setting (Time and Place):
Problem or Goal:
Event 1:
Event 2:
Event 3:
Event 4:
Event 5:
Solution:
Story Theme or Moral:

Here is the story map filled in for *The Three Little Pigs:*

Story Map

Main Characters: Mother Pig, three little pigs, Big Bad Wolf

Setting (Time and Place): Woods, make-believe time and place

Problem or Goal: Pigs wanted to be independent and have own house.

   Event 1: Mother Pig sends three little pigs out to build their own houses.

   Event 2: First little pig gets some straw and builds a straw house. Big Bad Wolf blows the straw house down.

   Event 3: Second little pig gets some sticks and builds a stick house. Big Bad Wolf blows the stick house down.

   Event 4: Third little pig gets some bricks and builds a brick house. Big Bad Wolf cannot blow the brick house down.

   Event 5: Big Bad Wolf runs off into woods (or gets scalded coming down the chimney, depending on how violent the version of the story is).

Solution: Pigs live happily ever after in strong brick house.

Story Theme or Moral: Hard work pays off in the end!

When using story maps to develop a sense of story structure, it is necessary to work through several of them with the children first. For readers who are having trouble comprehending, it is not enough to distribute story maps to have them complete. After reading a story, display the story map on an overhead projector. As you complete the map, think aloud so the thought processes you use are visible to children. Teacher think-alouds provide the expert model many struggling readers need to develop the thinking strategies that underlie good comprehension.

Once children understand the elements and how to fill them in, they can complete story maps in small groups and then independently. It is important to have children read the whole story before completing the map and to help children see that the map is a device that will help them determine and remember important elements in a story.

There are many variations on the basic story map. Teachers create their own variations to suit the age and sophistication of the children they are teaching. For example, this plot relationships chart created by Barbara Schmidt and Marilyn Buckley (Macon, Bewel & Vogt, 1991) might be easier for children to complete than the more encompassing story map.

Plot Relationships Chart			
Somebody	Wanted	But	So

Sample Plot Relationships Chart			
Somebody	Wanted	But	So
The three little pigs	to live in their own houses and be independent	the first and second pigs built straw and stick houses which the wolf blew down	the third pig built a brick house that the wolf couldn't blow down

"The Beach Ball" is not a story map but using this format helps children develop all the important concepts and can lead to the development of written story maps. The beach ball has a question written in black permanent marker on each colored stripe of the ball. The questions are:

- What is the title and author?
- Who are the main characters?
- What is the setting?
- What happened in the story?
- How did it end?
- What was your favorite part?

After reading a story, the teacher and children form a large circle. The teacher begins by tossing the ball to one of the students. The first student to catch the ball can answer any question on the ball. That student then tosses the ball to another student. This student can add to the answer given by the first student or answer another question. The ball continues to be thrown to various students until all the questions have been thoroughly answered. Some questions such as: *What happened in the story?* and *What was your favorite part?* have many different answers. The beach ball is a favorite comprehension follow-up for the children in all the classrooms in which it is used, including intermediate-aged children. In classrooms in which the teacher regularly uses the beach ball to follow-up story reading, children begin to anticipate as they read the answers they will give to the questions on various stripes. These children have developed a clear sense of story structure and their comprehension (and memory!) increases as they organize what they are reading and thinking around those colored beach ball stripes.

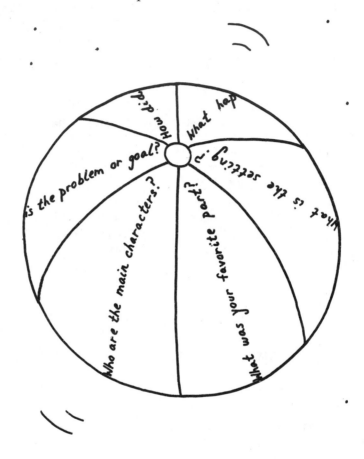

Questioning the Author-QTA

When we read, we don't just "understand what the author is saying," rather, we "figure out what the author means." This might sound like a picky distinction but helping struggling readers put this distinction into practice as they read makes a huge difference in their comprehension. If you have ever taught students who read a passage carefully and then tell you they can't answer the questions because "It didn't say!" you have experienced the reason students need to have their reading guided by a constructivist strategy such as Questioning The Author-QTA. The word "constructivist" is currently in danger of death from overuse, but it is a simple and powerful concept. When we read, we use the author's words to construct meaning. The meaning is more than what the author said. Authors can't tell us everything. They assume we know some things that we will connect to what they are telling us. They assume that we will form some opinions based on what they tell us and what we know. Our initial assertion was that reading—at its heart—was thinking means that reading is a constructive activity. Readers construct meaning by understanding what the author is saying, figuring out what the author means and forming opinions based on the author's meaning and what the reader already knows. This description of QTA is based on an excellent book by Isabel Beck, Margaret McKeown, Rebecca Hamilton, and Linda Kucan (1997), which gives detailed examples of lessons, suggestions for planning and implementing lessons and results of its use in several classrooms. If our brief description intrigues you, we highly recommend you read their practical and clearly written book.

There are several things that distinguish QTAs from other comprehension-fostering formats. The most important differences to us are that the instruction goes on not before students read or after students read but as students are reading, and that the teacher's job is to pose queries that foster meaning construction, not ask questions to assess if that meaning construction took place. To plan a QTA lesson, the teacher carefully reads the text and decides (1) what the important ideas are and what problems students might have figuring out these ideas; (2) how much of the text to read in each segment before stopping for discussion; and (3) what queries to pose that might help students construct meaning from the text. A clear distinction is made between queries—which lead the students to think and construct questions—which usually assess whether or not they have been able to think or construct. The teacher's job in a QTA is to pose the types of queries that will help students use what they know and figure out what the author means. Having decided on important ideas and segmented the texts, teachers plan both initiating and follow-up queries. Here is an adapted example taken from Beck et al. as students are about to read and construct meaning for a social studies passage about how Pennsylvania was formed.

The teacher and students are seated in a circle or horseshoe shape so that they can all see each other. They all have copies of the book open. For this lesson, the teacher has decided that the first segment to be read is just the first sentence. She tells the students to read the first sentence to themselves:

> The shape of the land in North America has changed over millions of years. (p. 51)

And then poses a typical initiating query,

> "What do you think the author is telling us?"

Initially, students may want to respond by just reading the sentence aloud, but the teacher responds by saying,

> "Yes that's what the author says but what is the author trying to tell us?"

The teacher then poses the follow-up query designed to help them connect information learned in previous chapters.

> "What have we already learned about the different kinds of shapes land can have that we need to connect here?"

The second segment contained many sentences and ended the paragraph. (It is important to note that the segment division is not determined by paragraphs but by ideas. Sometimes you want to make sure students are constructing meaning from a single sentence and sometimes you may want them to read several paragraphs. The teacher segments the text so that students stop at points where they need to construct important meanings.) This segment developed the concept of glaciers and the teacher's initiating query after students had read this segment to themselves was:

"What is the author telling us about snow and ice and glaciers?"

The QTA continued with the teacher telling the students how much to read and posing both initiating and follow-up queries until students had worked together to construct meaning for this difficult and complex text.

Children often think that authors are infallible! In doing QTAs with children, teachers point out that authors are not perfect! Sometimes they don't write very clearly. Sometimes they assume we know lots of things that we don't know, and so they don't tell us important facts. Children who engage in regular QTAs learn that when you are reading, you try to figure out what the author means—not just remember what the author says. They are then on the path to constructing meaning and active reading.

Sticky Notes

QTA lessons are powerful because the instruction is given "on line" when the students are actually engaged in the reading. Another way to promote thinking while reading is to encourage readers to take notes, highlight important information, put question marks next to things not understood, and so on. This is what most of us do when we read with pen in hand. In fact, at this moment, you may be reading this book pen in hand, underlining, annotating, etc. But, many students never learn to do what all good readers do because they don't own the book. The book is loaned to them and "no marks in the book" is one of the cardinal rules of public education at all levels!

If you want to promote students' thinking by having them make notes as they read, consider giving them several small sticky notes. Demonstrate how they should use these notes to mark particular places in the text that they want to go back to during the follow-up discussion. Show them how they can write just a word or two or a question mark or explanation point on the note and then place it where that thought, response of confusion occurred in the text. Sometimes, you might focus them on a particular strategy and ask them to look for specific things to mark with sticky notes—reasons why something occurred; examples of figurative language; strong persuasive words, etc. Even when you have given them some purpose for their sticky notes, make sure that they understand that the notes should always be used to mark their own personal responses and confusions. If you have given them specific things to mark, follow-up on that first and then ask,

"Now, what other things did you mark because you thought they were important or interesting or made you think of something in your life or because they
were confusing?"

Some teachers give children two different colors of sticky notes on those days
when they want both strategy-specific and personal responses.

Listening/Reading Transfer Lessons

Listening/Reading Transfer lessons (Cunningham, 1975) were designed specifically to help children learn to do the same kind of thinking while reading as
they do while listening. When reading, readers must simultaneously identify
words and think about meaning. Listening, however, allows listeners to devote
all of their attention to thinking about the meaning of what is being read.

Listening/Reading Transfer lessons (L/RT lessons) can be used to teach
any strategy. They work equally well with story and with informational text.
Imagine, for example, that a story or book you want the children to read is rich
in figurative language. You decide that this is a great opportunity to help children become sensitive to how authors use figurative language in order to make
their stories come alive.

To begin the lesson, you alert the students to the prevalence of figurative
language in everyday speech. You might say something like:

> My son Michael has just turned 17 and his stomach is a *bottomless pit*. He
> comes to every meal as *hungry as a bear* and gobbles down three helpings
> of everything. In spite of all he eats, he stays as *thin as a rail.*
>
> Use a real-world example such as this to help children identify figura-
> tive language and realize that it plays an important role in our daily commu-
> nication with each other.

Next, read a story to the children that is rich in figurative language, stopping when it's appropriate to identify and discuss how vividly it communicates ideas. Picture books often have lots of figurative language and even in
the intermediate grades, children enjoy hearing a wonderful picture book
read aloud.

If the selection you are going to have the children read is a long story or
a chapter book, you could use the first part of the story or the first chapter of
the chapter book for the listening part of your L/RT lesson. This has the added
advantage of getting your children interested in the story or book, getting the
character names pronounced, and getting the setting and problem established.
The first part of a story or book is always difficult until the reader can "get into
it." Reading this first part to the children is a way of making your reluctant
readers less reluctant.

Once you have completed the listening portion, have the children read a
certain portion. Be sure they understand that you want them to do the same
thing while reading that they did while listening. It is critical that you make
this point explicit because many stuggling readers, even in upper grades, believe
that reading is "saying the words." Their lack of comprehension is not because

they are unable to think about what they are reading, but rather because they are not in the habit of thinking while they read. Say something like:

> When you listened to me read, you found many examples of figurative language and you used this language to enjoy and understand more clearly what the author was saying. Expressions such as *scared stiff, stubborn as a mule,* and *lightning fast* helped you form vivid pictures in your mind. When you read to yourself, you find many more expressions that make the words come alive for you. Be on the lookout for these expressions and notice how they help you form clear mental pictures. After you have all read the story, you can point out some examples of figurative language and how that language makes the story come alive. Try to do the exact same kind of thinking and visualizing while you read as you did while you listened.

Once the children have read and you have let them point out examples of figurative language and have let them explain how this helped them enjoy the story, conclude the lesson by once again pointing out that when we read, we do the same kind of thinking as we do when we listen. You might also suggest that they experiment with figurative language in their own writing.

Another L/RT Example

L/RT lessons, like most good lesson formats, have infinite variations on the basic theme. You can use them to teach any important reading strategy. Here is another example:

Strategy: Drawing conclusions.

Real World example: Walk into the classroom one morning and act angry. Slam books around. Give children "piercing looks." Answer questions abruptly. After a few minutes of this unusual behavior, ask children what kind of a mood you appear to be in. Help them understand that you didn't have to tell them how you felt directly. Rather, they concluded that you were not in a good mood based on your actions.

Listening: Read a picture book or the first part of a story or book and stop at appropriate places to ask them what they can conclude or "figure out" that the author has not said. Have them explain what clues they used to draw certain conclusions.

Reading: Have them read and stop at appropriate places. Lead them in a discussion of conclusions they drew and clues they used.

Strategy: Help them become aware that we draw conclusions or figure things out all day in our everyday lives. We also draw conclusions when we listen to someone read and do the same kind of "detective" thinking when we read to ourselves.

L/RT lessons can be combined with a KWL, Graphic Organizer, Story Map, Feature Matrix, QTA or Sticky Notes. To do this, you would plan two parallel lessons using these formats. In the first lesson the children would listen, and in the second they would read. Again, be sure to hammer home your "We do the same kind of thinking while reading and listening" message to ensure the maximum amount of transfer. Remind yourself that your students "think" all the time. Your job is to help them get in the habit of using whatever thinking strategies they have while they read. Using many variations of L/RT lessons will help your students to do this.

Draw It/Act It Out

Understanding what one reads is more than just being able to generate questions, answer questions, or fill out a feature list. While each of these activities is useful and each has a role in fostering students' abilities to understand what they have read, none really gets at the reader's personal response to what was read. Langer (1995) discusses the notion of "getting into" a story, identifying with the characters, losing oneself in the plot and setting, experiencing the moods of the characters, and so on.

Many children who have found learning to read difficult have a hard time "getting into" a book, the characters, and the story line. They read passively, with little personal involvement in the story. This type of reading is often indicated by an adequate literal recall of facts but little ability to engage in hypothesizing about character motives, future action, or having difficulty visualizing characters and settings. To break students out of this response mode, we need to develop visualization and foster involvement.

Visualization is simply the ability to create mental pictures of characters and scenes—adding in all those little details that authors have left unsaid. Engaging students in artwork after reading—creating sketches of characters or settings they have just read about—is one strategy for fostering visualization.

I See What You Mean!

Steve Moline's *I See What You Mean* (Stenhouse, 1995) is an excellent source for all kinds of visual responses to reading. The book is chock-full of practical ways to have students construct graphic organizers such as diagrams, webs, flowcharts, time lines, and graphs, along with lots of student samples.

Having students "Act it Out" is another way of promoting active reading. Unfortunately, some teachers think of having students act or draw as "big productions" and thus, these powerful motivators are denied to the very kids that most need to see reading as "something interesting." There are many ways

Children of all ages enjoy acting. This enjoyment can be transferred to reading when reading and acting out are connected in the classroom.

to have students respond to reading by acting or drawing that require little time and preparation. Here are a few of the many possibilities to get you thinking about ways you can involve your students.

Draw Something

Having children draw, in response to reading, is one sure way to help them visualize or imagine. The best thing to have them draw is something that is not pictured. On some days, you may want them to draw something specific:

- the person who saved the boy
- one of the houses built by one of the pigs
- the beach after the hurricane

Other times you may want to allow their responses to be more personal and ask them to draw:

- the character you think you are most like
- the character you liked most or least
- the most interesting part of the story
- the place you would like to visit
- something you would draw if you were asked to illustrate the story

While it is certainly not true that all children who are poor readers have artistic talent, some do, and many who do not "have artistic ability" like to draw. Incorporating drawing can be one way to guide the children to think about their reading. Drawing is a nice "change of pace"—a way of demonstrating that reading is not a low-level, literal question/answer process. It is a powerful motivator for many struggling readers. Try to schedule time for children to explain their drawings to you or other children.

Do a Play

Children of all ages enjoy being in a play and there are wonderful stories for children already written in play format. Recasting a story as a play can also be a powerful reading/writing activity, especially if the children create the script and stage directions from the original story. Not only do children have to write, they also have to read carefully to transform ideas into action.

Most basal readers have at least one or two plays. Children's magazines, including *My Weekly Reader* and *Sprint* (Scholastic) often contain plays for children to do. *Take Part Starters, Grades 2–3* and *Take Part Plays, Grades 3--6* (Sundance) are play versions of favorite tales and stories, including *The Clever Little Tailor; Robin Hood, Treasure Island,* and many others. Curriculum Associates publishes some plays including fables, fairy tales, and others in the *Primary Reader's Theatre* series.

When having struggling readers do a play, remember that doing repeated readings is a very powerful way to help children develop oral-reading fluency and an understanding of characters. It helps their reading more if they don't memorize lines but, rather, read, and reread their parts until they can read them fluently.

Some teachers don't do plays because there aren't enough parts for everyone or they don't know what to do with the children who are not in the play while the players are preparing. Most children enjoy preparing to do the play and then watching each other do it. If you have a play that requires seven actors and you have 24 children in your class, divide your class into three groups of eight, putting a director and seven actors in each group. Let all three groups prepare and practice the play simultaneously (a true three-ring circus!). Then let each "cast" put on the play for the others.

If you have children do plays, remember that the purpose of this activity is for them to become more active readers, to visualize characters, to do some repeated readings, and for their enjoyment from being in the play to get transferred to reading. "Doing it" is what matters, not how professionally it is done. Props, costumes, and scenery should be nonexistent or very simple. Take a "process attitude"—the play helps develop important reading processes—not a "product attitude" and you will develop a new appreciation for plays.

Some teachers find that letting children make a simple mask to hide behind (using a paper plate and popsicle stick) can help diminish shyness and stage fright. This is especially true for ESL children, who are less self-conscious about their language when they have something to hide behind!

Act Out a Story

Acting out a story is another way to help children think actively and to visualize as they read. The best stories for acting out are the ones that you can visualize as plays. Everyone should have a part, as they did in the plays. Many teachers write down the characters' names along with a number to designate acting cast on little slips of paper:

First Little Pig 1	First Little Pig 2	First Little Pig 3
Second Little Pig 1	Second Little Pig 2	Second Little Pig 3
Third Little Pig 1	Third Little Pig 2	Third Little Pig 3
Mama Pig 1	Mama Pig 2	Mama Pig 3
Wolf 1	Wolf 2	Wolf 3
Man with sticks 1	Man with sticks 2	Man with sticks 3
Man with straw 1	Man with straw 2	Man with straw 3
Man with bricks 1	Man with bricks 2	Man with bricks 3
Director 1	Director 2	Director 3

The teacher then explains to the students that there will be three groups acting out the story and that they will all have parts. She explains what the parts will be and that she will pass out the slips after the story is read to determine what parts they will have. She encourages them to think about what all the characters do and feel because they might end up with any of the parts. After the story is read and discussed, the teacher hands a slip of paper to each child randomly. (This procedure of letting chance determine who gets starring roles and who gets bit parts is readily accepted by the children and easier on the teacher—who won't have to try to decide who should and could do what.

Sometimes, the most unlikely children are cast into starring roles and astonish everyone—including themselves!) The children then form three groups and whoever got the director slip in each group helps them act out the story. The teacher circulates among the groups, giving help and encouragement as needed. After 10–15 minutes of practice, each group performs their act while the other ones watch. Just as they enjoy doing a play, children generally enjoy acting out a story. Teachers who keep their focus on the "process" children go through as they read and act out stories will enjoy this activity and will not worry too much about the product. Acting out stories is designed to turn the children into avid readers—not accomplished actors.

Make a Scene!

While full-blown plays may seem a bit daunting for children and teachers (and take time), there is a variation on this theme that is often easier for children and can be quickly incorporated into many lessons. Rather than acting out a full play, have the children recreate a single scene. Scenes can be done by individuals, pairs, or small groups. They simply require the readers to select a scene, transform it into a script (not necessarily written out), briefly rehearse it, and then present it. No props, no costumes, just reenactment! The scene can be as short as a single exchange between characters, or can even be a single sentence delivered in the appropriate voice. Children who can literally become Richard Best from *The Beast in Ms. Rooney's Room* (Pat Reilly Giff) or the sassy little brother in *Island of the Blue Dolphins* (Scott O'Dell) demonstrate an understanding of the story and the characters.

Overhead Transparencies for Creative Dramatics

Creative Teaching Press publishes *Overhead Transparencies for Creative Dramatics*—a book of transparencies and simple headband patterns that make acting out a story a snap. The colorful transparencies become the scenery. When they are projected from the back of the room, children can actually move in front of them. The headbands are their "costumes" and help lend reality to the acting. They produce these books of transparencies and headbands for most of the classic fairy tales and for tall tales, myths, and fables as well.

The "Oprah Winfrey" Strategy

This is another technique that fosters involvement. To use it, several children must be reading the same book. You play the role of Oprah (initially) and interview them about their lives and roles. For instance, after reading *Anastasia at Your Service* (Lois Lowry), assign students the roles of Anastasia, Mrs. Bellingham, and her granddaughter—Daphne (we could also add Mr. and Mrs. Krupnik, Sam, and perhaps the surgeon or the maid). Now, just like Oprah, invite the students to appear on your "show." Arrange chairs alongside your desk, facing the rest of the class. Seat the "guests," with Anastasia next to your desk, and welcome them.

Begin with broad questions—"Tell me a bit about yourself, Anastasia." "What seemed to be the problem?" Then move to other characters for verification—"Do you agree with her, Daphne?" "What else would you add, Mrs. Bellingham?" You might even turn to the audience for questions, especially if some members have not read the book. Basically, like Oprah, you let your guests tell their stories. Ideally, readers transform themselves into the characters, taking on mannerisms and speech patterns that seem appropriate. You may want to model this transformation yourself by letting a student take Oprah's role while you become Mrs. Bellingham or another character. This activity can be brief (3–5 minutes is all most guests get on talk shows!) and takes little time to set-up after the initial exposure. The activity provokes thought about the characters and their motives, attitudes, and personalities. In short, it is a wonderfully innovative way to foster thinking and involvement while reading.

GUIDED READING FOR BEGINNING READERS

When children are just beginning to read, they need to read some books and stories at just the right level and have a teacher there to support them as they problem solve what to do about unfamiliar words and concepts. To do a guided reading lesson for beginners, it is important to choose a book or story that will be at just the right level for most of the children. The teacher calls the group of four to six children together and guides them to apply their reading strategies as they read a book. The kinds of strategies taught during a small group guided reading lesson are the same ones taught working with the whole class but because there are fewer children, the teacher can monitor how well they are applying the strategies and coach them to use what they know at the right time. Here is a description of what a small-group guided reading lesson might look like for beginning readers of any age.

The teacher gathers the group—which changes from day to day—together and introduces the book or story the children will read that day. The teacher reads the title and author and gives a brief description of what the book is about. Together, the teacher and children take a "picture walk" looking at all the pictures. The teacher helps the children use the pictures to build important concepts by asking questions such as:

"Do you know what this (pointing to ax) is called?
"What does it look like he is doing here?"
"What holiday does it look like they are celebrating?"

Based on the responses of the children, the teacher confirms their responses and/or suggests words and phrases.

"We can call it a hatchet. We can also call it an ax. Have you ever heard someone say they cut the wood with an ax?"
"Yes, it looks like he is fixing a flat tire. He uses the jack to hold the car up."
"Yes, they are having Thanksgiving dinner."

Sometimes, once the targeted word has been used by the children or suggested by the teacher, the teacher leads the children to look at the print on the page and see if they can find a word that would be especially difficult for them to decode on their own.

> "Let's say *Thanksgiving* together. Will the word *Thanksgiving* be a little, short word or a big long word? Yes, *Thanksgiving* will probably be a long word. What two letters do you think *Thanksgiving* might begin with? Say *Thanksgiving* again. What three letters do you expect to see at the end of *Thanksgiving*? Now, look at the print and see if you can put your finger on a word that might be *Thanksgiving*."

The introduction should be brief but should help students use the pictures to anticipate what they will be reading about, plant some new words, and help them locate any words that might prove impossible for most to figure out when they encounter them while reading.

Once the introduction is completed, the teacher asks the students to read the book or story to themselves. The children read silently or in whisper voices—whichever way they can and as the children read the teacher "listens in," noticing how children solve the reading problems that occur and occasionally intervening to coach an individual child. The teacher does not tell children words but gives them support such as:

> "Read that sentence again. Did that sound right to you? Look at this word you called *play*. What other word that begins with *p-l* would make more sense in that sentence?"
>
> "You said, 'He grabbed the purse.' That made sense but what letters would you expect *grabbed* to begin with. Right, *grabbed* would begin with *g-r* and the word begins with *s-n*. Can you think of a word that means grabbed but begins with *s-n*?"

When the children have completed reading the selection on their own with individual coaching by the teacher as needed, the group will talk about the book—what happened, what was funny, what they liked, etc. Particular parts of the book that were troublesome for several children may be revisited. If time permits, parts of the book may be read aloud either by individual children or together by the whole group.

Guided Reading

The clearest and most thorough description of how to carry out guided reading lessons with small groups of beginning readers is contained in *Guided Reading: Good first teaching for all children* by Irene Fountais and Gay Su Pinnell (1996). Anyone teaching beginning readers will want to read and reread this excellent source. In addition to teaching strategies, *Guided Reading* contains a list of hundreds of popular tradebooks with estimated difficulty levels.

ORGANIZING FOR GUIDED READING

The varying reading levels found in every classroom are the reason that guided reading with basal readers has traditionally been carried out with three groups of children grouped by reading achievement. Teachers put children in reading groups because they recognize that not all children read at grade level. Achievement groups have been the most common way to meet the inevitable individual differences. Unfortunately, achievement grouping for reading creates as many problems as it solves. Research suggests (Juel, 1988) that the children who are put in the bottom group in first grade usually remain in that group throughout elementary school and almost never "catch up" to grade level. As bottom-group children move up through the grade levels, they become increasingly "resistant" to reading instruction. They become less and less "involved" in reading and are likely to move through assigned material with little reaction or response. Everyone—the teacher, the parents, the children in other groups, and the bottom-group children themselves—view the bottom-group children as "children who can't read well." This perception seems to become a self-fulfilling prophecy.

The self-fulfilling nature of the reading group assignment is reinforced by the decision to slow the pace of curriculum coverage for the bottom groups and increase the pace of coverage for the top groups (Allington, 1991). In the traditional three-group first grade classroom teachers may, for instance, decide that the top group will complete the first grade readers (preprimers, primer, and first reader) and move into the second grade reader before the end of the school year. The middle group is paced so that they finish (or nearly finish) the first grade readers. The bottom group, however, is paced to complete only the preprimers and the primer and to begin the first reader in second grade.

The net result of this pacing is that top readers learn more about reading and have the opportunity to engage in substantially larger amounts of guided reading activity. Those in the bottom group simply learn less and read less. Stanovich (1986) has labeled this the "Matthew Effect" (a Biblical reference) whereby the rich get richer and the poor get poorer as a direct result of the planning and instructional decisions made by the teacher.

Even if there was some way to convince the bottom-group children that they were becoming good readers, even though they were progressing more slowly (and there does not seem to be!), there is another major problem with achievement grouping. When there are three groups in the classroom, the teacher must teach reading three times to three different groups. While the teacher is teaching one group, the others must be kept busy with some quiet occupation so as not to distract the teacher and the group she is working with. In traditional classrooms, children have often spent two-thirds of their reading time completing some kind of seatwork. There is little evidence that their reading/writing abilities are increased by doing the worksheet-type activities that pervade most classrooms. In fact, research (McGill-Franzen & Allington, 1991) suggests that if children spend too much time working on seatwork activities, their achievement actually suffers. Seatwork activities are particularly ineffective for struggling readers because they need larger amounts of real reading and writing, as well as more instruction and interaction with teachers and peers.

Putting the children into fixed groups for reading is a logical attempt to solve the very real problem of differing reading/writing proficiencies of the children. The poor self-concept of the bottom-group children and the wasted time spent in seatwork activities, however, mitigate against this attempted solution ever working in reality. No matter how good our instruction, some children are going to read more widely and more proficiently than other children; nevertheless, we cannot continue to organize our classrooms in ways that exaggerate these differences. Here are some ways teachers organize their reading instruction to provide for childrens' varying levels without putting them in fixed groups.

Vary Materials Used for Guided Reading

What to have your children read for the lessons in which you are guiding the development of their reading/thinking strategies is a complex and important issue. Basal readers have traditionally served this function and they are a convenient source for multiple copies of varied literature. In addition, basal manuals usually have teaching suggestions that help you determine which strategies you might focus on and that give you some guidance about how to teach these strategies. There are, however, some serious problems with using one basal reader for all of your guided reading lessons.

The first problem with basals is that their selections are generally chosen to be readable by average readers at a specific grade level. If you use one basal all the time for your children, your brightest children are never going to be challenged to read something that "they have to work at." A bigger problem is that the children on whom this book is focused—struggling readers—are typically not able to read as well as the other children in your room. Too often they find themselves facing material that is simply too hard for them to read. Even with teacher assistance, the readers still struggle. All children benefit from large amounts of easy reading coupled with opportunities to read more difficult material. A steady diet of difficult material is discouraging and can slow development of the reading proficiency.

One way that many teachers solve the "One size does not fit all" problem is to divide the time each week for guided reading between grade level and easier selections. Imagine that you are going to spend 30–40 minutes each day in some kind of guided reading format. Choose your selections so that on two or three days, the class is reading something on grade level and on the other two or three days, the class is reading something much easier. On the days when you are reading in the grade level selections, support your struggling readers by having the class partner read the selection. Ideally, your struggling readers would be assigned to better readers who are also friends of theirs.

The notion of alternating between easier and harder reading is readily accomplished in most classrooms and can be done with a wide variety of reading materials. One first grade teacher has reading partners **read** from the grade-level basal on Monday, Tuesday, and Wednesday, and **read** from easier levels of an old basal series every Thursday and Friday. In addition to basals, children can read from class magazines, such as the grade-level magazines, *My Weekly Reader* and (the easier) *Sprint Magazine,* or can alternate between tradebooks and basal reader selections, or between more and less difficult tradebook selections.

To make this approach work, you must find reading material that is of interest to the children in your grade but is easier to read. Fortunately, we do have a good variety of high-low material available for schools today. These easier materials provide struggling readers with reading experiences that are at their instructional level.

Use a Variety of Partner Reading Formats

Children accept that some of their friends are better ball players and better artists. In real life, friends often help each other and learn from each other. Partner reading allows friends to help each other read just as they help each other with numerous other activities.

For partner reading to be effective, children need to learn a variety of ways to do it. On some days that are designated as "take turn" days, the partners take turns reading the pages, and helping each other as needed. On other days that are designated as "ask question" days, the partners read each page silently and then ask one another a question about each page before going on to the next page. On sticky note days, the partners are given sticky notes to mark things they want to remember. They have a limited number of sticky notes and must decide together where to put the notes to mark what they find most interesting, important, or confusing. Occasionally, the teacher declares a "you decide" day in which the partners can decide to read together in any way they wish. Having these different kinds of partner-reading formats over the course of the week provides some variety in the reading. It also ensures that children engage in both silent and oral reading.

Meet with Small "Coaching" Groups While Others Read the Selection Individually or with Partners

On some days, you may want certain children to read the selection on their own, while others read it with partners, and you meet with small "coaching" groups and guide their reading. This "three-ring circus" is not as difficult to achieve as you might suspect. First, explain to your students that there are advantages to all three types of reading. When they are reading by themselves, they can read at their own pace and focus on just their own ideas. When they are partner reading, they have the advantage of getting help when they need it and they have someone to share ideas with. Explain that you, the teacher, like to read with a small group so that you can see how they are progressing and help them apply the strategies they are learning. Second, make sure children know how to read with their partners and what kind of partner format you want them to use on this particular day. Finally, you need some kind of an organizational chart so that children can see quickly how they will read the selection that day and not waste time waiting for you to get everyone in the right place. Here is a Three-Ring Circus chart one teacher uses to let students know how they will be reading. On days when the teacher wants to have a three-ring circus organization, she places cards with the children's names in the appropriate ring.

Three-Ring-Circus

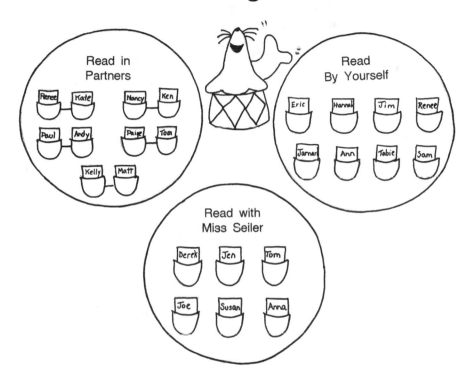

Use "Choose Your Book" Groups

For some guided reading/thinking lessons, you will want all the children to read the same text so that you can guide their thinking before they read and can follow-up after they read. There are instances, however, when you can set things up with the whole class and let the children choose to read from three or more books or stories.

In one fifth grade classroom, for example, drawing conclusions was the thinking strategy that the teacher wanted the children to focus on. She found three mysteries that she thought the children would enjoy and that (being mysteries) would lead the reader to try to "figure things out." She gathered the class together to talk about the mysteries that they had read and watched on TV. She then read the first chapter of each of the three mysteries to them, had them decide what the mystery was, and had them list some of the clues that they heard in the first chapter.

She explained that they didn't have enough books or enough time for everyone to read all three mysteries, but that she wanted approximately a third of the class to read each mystery. Each day they would read a chapter in their mystery by themselves or with a partner and would then get together with the group that had read the same mystery to summarize the clues and their discoveries. The children then wrote down their first and second choice of mystery books and the teacher assigned them to a mystery, making sure that everyone got their first or second choice and also trying, when possible, to assign the best readers to the hardest mystery and the poorest readers to the easiest mystery.

In a short time, all of the mysteries were solved. The children enjoyed all three stories—not just the one they had read. Many children then chose the mysteries they had not read and read them during self-selected reading time, in spite of the fact that they knew "who done it"! Even some of the struggling readers chose to read the harder mysteries and (with their increased knowledge of mystery story structure and their prior knowledge and vocabulary gained from listening to the daily mystery summaries) were able to read them successfully.

Importance of Readable Text

Having children read something in which they can recognize almost all of the words is critical to their reading development. Experts agree that the child must be able to successfully and independently read at least 95 percent of the words in a story and have good comprehension. If these percentages seem high to you, apply it to your own reading. Most books that adults read have about 400 words on a page. If you only know 90 percent of the words, you would have to stop and try to figure out 40 words. Even if you knew 95 percent of the words, you would still have to stop and think about 20 words on every page. When you think about this, it makes sense that children need lots of easy reading and repeated readings in order to become good and avid readers.

Letting children choose from among three similar books or stories is an excellent motivator for reading. Most people like to make choices, and children will often choose to read what they didn't get to read after they hear about it from the other groups. The problem, of course, has been in finding multiple copies of three similar books or stories. With good books becoming more available in classroom libraries, this problem is becoming less serious in some schools. Resourceful teachers are also looking through old basal readers for similar types of stories on different reading levels—stories about the old west, tall tales, biographies, etc., and are making **skinny books** to make "Choose Your Book Groups" a more frequent possibility.

ALTERNATIVES TO ROUND-ROBIN READING

Round-robin reading is the practice of having every student sit with a book opened to the same page while one student after another reads aloud. The inefficiency and boring nature of round-robin reading is one thing everyone agrees on and yet the practice persists. We think it persists because it is what most of us remember from our childhood and we can't quickly call up alternatives. So, here are some alternatives. If you find yourself slipping into round-robin reading because you can't think of an alternative quickly, post this somewhere until these become as automatic to you as round-robin reading:

Everyone Read to . . . —ERT . . .
This is the simplest alternative and should be used regularly. The teacher tells students how much to read. They read that segment and then the teacher follows-up on whatever purpose was set by asking: "What is the author telling us?" or "What new things did you learn?" or "What seems to be the problem in this story?" or "What did you find out was making the sky so dark?" Children tell in their own words what they read and then everyone goes on to the next segment. For older children, Everyone Read to . . . is usually silent reading. Because children must develop some reading fluency before they can "read it in their minds," this ERT . . . time is often not silent but, rather, what we call "whisper" reading. In ERT . . . everyone is reading the text for themselves in whatever way is appropriate in order to find out specific things they will then share with everyone.

Sticky Note Reading
This is like ERT . . . but children have sticky notes to mark what they find interesting, important, or confusing. Everyone is reading each selection in whatever way they can and are returning to various places in the text where someone wants to point out something they have noticed.

Choral Reading
Choral reading works best for poetry and refrains. The whole class can read or you can vary it by alternating the girls and boys or alternating by rows or tables. Children enjoy choral reading and it does give them fluency practice.

Echo Reading
In echo reading, the teacher reads first and then children become the echo and read it back. As they echo read, they try to match the teacher's emphasis and fluency.

Partner Reading
Partner reading has already been described. Remember to vary the format used and think about who would like to work with whom.

Summary

Some children find learning to read and write difficult. These children often fail to "discover" effective reading strategies. The struggling readers we focus on in this book are children who, most likely, need access to substantial amounts of high-quality teaching. These are the children that, too often in the past, have learned to call words but who have never really learned to read or write. Although they would sometimes become "functionally literate," they would never become readers and would never develop any of the sophisticated reading strategies—especially the ones linked to thinking. In this chapter, we have tried to offer a framework for planning instruction that will develop more thoughtful readers—children who monitor their own reading for sense and who respond to characters, plots, problems, and information. Supporting these children as they learn to read means more than just making time and material available. Guided-reading lessons provide children with the assistance they need today in order to develop the proficiency to have a go at it alone tomorrow.

References

Allington, R. L. (1991). Effective literacy instruction for at-risk children. In M. Knapp & P. Shields (Eds.) *Better schooling for the children of poverty: Alternatives to conventional wisdom,* (pp. 9–30). Berkeley, CA: McCutcheon.

Beck, I. L., McKeown, M. G., Hamilton, R. L., & Kucan, L. (1997). *Questioning the author: An approach for enhancing student engagement with text.* Newark, DE: International Reading Association.

Carr, E., & Ogle, D. (1987). KWL plus: A strategy for comprehension and summarization. *Journal of Reading, 30,* 626–631.

Cunningham, P. M. (1975). Transferring comprehension from listening to reading. *The Reading Teacher, 29,* 169–172.

Dole, Duffy, Roehler, & Pearson, (1991). Moving from the old to the new: Research on reading comprehension instruction. *Review of Educational Research, 61,* 239–264.

Fountais, I. C., & Pinnell, G. S. (1996). *Guided reading: Good first teaching for all children.* Portsmouth, NH: Heinemann.

Johnston, P., & Allington, R. L. (1991). Remediation. In Barr, R., Kamil, M., Mosenthal, P., & Pearson, P. D. (Eds.) *Handbook of Reading Research, vol. 2* (pp. 418–452). New York: Longman.

Juel, C. (1988). Learning to read and write: A longitudinal study of 54 children from first through fourth grade. *Journal of Educational Psychology, 80,* 437–447.

Langer, J. A. (1995). *Envisioning literature: Literacy understanding and literature instruction.* New York: Teachers College Press.

Macon, J. M., Bewell, D., & Vogt, M. (1991). *Responses to literature.* Newark, DE: International Reading Association.

McGill-Franzen, A. M., & Allington, R. L. (1991). The gridlock of low-achievement: Perspectives on policy and practice. *Remedial and Special Education, 12,* 20–30.

Moline, S. (1996). *I see what you mean: Children at work with visual information.* York, ME: Stenhouse.

Ogle, D. (1986). K-W-L: A teaching model that develops active reading of expository text. *The Reading Teacher, 39,* 564–570.

Pearson, P. D., & Fielding, L. (1991). Comprehension instruction. In Barr, R., Kamil, M., Mosenthal, P., & Pearson, P. D., (Eds.) *Handbook of Reading Research, vol. 2* (pp. 815–860). New York: Longman.

Pittleman, S. D., Heimlich, J. E., Berglund, R., & French, M. P. (1991). *Semantic feature analysis: Classroom applications.* Newark, DE: International Reading Association.

Stanovich, K. E. (1991). Word recognition: Changing perspectives. In Barr, R., Kamil, M., Mosenthal, P., & Pearson, P. D. (Eds.) *Handbook of Reading Research, vol. 2* (pp. 418–452). New York: Longman.

Stanovich, K. E. (1986). Matthew effects in reading: Some consequences of individual differences in the acquisition of literacy. *Reading Research Quarterly, 21,* 360–407.

4
GUIDING CHILDREN'S
WRITING/THINKING

I magine coming upon someone sitting, pen in hand, or with fingertips poised over a keyboard staring at a blank page or blank screen and you ask, "What are you doing?" The person will often respond, "I'm *thinking!*" Continue to observe and you will see the person move into the writing phase eventually, but this writing is not continuous. There are constant pauses; if you are rude enough to interrupt during one of these pauses to ask, "What are you doing?" the writer will probably respond again, "I'm *thinking!!!*"

Eventually, the writer finishes the writing, or rather, the first draft of the writing. The writer may put the writing away for awhile or may ask someone to, "Take a look at this and tell me what you think." Later, the writer will return to the writing to revise and edit it. Words will be changed and paragraphs will be added, moved, or deleted. Again, the writer will pause from time to time during this after-writing phase; if you ask what the writer is doing during this phase, you will get the familiar response, "I'M THINKING!"

We offer this common scenario as proof that the essence of writing is thinking and that even the most naïve writer knows this basic truth. Because writing is thinking and because learning requires thinking, students who write as they are learning will think more and, thus, will learn more.

In addition to the fact that writing is thinking, writing is hard! It is complex. There are many things to think about at the same time. There are such big issues as:

- What do I want to say?
- How can I say it so that people will believe it?
- How can I say it so that people will want to read it?

In addition to these big issues, there are a host of smaller, but still important issues.

- How can I begin my writing in a way that sets up my ideas and grabs the reader's attention?
- Which words best communicate these feelings and thoughts?
- What examples can I use?

- Do I need to clarify here or include more detailed information?
- How can I end it?
- Now, I have to think of a good title!

As if these grand and not-so-grand issues aren't enough, there are also a number of small details to worry about. Sometimes, these are taken care of during the after-writing phase, but often writers will think about them as they write. Some examples include:

- I wonder if this sentence should begin a new paragraph?
- Do I capitalize the word *state* when it refers to North Carolina?
- How do you spell *Beijing?*
- Does the comma go inside or outside the quotation marks?

We have not included this discouraging sampling of the "balls" that writers have to keep in the air as they perform the difficult "juggling" act of writing in order to discourage you. We included them to convince you that students need instruction, guidance, support, encouragement, and acceptance if they are going to be willing and able participants in writing. Unfortunately, writing instruction in schools often has focused primarily on the editing skills of penmanship, spelling, mechanics, and grammar. Schools used language books, handwriting books, and spelling books as the base for the writing curriculum. In these schools, children rarely had the opportunity to think, compose, or write. Instead, they spent most of their time concentrating on the skills.

Recently, many schools have moved away from commercial programs and have set out to create their own writing curriculum in which the emphasis is on writing. In addition, most recently published basal reader programs have added writing components. In most schools, children write more now than they did a few years ago, but there are still concerns about whether writing is actually being taught—especially thoughtful writing. There are also concerns about whether the writing that children are doing is broad and is representative of the various types of writing that are necessary in school and outside of school. Do children spend substantially more time composing stories than they do reports? Do schools actually teach how to search out, gather, and organize information for reports? Are children learning how to revise? Are children learning to spell?

In this chapter, we cannot provide full answers to all of these questions, but we present a broad view of writing and a clear view of how to develop struggling readers' writing ability. Children struggling to become literate are the very children who need the most opportunities to write and who need the best writing instruction across the elementary grades. This chapter is focused on these children.

In Chapter 2, we emphasized the importance of daily self-selected writing. The opportunity to write daily is especially critical for children who come from homes where they have few opportunities to see adults write or to actually write themselves. Writing every day helps develop thoughtful readers as well as thoughtful writers. The single most important thing you can do to help students become better writers is to provide them with time to write, materials with which to write, and to demonstrate the process and the importance of writing to them. Once the children are writing on a regular basis, there are specific instructional activities you can use to develop their writing abilities. This chapter will describe five effective ways to guide children's writing and thinking.

SHARED AND GROUP WRITING

In the last chapter, we described shared reading as a process in which the teacher and the children read together. Shared writing is a process in which the teacher and children write together. Generally, the teacher leads the children to share ideas and then records the ideas as the children watch. Shared writing—like individual writing—can be used to write a wide variety of things. Regie Routman (1991), in her wonderfully practical, readable book, *Invitations,* includes this list of some of the possibilities (p. 60):

- wall stories and big books
- stories, essays, and poems
- original story endings
- retellings of stories
- class journal entries
- class observations of pets, plants, and science experiments
- shared experiences such as field trips and special visitors
- class rules and charts
- weekly newsletter to parents
- news of the day
- curriculum-related writing
- reports
- informational books
- evaluations of books and activities

Language Experience Approach

Shared writing is similar to language experience in that the teacher writes as the children watch, but it has one important feature that is different. One of the cardinal principles of language experience has always been that the teacher should write down exactly what the child said. R. V. Allen and Allen (1966), Stauffer (1980), and others, who promoted language experience as an approach to beginning reading and writing, argued that children must learn that the things they say can be written down and then read back. This important learning could only occur if the child's exact words were recorded. The problem for teachers arises when a child's spoken dialect differs from standard written English. Teachers find it difficult to record sentences such as:

- I ain't got no sisters.
- I done broke my foot.

Most teachers, when working with individual children, however, will write down the sentences just as they are spoken because they realize that the child will read the sentence the way it was spoken. If the sentence,

I ain't got no sisters.

is changed to the standard,

I don't have any sisters.

then the child, remembering what was said, will read the word *don't* as "ain't," the word *have* as "got," and the word *any* as "no." Likewise, if the child's spoken sentence,

I done broke my foot.

is changed to the standard,

I broke my foot,

then the child, remembering what was said, will say the word *done* while looking at "broke," the word *broke* while looking at "my," the word *my* while looking at "foot," and will run out of written words before finishing the spoken sentence. If language experience is being used with an individual child to help that child understand what reading and writing are and to show that the child can write and read what he or she can say, then the child's exact words must be written down. To do anything else will hopelessly confuse the child about the very things you are trying to clarify by using individual language experience.

Shared Writing

The situation changes, however, when you are working with a class or a small group of children. The group invariably includes children who use a variety of different language structures. Recording sentences when you are working with children whose language usage varies can lead to confusion, and sometimes ridicule from the children whose spoken language is closer to standard written English. In addition, the charts, letters, books, etc. that you create during shared writing are apt to be displayed in the classroom and/or sent home to parents. It is difficult to explain to parents why nonstandard usage should be written down; there have even been examples of teachers being accused of "not knowing how to write good English."

Shared writing differs from language experience because the teacher and the children all "share" the construction of the writing. In creating a daily entry for the class journal, the teacher asks the children what important things they think should be included. She listens to all suggestions and accepts whatever kind of spoken dialect children use. After listening to the suggestions she records them, using standard written English and imposing some kind of order and cohesion. She then reads aloud the sentences she has written. Because the teacher listens to the suggestions of many children and then records the "gist" but not the "exact words" of any child, the problem of recording and reading nonstandard usage does not occur.

Likewise, shared writing provides the opportunity to rework awkward constructions that students may offer. Most teachers would not write down verbatim sentences such as:

- We was going there then but then we didn't until the next day.
- Well, a lizard is one of those, ah, reptile things, I think.

By reworking these sentences collaboratively aloud with students, the teacher models the shift from oral to written language and the editing process that all writers must learn.

Both shared writing and individual language experience are valuable tools to use with children whose reading and writing experiences have been limited at home and at school. In individually-dictated language experience situations, children's exact words should be written down. To do otherwise is to defeat the purpose of individual language experience. When working with a group to create something for public consumption, however, shared writing in which all the children share ideas and the teacher writes a composite seems to be the best alternative.

Group Writing

A natural offshoot of shared writing is group writing. Group writing works especially well with descriptive and other informational writing genres. Children, who have been regularly engaged in coming up with ideas and helping the teacher create a readable, cohesive piece that represents all of their ideas, know how people can work together to share writing. When you want students to write communally, there are a variety of ways to organize.

The easiest way to have children work together is to give them some kind of writing task occasionally and tell them that since "two heads are better than one," they can work with a friend. Let the friends negotiate whether one person will write the first draft or whether they will take turns. Usually, one child will write and share what has been written while the other creates, listens, and offers editorial comment. Encourage the partners to brainstorm ideas first and then to talk about the best way to put these ideas in writing. Normally, if the children get to choose a friend to write with, they have little difficulty deciding who will do what.

You might also assign students to work together in groups of three in which one person records the ideas of the entire group. This communal writing seems to work best if everyone contributes ideas that are jotted down by one or more students, and then another student produces a first draft and reads it to the group. All group members can then suggest ways to make the writing better or more clear. Finally, the third member of the group could complete the editing and could revise the first draft into a final draft form.

For a lengthy piece, students might divide up the sections. They would first plan which parts each person would write and set some guidelines about the content and the writing style. Each person would then write his or her part and everyone in the group would respond to it. The group would work together to produce a draft that they all contributed to.

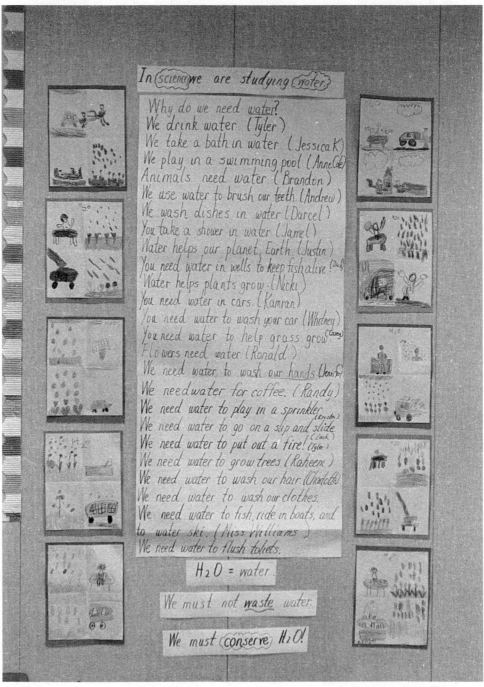

Here is a shared writing chart that was created in one primary classroom as the children studied about water.

WRITER'S WORKSHOP

Writer's Workshop (Graves, 1995; Calkins, 1994) is the term most commonly used to describe the process of children choosing their own topics, writing, revising, editing, and publishing. In Writer's Workshop, we try to simulate as closely as possible an atmosphere where real writers write and to help children see themselves as "real authors."

Writer's Workshop usually begins with a minilesson during which the teacher writes. Next, the children write. As the children write, the teacher helps children who have chosen a piece to revise and edit. Writer's Workshop usually concludes with an Author's Chair in which children read their writing and get responses from the other "writers" in the room. Here is an example of how one teacher conducts her Writer's Workshop.

The Minilesson in Which the Teacher Writes and Edits

Writer's Workshop in this classroom begins in the same manner every day. The teacher sits down next to the overhead and the children gather on the floor around her. They are eager to see "what she will write about today!" The teacher holds her overhead pen and thinks aloud.

"There are a lot of ideas in my mind this Monday morning that I could write about. I could write about how cold it was at our house when the power went off and how it stayed off almost all day on Saturday." (Some children nod and look like they want to tell about similar situations at their houses over the weekend. Other children look puzzled. You can tell by looking at them that they had no electrical problems that weekend and are curious about what happened.)

"I could write about the visitor we are going to have this afternoon and the animals he will probably bring with him." (The children appear delighted at the prospect of someone coming who might bring animals. "What kind of animals?" they wonder.)

"I could write about the book I finished last night. I could write about the accident that I saw on the way to school this morning. I could write about running into Jamie at the grocery store on Friday afternoon and seeing her baby brother. So many things have happened since we left here on Friday afternoon that I could write about and share with you. It is so hard to decide!"

After sitting there in a "thinking posture" for a few more seconds, the teacher decides and begins to write. She puts her name in the left-hand corner of the paper and then writes the title in the center of the first line:

A Saturday Without Electristee

As she writes *electristee,* she says the word slowly, stretching out the sounds so they can tell that she is trying to figure out how to spell it. The teacher continues writing. From time to time, she stops as if to think what to say next. She invent-spells some words and looks up at the classroom word wall to find out how to spell others. She leaves out some punctuation marks, an important word or two, and some capital letters. The children watch her very carefully and you can tell from their shaking heads and pointing fingers that they notice many things that will need "fixing." When the teacher finishes writing, she says, "Now, when I finish writing, I always reread my writing to see if I said what I wanted to say." She then reads the paragraph aloud, filling in one word she left out and changing a few capitals, but otherwise not finding several things that need fixing.

Next, the teacher reminds the children that this is a good "draft"—not perfect but good. She can read it and it makes sense. "If I wasn't going to publish this, it would be just fine the way it is. If I wanted to read it when it was my turn in the Author's Chair, I would be able to read it to you. But, what do I need to do if I decide to make this into a book or decide to put it on our writer's board or in our class newspaper?"

The children respond in chorus, "Choose a friend to help you edit it." "That's right, and I choose Ramona," the teacher responds as she hands Ramona a different color marker. Ramona proudly takes her place at the overhead projector. The teacher then points to a chart in the room and leads Ramona and the class to read each item that needs to be checked.

Editing checklist and date each item was added to list:

1. Name and date (9/3)
2. Title in center (9/17)
3. Sentences make sense (9/24)
4. Possible misspelled words (10/17)
5. Ending puncuation.?! (11/25)
6. Capitals in right places (1/14)
7. Stays on topic (2/14)

Ramona, with help from the class, pretends to be the friend and edits the piece. She looks for the name and date; she does not find the date, so she writes it in. She then writes a *1* on the bottom of the page to show that she checked for number 1.

The class agrees that there is a title and that it is in the center and so Ramona writes a *2* beside the *1*.

Ramona then reads all the sentences and finds that two of them don't make sense because there is a word missing. The teacher states what words she meant to include and Ramona draws a ^ and inserts them. She then writes a *3* to show that she checked for number 3.

Children who want Ramona to circle some words that "need checking" raise their hands. (This includes one word that is spelled correctly, which is fine since the editing friend is only supposed to help you find the ones you need to ask someone about or need to check in the dictionary if you can.) When the potentially misspelled words are circled, Ramona writes a *4* at the bottom.

The sentences are read again and a period is put at the end of one of them. Ramona and the class decide to change another period to an exclamation point. Ramona writes a *5* at the bottom.

Next, the class makes suggestions about a word that needs a capital letter. Ramona changes this and writes a *6* at the bottom.

Finally, Ramona asks what the topic was and if everyone thinks that the teacher's writing stayed on this topic. They agree that all of the sentences were about not having electricity on Saturday and Ramona writes a *7* at the bottom.

The teacher thanks Ramona and the class for all of their help and tells them that they have made her piece much easier for other people to read. She then reminds the children of the steps she went through in writing the piece.

First, she had to decide about what to write and then she had to think about what to say. She wrote the first draft as best she could, used the word wall when needed and "figured out" how some words might be spelled. When she had finished the piece, she reread it to see if it made sense and made a few more changes.

The teacher then reminded the children that they didn't need to choose a friend to help them edit every piece. The children knew that editors—friends and teachers—were needed when a piece was going to be made into a book or published in the class newspaper. If they were going to publish a piece, they should choose a friend who would read the piece for the seven things they had learned so far.

The teacher drew their attention to the dates next to each item on their editing checklist and asked if they remembered what these dates meant. The children responded that the date was the first day that they had added this item to the checklist. The children were clearly proud that at the beginning of October they were only checking for three things. Now, they had learned seven things to check for. They also wanted to know when they could add the eighth thing. The teacher reminded them of the juggling analogy she told them about in the beginning. A juggler learns to juggle by first juggling one or two items and then gradually adds one more when ready. She pointed out that they had only been reading to see if the piece stayed on the topic for a few weeks, and that they would have to get very good at this before adding item number eight.

Why Modeling and Demonstration Are Critical for Struggling Readers

Many teachers who have tried to get struggling readers involved in the writing process express frustration with the limited abilities and the unwillingness of the children to write and edit. We believe that teacher demonstration of the writing process steps is the critical factor in establishing a successful Writer's Workshop with struggling readers. Children who watch the teacher think aloud about what topics to write on and about what to say are much less apt to complain. "I ain't got nothing to write about." Children who watch the teacher invent-spell some words and leave out some words, punctuation, capitalization, etc. have more than just our word for the fact that first drafts are never perfect. Children who watch the teacher organize (and reorganize) information while composing will develop a better "feel" for organizing their own work. Children who use a gradually-added-to-checklist to help edit a piece written by the teacher learn how a first draft can be improved if it is going to be published.

The Children Write

After this minilesson (which takes longer to describe than it actually takes to do!), the children begin working on their writing. Some children get their writing notebooks and begin a new piece. Other children continue working on the piece that they started yesterday. The children are encouraged to write about anything they choose to write about, but the teacher's musing about what she might write about and her piece itself clearly remind the children of things they want to write about. Several children whose homes had also been without electricity on Saturday write about what it was like at their house. Although the teacher didn't write about meeting Jamie and her baby brother at the grocery store, Jamie was stimulated to describe this encounter.

Publishing

Once children have produced at least three to five first-draft pieces, they choose one they want to publish. They get advice from others and revise their writing to make it as clear and interesting as possible. They choose a friend to help them with the editing. They conference with the teacher, who helps them with the final editing.

Depending on the length and type of piece written, the teacher helps the child to decide which way to publish it. Some pieces become books that are complete with illustrations, dedications, and "about the author" pages. Other

The teacher is helping one boy to edit a piece.

Another boy is using the class-created editing checklist to edit his own piece before taking it to the teacher/editor. The girl has had her piece edited and is now copying and illustrating it to put on the Writing Board.

Here are some of the books published in one classroom. Parent volunteers assembled the blank books with a Dedication page at the beginning and an About the Author page at the end. Children copy their revised/edited piece into these books and then illustrate them. These child-authored books are popular reading choices during self-selected reading.

pieces are copied or typed on the computer and are displayed on the writing bulletin board.

Sharing in the Author's Chair and Beyond

In addition to demonstrations by the teacher, opportunities for the children to share and publish their own writing are critical. In the classroom just described, the writing part of each day ends with some of the children sitting in the "Author's Chair" and reading something to the class. Sometimes, they read a "published" piece. More often, they read from a first draft that they have just written. After each child has read, he or she calls on class members to tell something that they liked about the piece. The author can also ask if there are any questions and can elicit suggestions to make the piece better. During Author's Chair, the focus is exclusively on the message that the author is trying to convey. Here again, the role of the teacher model is extremely important. Useful comments include:

- I love the way you described . . .
- I wondered why the character . . .

- Your ending really surprised me.
- The way you began your story was . . .
- I could just imagine . . .
- I thought this was a true story until . . .

If the children hear the teacher responding to their message, they respond similarly.

It is important that students' writing be valued; the best evidence of this is found in classrooms where their compositions are routinely displayed. When wall space, bulletin boards, and clotheslines display compositions, children realize that they may have an audience beyond the teacher. In many schools, there is an author's night scheduled each semester. Parents are invited to read and comment on the compositions students have created and selected for display. These compositions are arranged on tables and racks in classrooms, in hallways, and are posted about the rooms as well. Each composition has a comment sheet alongside it; parents and other children may read it or react on it (of course, parents first locate their child's work). This event allows parents to see how children develop over the elementary years and how their child is developing in particular. Often, it helps upper-grade teachers see how far children have come and helps primary grade teachers see the development of previous students several years later.

Allocating Time for Writer's Workshop

Many teachers find it difficult to decide how much time and effort should be allotted to first drafts and to revising, editing, and publishing. While the actual amounts may vary with the ability and age of the children, elementary children should usually spend more time writing their first drafts than they spend publishing them. In any case, the extremes should be avoided. Not every first draft should be taken through the revise, edit, publish cycle because this would greatly diminish the amount of time children would have for producing first drafts. On the other hand, children who never take a first draft through this cycle may learn that the first draft is a final draft! A balance is required if children are going to learn that first-draft writing is not expected to be perfect, while at the same time learn how to take a first draft and transform it from "sloppy copy" to the "polished and published" product.

The critical factor will be the time allocated for writing and how that time is organized. For older children, two or three one-hour periods each week may be better than daily 30-minute periods, even though the total amount of time allocated is similar. Good writing takes time and writing longer pieces takes time. If we routinely schedule relatively short periods for writing, we should expect relatively brief pieces of writing. If we want children to involve themselves in their writing, to research topics, to organize and reorganize, and to share and respond, we will need to allocate longer periods than have traditionally been available in elementary schools. Of course, we should have substantial flexibility and should plan frequent writing opportunities—many of which can be brief. But we also need to plan extended writing periods, especially as children move into the intermediate grades.

This child is sharing a first draft piece as he reads in the "Author's Chair."

Finally, when considering time, we must remember that good writing often takes more than one day. Children who think they should begin a new piece every day and magically finish it in whatever time is allocated produce short, shallow pieces. During process writing, children learn that some pieces take many days to complete. The teacher models this during the minilesson that begins Writer's Workshop. On some days, the teacher does not finish the piece in the allotted time. "Stay tuned tomorrow," says the teacher as he puts the just-begun piece away. When tomorrow comes, the teacher models another important writing strategy—rereading what you wrote yesterday so that you can figure out where you were and continue. The most effective teachers "practice what they preach." If you want your students to be willing to lay aside a piece until tomorrow and to know how to reread to get back into that piece, make sure some of your pieces require you to do the same.

FOCUSED WRITING

During Writer's Workshop, children choose their own topics as well as the type of writing they want to do. They come to think of themselves as writers and develop writing fluency and confidence. We do, however, need to teach children how to write specific forms. In addition to stories, children need to learn how to write short reports, business and friendly letters, and essays. Many children enjoy writing poetry and there are many types of poetry that don't have to rhyme. In many states, children are tested on their ability to do specific writing—narrative, descriptive, persuasive, and so on—at specific grade levels. Demonstration is once again the most effective teaching strategy for teaching children specific forms. Here is a sample focused-writing lesson in which children learn to write a friendly letter.

Modeling and Demonstration

The teacher of this class has a good friend who is teaching in a faraway state. The two teachers talk regularly on the phone and have both been concerned about giving their students "real" reasons to write. One of them remembers having a pen pal whom he never met but with whom he corresponded for years. The two teachers decide that, although this is a rather old-fashioned idea, their children would probably still enjoy having their own pen pals. The class is indeed excited about the idea and this is their first letter-writing experience. The teacher wants them to learn the correct form for a letter, while at the same time making sure the emphasis is kept on the message to be communicated.

The lesson begins with the teacher asking the children what kinds of things they would like to know about their pen pals. He records these questions on large index cards.

- How old is he/she?
- What is school like there?
- Do they have a gym?
- Do they have a lot of homework?
- Do they have a soccer team?

- Does he/she play soccer?
- Does he/she play baseball? football? other sports?
- Is it cold all the time?
- Does everybody ski?
- What does he/she like to eat?
- Do they have video games?
- Do they have a mall?

It is clear that the children have many things they would like to know about their new pen pals. The teacher then helps them organize their questions by beginning a web like this:

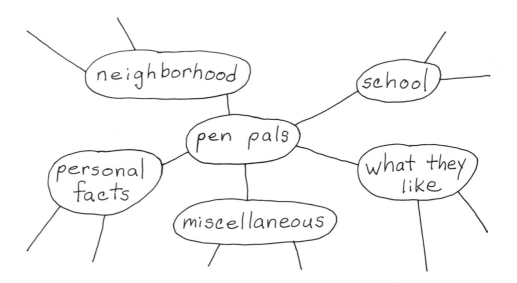

The children help decide where the questions they have already come up with should go, and then come up with some more questions that are also written on index cards and put in the correct places.

On the following day, the teacher and the children review the web and the teacher points out that if these are some of the things they would like to know about their pen pals, they are probably also some of the things their pen pals are wondering about them. He explains that they can't possibly include all of this information in the first letter, but that they will be writing back and forth all year. As the year goes on, they will share and learn these kinds of things and many things they haven't even thought of yet.

The teacher then goes to the overhead and leads the children through the process of writing the first letter. He explains that since this letter will be read by their pen pals, and probably by many other people, each letter must be as correct and readable as possible. Today's task is to get a good first draft that they will edit and recopy or type tomorrow. The teacher then explains and models for the children how and where they put the inside address, date, and greeting. The children watch as he does each step at the overhead. They then do the same on their papers.

Once these formalities are over with, the teacher leads them to look at the web and decide what to write about in the first paragraph. The class decides that they should write about their personal facts. The teacher agrees and has them put their pencils down to watch as he writes a paragraph that gives some personal facts about himself.

Editing as You Go

After writing this first paragraph, the teacher reads it aloud, changing a word and adding another word in order to model for the children that when we write, we read and change as we go along. He points out the paragraph indentation and has the class notice that his paragraph has four sentences. The teacher then instructs the children to write their first paragraph, telling some personal facts about themselves. He reminds them that we always write first drafts on every other line so that we have space to add or change things later.

The Children Write

The children begin to write their paragraphs. As they write, they glance at the web on the board and at the teacher's letter on the overhead. It is clear that even though these children are not very sophisticated writers, the demonstration they have observed along with the displayed web and letter provide the support they need to get a first draft of their paragraph.

When most students have finished their paragraph, the teacher reminds them that good writers stop occasionally and read what they have written before moving on. He then waits another minute while each child reads what has been written. He is encouraged to see them making a few changes/additions they have noticed in their own rereading.

The process of the teacher writing a paragraph, reading it aloud and making a few changes/additions, and then giving the children time to write their own paragraph continues that day and the next as the teacher and the children construct paragraphs with information from the categories on the web. After each paragraph, the children are reminded to reread and make any changes/additions they think are needed. The teacher is encouraged to notice that when they get to the fifth paragraph, many children are automatically rereading and changing without being reminded to do so.

Finally, the teacher suggests possible closings and shows the children where to put the closing. As they watch, he writes a closing on his letter and then they write one on theirs. This completes the first draft of the letters.

Revising to Publish

The next day, the teacher helps them polish their letters. He puts them into sharing groups of four children and then has each child read her or his letter to the others. Just as they do for Author's Chair, this sharing is totally focused on the message. Listeners tell the author something they liked and the author asks them if anything was not clear or if they have suggestions for making it better. When everyone in the group has had a chance to share, they make whatever additions/revisions they choose to. Children can be seen crossing things out and inserting additional information. As they do this, it becomes apparent why it is critical to write the first draft on every other line.

A Final Edit

Now that the letters are revised and the children are satisfied with their message, it is time to do a final edit. During Writer's Workshop, the children are accustomed to choosing a friend to help them edit a draft that they are going to publish, so they just tailor this process to letters. They refer to the editing checklist displayed in the classroom and decide that the things they usually edit for are still valid, but that they need to change number 1 to correspond with letter editing. Number 1 had been "Name and date." They decide that for letters, number 1 should be "Address, date, greeting, closing." The children then pair up with a friend and read for each thing on the checklist together. When they have finished helping each other edit, they share their drafts with the teacher during final editing.

Publishing the Letter

On the following day, they choose some "stationery" from a motley collection (contributed by parents and purchased in bargain bins) and copy the letters in their most legible handwriting. Finally, the teacher demonstrates how to put the address and the return address on the envelopes. (Even though he intends to mail them all to the pen pals' school in one big envelope, he wants children to learn how to address envelopes and knows the pen pals will feel that they are getting a real letter when it comes sealed in a real envelope.) The letters are mailed and their writers eagerly await their replies. Next week, in a faraway city, this process begins again as the teacher's friend takes her class through the same steps of learning to write letters so they can write back.

　　　The procedure just described is not difficult to carry out, but it does take time. Most classes would spend at least five 45-minute sessions going through the brainstorming, webbing, modeling, first drafting, revising, and editing. When you get the letters sent off, you may think, "Never again!" But, what you must keep in mind is that the first time you do anything is always the hardest—for you and the children. A month later, when the children have gotten their letters back and are ready to write again, the process will be much easier and will go much more quickly. After three or four letters, most children will know how to organize information and will write an interesting and correctly formed letter with a minimum of help. By the end of the year, they will be expert letter writers and will have gained a lot of general writing skills in the process.

Other Examples of Focused-Writing Lessons

The procedure just described for learning to write friendly letters can be used for any writing format you want children to learn. Imagine, for example, that you think they would enjoy writing cinquain poetry. There are many different ways to create cinquains. Perhaps the easiest way for elementary children is the form shown here:

Teachers
Smiling, worrying
Smart, busy, perky
They love their children.
Teachers

As you see, the first and last lines are the same word—the subject of the poem. On line two, you write two *-ing* words. On line three, you write three adjectives. On line four, you write a four-word sentence or phrase.

To teach children how to write cinquains, draw lines to show the form of the cinquain, and duplicate this on paper for the children and on an overhead for your use:

Decide on a subject for the cinquain. (They make very impressive Mother's Day cards, but do expand the concept of "mother" to include a grandmother, an aunt, or whoever the primary female caretaker is!) Let children watch you write the noun on the first and last lines. Have them write the same noun on their first and last lines.

Mama

Mama

Next, have them brainstorm words that tell what mothers do that end in *-ing* and list these on the board:

| working | talking | driving | cooking | baking |
| thinking | worrying | fussing | cleaning | singing |

Choose two of these *-ing* words and write them on your second line. Tell children to write two *-ing* words on their second line. Tell them that they can choose from the brainstormed list or can come up with any two on their own.

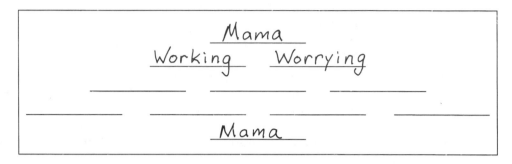

Next, brainstorm descriptive words for line three and write these on the board:

busy	pretty	sweet	soft	perky
smart	organized	lonely	worried	careful
tall	short	Black	proud	perfect

Write three descriptive words on your third line. You may want to use one or two words that are not on the brainstormed list in order to be sure your children understand that the list is just to give them ideas, not to limit their ideas.

> Mama
> Working   Worrying
> Busy   Black   Beautiful
> _____ _____ _____ _____
> Mama

For the fourth line have children brainstorm four-word phrases or sentences:

- She works too hard.
- She loves you best.
- My mama is best.
- I love her best.
- She makes me laugh.
- Always in the kitchen.
- Some kids have two!

Write one of these or write another four-line phrase or sentence on your fourth line and have the children write one on theirs.

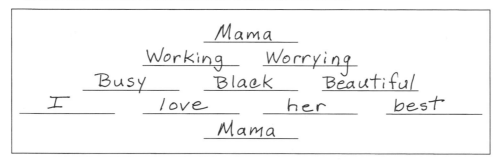

The cinquains are now complete. Let several children read theirs aloud. They will be amazed to discover that, although the topic was the same and they all worked from the same brainstormed list, each poem is different.

Once children have one cinquain written, let them make up another one on the same topic. You may then want them to choose one to use as the text on a Mother's Day card. If so, have them share, revise, and edit in the usual manner.

To get reluctant writers involved, oral histories or personal memoirs are wonderful long-term writing projects because they tell about families or themselves (familiar topics). To begin, you will want to locate an oral history to share with the class or invite a member of the community (the principal?) to be your subject for a class oral history project. Interview the subject, tape record the interview, take notes, and have the children take notes also. After the interview, create a group summary using your notes, their notes, and the tape if there is a problem. Memoirs abound in children's literature, Elizabeth Fitzgerald Howard's, *Aunt Flossie's Hats (and Crabcakes Later)* and Cynthia Rylant's, *When the Relatives Came* are two of the wonderful examples of this genre. Again, after reading and discussing these published memoirs, the teacher may create her own, or perhaps create a class memoir based on a collective experience. Now children can begin to plan their own memoirs.

Focused Writing Using Paragraph Frames

Another way to teach children specific writing forms is through the use of paragraph frames. These frames are especially helpful in teaching children to use connecting and transition words that show the relationships in various text structures. Cudd and Roberts (1989) suggest that teachers begin by demonstrating for children how to write a particular type of paragraph. Their example for a first lesson suggests using a sequence relationship because much of what children write has a sequential relationship and because children find this an easy one to compose. Here are the steps (adapted) they suggest going through for the demonstration lesson:

1. As the children watch, write a simple paragraph about a topic that lends itself to sequential ordering. Use clue words such as *first, next, then, later, finally.*
2. Copy the sentences on sentence strips and mix them up.

Lots of Different Things We Write

There are a variety of writing genres ranging from very informal (e.g., grocery lists) to very formal (such as term papers). The following list provides a starting point for thinking about the many different types of writing tasks that we might offer students. Too often we have only offered students a very narrow range of writing opportunities that have been limited in both frequency and variety.

Description	Article	List	Log
Directions	Report	Comparison	Play
Invitation	Summary	Advertisement	Editorial
Story	History	Interview	Obituary
Diary	Journal	Letter	Memo
Jingle	Verse	Song	Poem
Captions	Headline	Chart	Notes

3. Reread the original paragraph and discuss the sequence and the sequence words with the children.
4. Have children arrange the mixed up sentence strip sentences in the correct order and read the paragraph.
5. Have students copy the paragraph and illustrate it to show the sequence of events.

Once children understand how a sequential paragraph is written, the teacher can present them with a sequence frame, such as the following:

Mother box turtles prepare for their babies in a very interesting way. First,

_____

_____ . Next, _____

_____ .

Finally, _____ .

After this, _____ .

Example from Cudd, Evelyn T., & Roberts, Leslie L. (1989, February). Using writing to enhance content area learning in the primary grades. *The Reading Teacher, 42*(6), 392–404.

Using a shared writing technique, the teacher and the children compose the sentences that will fill in the frame. Each child then copies this completed paragraph and illustrates it.

Once children have seen the filling in of the frame modeled to them, they are ready to move toward writing their own sequentially ordered paragraphs independently. At this stage, the teacher provides the frame and the students fill in the appropriate events. The final move to independence occurs when students are able to use sequence words and create their own sequentially-ordered paragraphs.

Cudd and Roberts provide many examples of the different types of structures children might learn to write by using paragraph frames.

Mother box turtles prepare for their babies in a very interesting way. First, she looks for a safe place to burry her eggs. Next, she digs a hole so it will be moist for her eggs. Finally, she lays her eggs; burrys the hole, and then tamps it down. After this, the mother turtle leaves her babies on their own.

Example from Cudd, Evelyn T., & Roberts, Leslie L. (1989, February). Using writing to enhance content area learning in the primary grades. *The Reading Teacher, 42*(6), 392–404.

Although these frames have been suggested for use by beginning writers, we have had a great deal of success using them with older children who have difficulty writing or who "hate to write." Learning how to use transition words and connecting words allows them to write something that sounds very "sophisticated." In addition, many older children who have had a history of failure in reading and writing are interested in learning about real things—things in real life. They can be lured into reading and writing by exploring informational books with lots of pictures on a topic that is of interest to them, and then making a book of their own to display what they have learned. They can also write their own informational text on topics they know a lot about. (One boy in a rural school wrote about how his family made maple syrup; another wrote about how to smoke fish to preserve them.) Using the frames to help them structure their writing allows them to produce a much better product that they can be proud of. In addition, reading comprehension is enhanced as students become more familiar with different text structures.

Bats are unusual animals for several reasons.

First, _____ .

Second, _____ .

Third, _____ .

Finally, _____ .

As you can see, bats are unique in the animal world.

Illustrate with a picture of what you
consider to be the most unusual thing
about the bat.

Example from Cudd, Evelyn T., & Roberts, Leslie L. (1989, February). Using writing to enhance content area learning in the primary grades. *The Reading Teacher, 42*(6), 392–404.

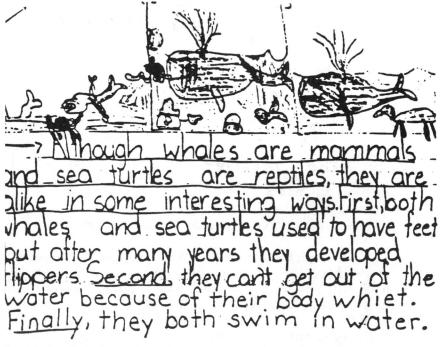

Although whales are mammals and sea turtles are reptiles, they are alike in some interesting ways. First, both whales and sea turtles used to have feet but after many years they developed flippers. Second, they cant get out of the water because of their body whiet. Finally, they both swim in water.

Example from Cudd, Evelyn T., & Roberts, Leslie L. (1989, February). Using writing to enhance content area learning in the primary grades. *The Reading Teacher, 42*(6), 392–404.

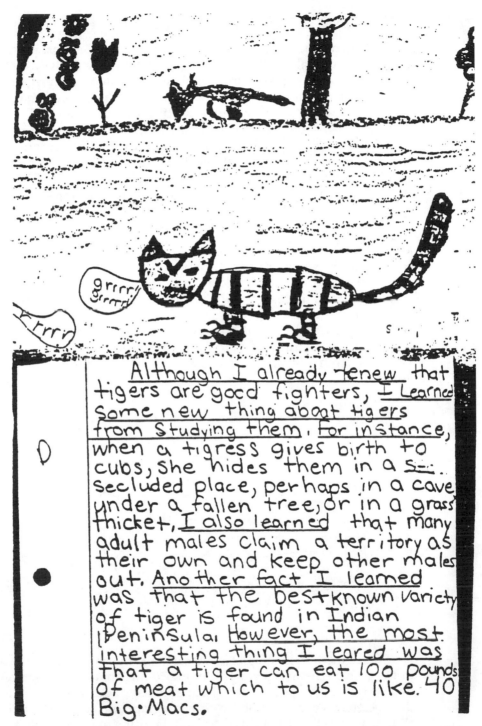

Although I already knew that tigers are good fighters, I learned some new thing about tigers from studying them. For instance, when a tigress gives birth to cubs, she hides them in a s... secluded place, perhaps in a cave under a fallen tree, or in a grass thicket. I also learned that many adult males claim a territory as their own and keep other males out. Another fact I learned was that the best known variety of tiger is found in Indian Peninsula. However, the most interesting thing I leared was that a tiger can eat 100 pounds of meat which to us is like 40 Big Macs.

Example from Cudd, Evelyn T. (1989, December). Research and report writing in the elementary grades. *The Reading Teacher, 43*(3), 268–269.

FOCUSED WRITING BEFORE, DURING, AND AFTER READING

Children who write become better readers. One of the most powerful connections you can make is through reading and writing (Spivey, 1997). Children who read something, knowing that they will write something, are more likely to read with a clear sense of purpose. Children who use information from their reading to write produce better writing because they have more to say. Research has shown a clear benefit from connecting reading and writing (Shanahan, 1988). It has also shown that a writing program that includes instruction in specific informational text structures improves both writing and reading comprehension (Raphael, Kirschner, & Englert, 1988). In this section, we will describe a variety of structures for focused writing that connect reading and writing.

Graphic Organizers

In Chapter 3, we described a variety of ways to guide children's reading so they would learn how to think about the different types of reading. One type of guided-reading lesson involved having the students construct or fill in various types of graphic organizers. The webs, charts, diagrams, timelines, etc. that you and the children constructed to organize the information learned from reading are marvelous springboards for writing. Remember the web from the previous chapter that the students used to describe Amanda?

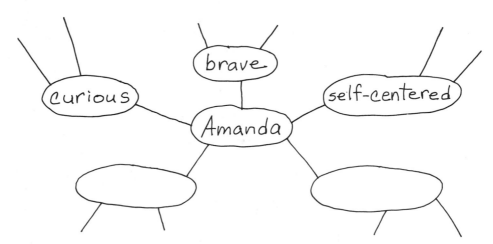

Once the web is complete, you can have the children use the information in the web to create a character summary for Amanda. To demonstrate how you do this, choose one of the adjectives that best describes her and let the children listen and watch as you create a paragraph on the board or on chart paper. When teachers think aloud as they model writing in front of the class, they provide powerful lessons about the writing process.

After children watch you write and listen to you think aloud about how best to combine your ideas, point out to them the features of your paragraph that you want them to use:

- The paragraph is indented.
- All sentences begin with capital letters and end with a period.
- The name *Amanda* is always capitalized.
- The first sentence tells the most important idea—that Amanda is curious.
- The other sentences are details that show how curious she is.

Now each child should write a paragraph about Amanda choosing any one of the remaining adjectives on the web (or an adjective that is not on the web that they think best describes her). Their paragraphs will all be different but should follow the form demonstrated in your paragraph.

This type of guided writing, in which children use the information they have obtained from reading and have recorded it on some type of graphic organizer and who then follow a model that they watched the teacher create, is extremely effective for struggling readers. Almost all children will produce interesting, cohesive, well-written paragraphs and be proud of what they produce. With enough lessons such as this one, all children can learn how to construct paragraphs. This ability to create well-formed paragraphs is the basis for all different types of writing.

Almost any information recorded in graphic organizer fashion can be used for reading/writing lessons. In the previous chapter, you saw a web that children would use to organize the information read in an article about birds.

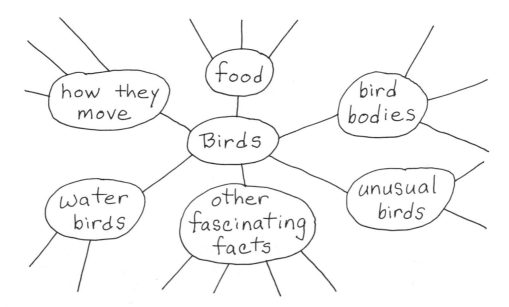

> *Amanda is a very curious little girl! She always wants to know everything about Miss Morgan. One day she followed her home to find out where she lives and what her house looks like. She is also positive that Miss Morgan will marry Mr. Thompson who teaches next door. Miss Morgan isn't sure what she thinks about that! Who knows what Amanda will try and find out next!*

Here is a paragraph describing Amanda as a curious person. The children watched as the teacher wrote this paragraph. Using this paragraph as a model but using their own ideas, each child then chose the adjective he or she thought best described Amanda and wrote a descriptive paragraph.

You also saw how information about birds could be recorded in a feature matrix.

Once these graphic organizers are completed, you can use them to have the children write about birds. Based on the web, the teacher would model how to write a descriptive paragraph about the different foods birds eat. Each child would then choose another one of the subtopics—bird bodies, ways birds move, etc.—and would write a descriptive paragraph about that topic. Based on the information about particular birds from the feature matrix, the teacher would model how to write a paragraph about one of the birds and then let each child choose one of the other birds and write and illustrate a descriptive paragraph about it. After each child writes about one of the birds, the children might work in groups to revise, edit, and produce a book about birds.

Birds						
	fly	swim	build nests	lay eggs	have feathers	molt
robins						
whippoorwills						
penguins						
ostriches						

Lessons in which graphic organizers are constructed and then used based on reading as a basis for writing are particularly important and effective for children whose first language is not English. Watching the teacher use the information from the graphic organizer to write something and then use the model they have watched the teacher write in order to construct their own piece of writing is an extremely powerful way for these children to increase their control of the English language. If your class contains many children whose English is limited, lessons such as these should occur on an almost daily basis in your classroom.

Research

Another way to connect reading and writing is to have children do research to find the answers to questions. Many struggling readers find research an impossible task, but it can be structured so that they succeed. They gain a great sense of control and power when they can find and report information. The easiest, most manageable research format for struggling readers and writers is QUAD (Cudd, 1989). QUAD stands for *QUestions, Answers, and Details*. Children first decide on a topic that they want to research and then fill the topic in on the top of their QUAD sheet. Next, they come up with some questions to which they hope to find the answers. They take this QUAD sheet with them to the library and record answers and details in the appropriate spaces. Finally, they add the references they used at the bottom.

Name A. W.

Topic: Kangaroos		
Questions	Answers	Details
1. Do kangaroos hibernate?	no	groundhogs, dormice, and bears do
2. What kinds of food do they eat?	plants	grass, grain, leaves, and twigs
3. How far can they jump?	30 feet 1 jump	
4. Do kangaroos live in one part of Australia	no	they also live in South America
5. How many different kinds of kangaroos are there?	50 or more.	gray kangaroo, red kangaroo, and tree kangaroo
References: Childrens' Britannica	Kangaroos	Book of Knowledge

Example from Cudd, Evelyn T., & Roberts, Lesle L. (1989, February). Using writing to enhance content area learning in the primary grades. *The Reading Teacher, 42*(6), 392–404.

Children can work in pairs or small groups to research the answers to their questions. They can then share the results of their investigations with each other by reading the information right off the sheets. As children become more able researchers, you can help them take the information recorded on the QUAD sheets and turn it into a research report.

Response Logs

Many teachers find that an easy and natural way to connect reading and writing is to have students keep a literature response log. Children are encouraged to take some time after reading each day and record their thoughts, feelings, and predictions. From time to time, the children can be asked to share the responses they have written. This is often a good basis for promoting a discussion of divergent responses to the same story. However, Sudduth (1990) reported that many of her third graders didn't really know what to record in their literature logs. This was especially true of those children who were finding learning to read difficult. She outlined the step-by-step instruction that she took them through:

- At first, have the students read the same book. They can read this silently or with a partner or listen to a tape recording or to a teacher read aloud.

- Have specific stopping points in the reading and help the children verbalize what they are thinking and feeling.
- On chart paper or the overhead, record some of the students' responses and have them copy the ones they agree with into their logs. Use "frames" such as:

> I was surprised when _____.
> Since _____ and _____ happened, I predict that _____ will happen next.
> The story reminds me of the time I _____.

- As students understand the various open-ended ways in which they can respond to literature, move them toward independence. Continue the discussions but don't write down what they say. Rather, have them write their own personal entries following the discussions. Have the class brainstorm a list of log topics and frames, and display these so that students can refer to them when they need a "starter."
- Have students choose the book they want to read and do their own response logs. Divide the time available for self-selected reading into reading time and log-writing time, perhaps 20 minutes to read and 10 minutes to write. Once children are reading individual books, provide a time each week when they can share what they have written in a small group format.

Writing Before Reading

In most classrooms, writing occurs after reading and is used to help readers clarify and solidify what is learned and to help them respond to what they have read. There are equally compelling reasons for having children write before they read. You learned in Chapter 3 that reading is primarily thinking and that, while all children can think, they sometimes don't think while they read. You learned about a variety of useful guided-reading formats for getting children thinking before, during, and after reading. Writing before reading is another way to get children thinking.

This writing can be a "quickwrite" such as "2-minute fast facts." Imagine that your children are going to read an informational selection about reptiles. Make sure everyone has some paper and a pencil ready, set your timer for 2 minutes, and have the children list as many facts as they can about reptiles. Stress that they should get as much down as they can in two minutes—in abbreviated list form, not worrying about spelling, complete sentences, etc. When the timer sounds at the end of 2 minutes, have students draw a line to show where they finished and have them number the facts they came up with before reading.

Next, have the students read or listen to the informational article about reptiles. Do not let them write anything while they are reading/listening, but make sure that they know they will have 3 minutes to add to their list after reading.

When students have finished reading, set your timer for 3 minutes and let them add to their list of reptile facts. Once the timer sounds, have the students compare lists in small groups. Each group might list the facts most members knew before reading and which facts most members learned from the article. Each group could then write these "before" and "after" fact lists on a chart and share with the class.

This very simple procedure is used most effectively when the students are going to read on a topic about which they already have some prior knowledge. While making the 2-minute prereading list, they realize that they already know a lot and will get their prior knowledge activated and ready to help them think about the material they are going to read. They are always amazed at how much more they can list after reading. Children who use writing to tally up what they knew before and after reading soon learn that "there is a lot to be learned from reading."

Sometimes, you want students to do more extended writing before reading in order to sensitize them to the process of how authors create images, build suspense, flesh out characters, etc. Writing before reading can be an especially powerful activity when used with children who have difficulty "getting into" a selection. These are children who typically begin reading with little or no attempt at bringing up relevant prior background knowledge, children who do not generate predictions or questions as they read, and children who passively enter the reading activity and focus on getting it over with, rather than getting involved with it. These are the children who do better on factual questions than on responding to character motives. They are the children who remember names of the characters but find it difficult to answer questions such as, "Who does Russell remind you of?" (They often respond with, "I don't know" or "It didn't say" or "No one"). These are the children who find imagery difficult and who don't have good mental images of what the characters look like or how they might be dressed unless the story is illustrated or is explicit on these matters. These are the children who have not discovered what reading is all about.

Imagine that you want students to think about how authors use words to create a certain mood. You find a story in which a child is lost out in the woods at night. The fear that the child feels becomes tangible through the images that the author creates. You decide to use a writing activity in which the children write about a time that they, or someone they knew, were lost.

First you talk with the children about being lost and about the fears they experience. You then talk about how authors make things seem real by giving specific details and by using powerful words. Next, let them write about a real or imagined experience of being lost and have them try to make the terror become real for the reader. After writing, let them share what they have written and notice how they used specific details, powerful words, and images.

As you show them the story you have selected for them to read, tell them that this author had the same writing task that they did. She wanted to tell about a lost child and made it so real that the readers felt like they too were lost. Have them read and compare the language and images used by this writer to the ones that they used in their stories. After they have completed reading the story, discuss specific examples of the language used and the images created by the author. Put some of the sentences on the board or on chart paper. If they are excited by the story and the way that the author created the images of fear, they may want to revise their own stories using some of the "tricks" that were used by the author of the story they just read.

Writing During Reading

In the last chapter, sticky notes were suggested as a way to help students notice and mark interesting, important, or confusing spots in the text. The cryptic notes students write on sticky notes involves them in writing—and more importantly thinking— as they are in the very act of reading.

It is clear that readers make better writers and writers make better readers. You want your students' writing to be enriched (both in information and style) by their reading and you want them to read with the sharp eye of a writer. When you engage the children in a writing activity before, during, or after reading, you increase their facility with and affinity for both reading and writing.

WRITING "ON THE COMPUTER"

We have not mentioned computers yet, in spite of the fact that many people think they are "the answer" for helping struggling readers become literate. As you learned in Chapter 1, we don't believe there is any one answer and, while computers have enormous potential for literacy, it is still only "potential" in most schools with a high number of at-risk children. The first thing you might notice about computers in these schools is that there aren't many! Funding being what it is for public schools, computers are often paid for by PTA fundraising and this financial support is often lacking in schools that serve many children at risk for reading and writing failure. When you do see computers being used by students, the software is often the "electronic worksheet" variety. Often it is the children who are finding learning to read difficult, who are performing small skill tasks similar to what they might do on worksheets. Too often, these tasks have little or no relationship to the development of authentic reading and writing.

We do feel, however, that there is tremendous potential for children's literacy development if they can have access to computers and software that will support their writing. In our experience, children who have regular access to computers for word processing are more willing to write, write more, revise more, and feel more confident in their writing. Teachers of at-risk children should "go out on a limb" to get computer access for their children. They should then assign high priority to incorporating the available word processing software and to allocating their use of time to have children write "on the computer."

In addition to a normal word processing program that allows the children to write, edit, check spelling, etc., there are some writing programs that support writing in specific ways. Some of these programs help children organize their reports, others provide basic report structures, or writing frames, for children.

There is a whole generation of desktop publishing software that allows children to create very professional looking newsletters, reports, and announcements. Other software can produce charts, maps, and graphs. Programs are also available that allow children to scan pictures and place them in their reports. There are also artwork files that allow children to select illustrations, logos, and other visuals to spice up their stories, news reports, or announcements. In short, the explosion of computer-based word processing offers exciting possibilities for the future of writing in the elementary school.

Teachers who want to use computers to help children write should get a copy of Sonia Katzer and Christine Crnkovich's *From Scribblers to Scribes: Young Writers Use the Computer* (Teacher's Idea Press, 1991). It is clear that these two authors are real teachers who have worked out most of the nitty-gritty details for using computers with children. The book contains lots of easy-to-follow sample lesson plans and suggestions for scheduling and organizing. It also has a whole chapter on using computers with "Challenged Learners," which includes struggling readers as well as children with visual and physical impairments. This book is on our "must have" list if you want to do anything with writing and computers.

Some Excellent Writing Software

Here is a sampling of some of the best programs we have seen. Given the pace of development, by the time our book is published, these will probably all be replaced by better and newer programs. We include this list more for the purpose of illustrating the kind of writing support computers can offer students than for specific recommendations of software. Find the newest software that perform these (and yet unimagined) functions:

Print Shop (Broderbound). Allows children to produce cards, invitations, posters, etc. with "professional quality" layout and graphics.

Language Experience Primary Series (Teachers Support Software). Allows teachers/tutors to record stories and print out word lists, charts, etc. Allows children to choose their words to make new sentences and to illustrate what they have written. Synthesized speech available.

Pow! Zap! Ker-Plunk! (Queue). This program is a comic-book maker. It includes clip art, speech bubbles, and comic book backgrounds that enable children to produce books, cards, mobiles, and puppets.

Story Builder (American School Publishers), *Story Maker* (Scholastic), *Once Upon a Time* (Compu-Teach), *Monsters and Make-Believe* (Queue), *Snoopy Writer* (American School Publishers). All these programs help children learn how to form sentences, paragraphs, and stories and provide graphic support.

Story Starters: Social Studies and *Story Starters: Science* (Pelican). These programs include clip art and background related to science and social studies topics. Students can use the art and background to produce professional-looking books about U.S. history as well as animals, plants, weather, the solar system, and other science topics.

Thinking Networks for Reading and Writing (Think Network). Children learn about topics and then learn to use skeleton map outlines to create text that can be structured in a variety of ways.

Children's Writing & Publishing Center (The Learning Company). A simple desktop publishing program that allows children to create newsletters, stories, reports, etc. Includes 150 pictures and the ability to import graphics from other sources.

SUMMARY

Perhaps you have wondered about the role of skills in writing instruction as you have been reading this chapter. "What about grammar, mechanics, spelling?" "Don't they need to learn these disciplines?" are questions often asked by teachers of struggling readers. One look at their first drafts will often convince us that some kind of "skills instruction" is needed.

The concern that teachers have about teaching these skills is legitimate. Children need to learn not only how to express their ideas and feelings but also how to express them clearly and in ways that others can read. Decades of research (Langer & Allington, 1992), however, have made it clear that, if the goal of your skills instruction is improved writing, instruction must take place in the context of real writing. Children who put *were* and *was* in the correct blanks on worksheets and who demonstrate the ability to capitalize proper nouns on a test do not necessarily apply these skills to their own writing. In fact, we have far more children who know how to spell and punctuate than how to write thoughtfully and precisely. There is no shortcut to good writing. Children who find writing difficult will learn how to write well when they watch teachers demonstrate and "think aloud" about the writing and editing process day after day. They will learn how to take a first draft and polish it when they are given the time and the peer, teacher, or computer support to do so. They will learn to care about how well their writing communicates their ideas and how easily others can read it when it is regularly displayed, and when teachers focus more on the clarity and quality of the message than on the penmanship and spelling.

Although we believe that engaging struggling readers in lots of self-selected writing is the most important component of a strong literacy program, we do not believe that "just writing" is enough. In this chapter, we have outlined five instructional formats teachers can use for teaching the "skills" in the context of writing. Teachers who engage children in shared and group writing, who conduct Writer's Workshops, who do focused lessons in which children learn how to write specific forms, who connect reading and writing experiences, and who take advantage of whatever computers they have to support children's writing, will produce good writers—in every sense of the word "good"!

Teachers who engage children in lots of writing do not ignore the skills. Rather, they observe children's writing and decide which particular skills the children are ready to learn. Skills that are needed by many children are taught in a writing minilesson. Skills teaching also takes place on an individual basis when teachers are helping children edit and publish their pieces. In the next chapter, we will describe how teachers provide spelling instruction along with decoding instruction.

REFERENCES

Calkins, L (1994). *The art of teaching writing*. Portsmouth, NH: Heinemann.

Cudd, E. T. (1989). Research and report writing in the elementary grades. *The Reading Teacher, 43,* 268–269.

Cudd, E. T., & Roberts, L. (1989). Using writing to enhance content area learning in the primary grades. *The Reading Teacher, 43,* 393–404.

Graves, D. H. (1995). *A fresh look at writing*. Portsmouth, NH: Heinemann.

Langer, J., & Allington, R. L. (1992). Writing and reading curriculum. In P. Jackson (Ed.) *The Handbook of Curriculum Research*. New York: Macmillan.

Raphael, T. E., Kirschner, B. W., & Englert, C. S. (1988). Expository writing program: Making connections between reading and writing. *The Reading Teacher, 41,* 790–795.

Routman, R. (1991). *Invitations*. Portsmouth, NH: Heinemann.

Shanahan, T. (1988). The reading-writing relationship: Seven instructional principles. *The Reading Teacher, 41,* 636–647.

Spivey, N. (1997). *The constructivist metaphor: Reading, writing and the making of meaning*. New York: Academic Press.

Stauffer, R. G. (1980). *The language-experience approach to the teaching of reading, 2nd ed.* New York: Harper & Row.

Sudduth, P. (1989). Introducing response logs to poor readers. *The Reading Teacher, 42,* 452.

Van Allen, R. V., & Allen, C. (1966). *Language experiences in reading: Teachers' resource book*. Chicago: Encyclopedia Brittanica Press.

5
Developing Decoding and Spelling Fluency

(Commonly Called "Phonics"!)

Words are the building blocks of reading and writing. In order to read and write, children must learn to recognize and spell the most commonly used words quickly and automatically. For many children, this is not an easy task. The most frequently occurring words are meaningless, abstract, connecting words (*of, and, the, is*, etc.). Children use these words in their speech but they are not aware of them as separate entities. Read these sentences with a natural speech pattern and notice how you pronounce the italicized words.

- *What* do you want?
- Can I have a piece *of* pie?
- Where are *they*?

In natural speech, the *what* and the *do* are slurred together and sound like "wudoo." The *of* is pronounced like "uh." The *they* is tacked on to the end of *are* and sounds like "ah-thay." All children use the highly frequent words such as *what, of*, and *they* in their speech but they are not as aware of these words as they are of the more concrete, tangible words such as *want* and *pie*. To make life more difficult, many of these high-frequency words are not spelled in a regular, predictable way. *What* should rhyme with *at, bat*, and *cat. Of* should be spelled u-v. *They*, which clearly rhymes with *day, may*, and *way* should be spelled the way many children do spell it—t-h-a-y.

When you consider that the most frequently occurring words are usually meaningless, abstract words that may be irregular in their spelling or pronunciation and that children use but don't even realize are separate words, it is a wonder that any child learns to recognize and spell them! In order to read and write fluently, however, children must learn to instantly recognize and automatically spell these words. In this chapter, we will describe how using a word wall can help children learn these critical words.

In addition to learning to read and spell the most frequent words instantly, children must learn how to figure out the spelling/pronunciation of a word they do not know. All proficient readers have the ability to look at a regular word they have never seen before and assign it a probable pronunciation. Witness your ability to pronounce these made-up words:

bame   spow   perzam   chadulition

Of course you weren't "reading" because having pronounced these words, you wouldn't create any meaning. But if you were in the position of most young readers who have many more words in their listening/meaning vocabularies than in their sight-reading vocabularies, you would often meet words that were familiar in speech but unfamiliar in print. The ability to figure out the pronunciation of unfamiliar-in-print words rapidly would enable you to use your huge store of familiar-in-speech words and thus create meaning.

Before we continue, how did you pronounce the made-up word, *spow?* Did it rhyme with *cow* or with *snow?* Because English is not a one-sound, one-letter language, there are different ways to pronounce certain letter patterns; the number of different ways is limited, however, and with real words (unlike made-up words), your speaking vocabulary lets you know which pronunciation to assign.

Not only do readers use their phonics knowledge to enable them to read words they have not seen before, but this same knowledge also enables them to write. If the four made-up words had been dictated to you and you had to write them, you would have spelled them in a way that was reasonably close to the way we spelled them. You might have spelled the first one *baim* and the last one *chedulition,* but your "invented" spelling would have resembled our made-up spelling to a remarkable degree.

All good readers and writers develop the ability to come up with pronunciations and spelling for words they have never read or written before. Many poor readers do not. When good readers see a word they have never before seen in print, they stop momentarily and study the word—attending to print detail and looking at every letter in a left-to-right sequence. As they look at all the letters, they are not thinking of a sound for each letter because good readers know that sounds are determined by letter patterns, not by individual letters. Good readers look for letter patterns they have seen together before and then search their mental word banks looking for words with similar letter patterns. If the new word is a big word, they "chunk" it—that is, they put letters together that make familiar-sounding chunks.

Based on careful inspection of the letters and a search through their mental banks for words with the same letter patterns, good readers "try out" a pronunciation. If the first try doesn't result in a word they have heard and have stored in their mental word bank, they will usually try another pronunciation. Finally, they produce a pronunciation that they "recognize" as sounding like a real word they know. Then they go back and reread the sentence that contained the unfamiliar-in-print word and see if their pronunciation makes sense with the meaning they are getting from the context of surrounding words. If the pronunciation they came up with makes sense, they continue reading. If not, they look again at all the letters of the unfamiliar word and see what else would "look like this and make sense." Imagine a young child reading this sentence:

- The man was poisoned by lead.

Imagine that he pauses at the last word and then pronounces *lead* so that it rhymes with *bead*. Because that is the only similar real word he remembers hearing, his eyes then glance back and he quickly rereads the sentence. He then realizes that, "This doesn't make sense." He studies all the letters of *lead* again and searches for similar letter patterns in his mental word bank. Perhaps he now accesses words such as *head* and *bread*. This gives him another possible pronunciation for this letter pattern—one that is also recognized as a previously heard word. He tries this pronunciation, quickly rereads the sentence, realizes that it now "sounds right," and continues reading.

From this scenario, we can infer the strategies that good readers use to successfully decode an unfamiliar-in-print word:

1. Recognize that this is an unfamiliar word and look at all of the letters in a left-to-right sequence.
2. Search your mental bank for similar letter patterns and the sounds associated with them.
3. Produce a pronunciation that matches that of a real word you already know.
4. Reread the sentence to cross-check your possible pronunciation with meaning. If meaning confirms pronunciation, continue reading. If not, try again!

Had this unfamiliar-in-print word been a big word, the reader would have had to use a fifth strategy:

5. Chunk the word by putting together letters that usually go together in the words that you do know.

The strategies of looking at all the letters in a left-to-right sequence, matching letter patterns with pronunciations, chunking big words, and cross-checking are supported by numerous research studies (Adams, 1990) and by common-sense observations of what we—as good readers—do. Unfortunately, they are not what children are usually taught to do. Consider some of the traditional phonics instruction given to children:

- The *e* on the end is silent and makes the vowel long.
- When a vowel is followed by *r*, it is *r* controlled.
- When there are two consonants in the middle of a word that are not a digraph or a blend, divide between them.

This kind of rule-based, jargon-filled instruction is confusing to many children and does not represent what people actually do when they come to an unfamiliar word in their reading, or when they are trying to figure out how a word might be spelled. The traditional phonics rules are descriptions of how the letter-sound system works. They are not what you use when you need to pronounce or spell an unfamiliar word.

This chapter contains activities that teach children to do what good readers and writers actually do when they read or spell an unfamiliar word. (Many of these activities come from Cunningham, 1995, *Phonics They Use: Words for Reading and Writing,* which includes more detail and variation than can be described in this one chapter.) The chapter is divided into five sections. Activities in the first section are designed to help children build basic understandings about words and letter-sound patterns. These activities should play a major role in the literate home simulation kindergarten and should continue throughout first grade until children develop the essential understandings about words. It is possible that some struggling second and third graders might not have developed these critical concepts yet—particularly if they are just learning to speak English. These activities can be adapted for older beginning readers.

The second section contains activities designed to ensure that children develop an instant and automatic ability to read and write the high-frequency words. The third section focuses on the important skill of cross-checking meaning with letter-sound knowledge. Sections four and five help students learn the patterns essential for decoding and spelling. Activities in section four will help students decode and spell regular one- and two-syllable words.

The final section provides activities that help children learn to read and spell multisyllabic words. These activities are most appropriate for students in grades four and up but have also been used successfully with third graders who are tired of those "baby words" and are impressed with themselves when they start to acquire a store of "really big words!"

BUILDING A FOUNDATION FOR WORD AND LETTER/SOUND LEARNING

In preceding chapters, you learned about the most important part of the foundation for word and letter/sound learning. Instruction in kindergarten and beginning first grade must simulate the early reading/writing experiences of children from literate homes. Reading and writing materials must be omnipresent. Teachers must read from a variety of books and real-world materials. Children must be encouraged to "read" the predictable books, songs, and poems that are an integral part of their day. Their fledgling efforts at "pretend reading" and writing must be applauded and supported. All children can and should develop a clear understanding of what reading and writing are for, and the "Of course I can" attitude that is critical for their development as readers and writers.

Once children understand what reading and writing are for and are convinced that they too can join the literate community, there are some smaller—but still critical—understandings that children must develop. Children must learn the conventions and jargon of print. They must develop phonemic awareness. They must begin to learn letter names and the sounds often associated with letters.

Print is what you read and write. Print includes all the funny little marks—letters, punctuation, space between words and paragraphs—that translate into familiar spoken language. In English, we read across the page in a left-to-right fashion. Because our eyes can only see a few words during each stop (called a fixation), we must actually move our eyes several times to read one line of print. When we finish that line, we make a return sweep and start all over again. If there are sentences at the top of a page, a picture in the middle, and more sentences at the bottom, we read the top first and then the bottom. We start at the front of a book and go toward the back. These arbitrary rules about how we proceed through print are called *conventions.*

Jargon refers to all the words we use to talk about reading and writing. Jargon includes such terms as *word, letter, sentence,* and *sound.* We use this jargon constantly as we try to teach children how to read:

> "Look at the first word in the second sentence. How does that word begin? What letter makes that sound?"

Using some jargon is essential when talking with children about reading and writing, but children who don't come from literacy-rich backgrounds are often hopelessly confused by this jargon. Although all children speak in words, they don't know that words exist as separate entities until they are put in the presence of reading and writing. To many children, letters are what come in the mailbox, sounds are horns, bells, and slamming doors and sentences are what you have to serve if you get caught committing a crime! These children are unable to follow our "simple" instructions because we are using words that either have no meaning to them or have an entirely different meaning.

Phonemic awareness is not just another word for phonics. It is the ability to take words apart, put them back together again, and change them. A child's level of phonemic awareness is a very good predictor of beginning reading success. Phonemic awareness develops through a series of stages in which children first become aware that language is made up of individual words, that words are made up of syllables, and that syllables are made up of phonemes. It is important to note here that it is not the "jargon" that children learn. Five-year-olds cannot tell you that there are three syllables in *dinosaur* and one syllable in *Rex.* What many of them *can* do is clap out the three beats in dinosaur and the one beat in Rex. Likewise, they cannot tell you that the first phoneme in *mice* is *m-m-m . . .,* but some can tell you that you would have *ice* if you took the first sound off of *mice.*

Children develop this phonemic awareness as a result of the oral and written language they are exposed to during their preschool years. Nursery rhymes, chants, and *Dr. Seuss* books usually play a large role in this development. Lap reading, in which children can see the print being read to them, also seems to play an important role. Most children who have the luxury of being read to on demand will select a "favorite" book that they insist on having read again and again. They will ask questions about the words such as, "Where does it say, *snort?*" "Is that *zizzerzazzerzuzz?*"

Children also develop a sense of sounds and words as they try to write. In the beginning, many children let a single letter stand for an entire word. Later, they write more letters and often say the word that they want to write, dragging out its sounds in order to hear what letters to use. Children who are allowed and encouraged to "invent-spell" develop an early and strong sense of phonemic awareness.

ACTIVITIES FOR BUILDING THE FOUNDATION

There are many ways to help children learn the conventions and jargon of print; develop their phonemic awareness and teach letter names and sounds. Here are some that kindergarten and first grade teachers and children find to be effective and enjoyable.

Names and Other Concrete Words

Most kindergarten and first grade teachers begin their year with some get-acquainted activities. As part of these get-acquainted activities, they often have a "special child" each day. In addition to learning about each child, you can focus attention on the special child's name and use that name to develop some important understandings about words and letters.

To prepare for this activity, write all the children's first names (with initials for last names if two names are the same) in permanent marker on sentence strips. Cut the strips so that long names have long strips and short names have short strips. Each day, reach into the box and draw out a name. This child becomes the "King or Queen for a day" and the child's name becomes the focus of many activities. Reserve a bulletin board and add each child's name to the board. (Some teachers like to have children bring a snapshot of themselves or take pictures of the children to add to the board as the names are added.) Here are some day-by-day examples of what you might do with the names:

Day one   Close your eyes. Reach into the box, shuffle the names around, and draw one out. Crown that child king or queen for the day! Lead the other children to interview this child and find out what he or she likes to eat, play, or do after school. Does she or he have brothers? Sisters? Cats? Dogs? Mice? Many teachers record this information on a chart or compile a class book with one page of information about each child.

Now focus the children's attention on the child's name—David. Point to the word, *David,* on the sentence strip and develop the children's understanding of jargon by pointing out that this *word* is David's name. Tell them that it takes many *letters* to write the word *David,* and let them help you count the letters. Say the letters in *David*—D-a-v-i-d, and have the children chant them with you. Point out that the word *David* begins and ends with the same letter. Explain that the first and the last *d* look different because one is a capital *D* and the other is a small *d* (or uppercase/lowercase—whatever jargon you use).

Take another sentence strip and have children watch as you write *David.* Have them chant the spelling of the letters with you. Cut the letters apart and mix them up. Let several children come up and arrange the letters in just the right order so that they spell *David,* using the original sentence strip on which

David is written as a model. Have the other children chant to check that the order is correct.

Give each child a large sheet of drawing paper and have them write *David* in large letters on one side of the paper using crayons. Model at the board how to write each letter as they write it. Do not worry if what they write is not perfect (or even if it doesn't bear much resemblance to the one you wrote). Also resist the temptation to correct what they wrote. Remember that children who write at home before coming to school often reverse letters or write them in funny ways. The important understanding is that names are words, that words can be written, and that it takes lots of letters to write them.

Finally, have everyone draw a picture of David on the other side of the drawing paper. Let David take all the pictures home!

Day two   Draw another name—*Caroline.* Crown Caroline and do the same interviewing and chart making that you did for David. (Decide carefully what you will do for the first children because every child will expect equal treatment!) Focus their attention on Caroline's name. Say the letters in *Caroline* and have the children chant them with you. Help the children count the letters and decide which letter is first, last, etc. Write *Caroline* on another sentence strip and cut it into letters. Have children arrange the letters to spell *Caroline,* using the first sentence strip name as their model. Put *Caroline* on the bulletin board under *David* and compare the two. Which has the most letters? How many more letters are in the word, *Caroline* than in the word, *David*? Does *Caroline* have any of the same letters as *David?* Finish the lesson by having everyone write *Caroline.* Have everyone draw Caroline pictures and let Caroline take all of them home.

Day three   Draw the third name—*Dorinda.* Do the crowning, interviewing, and chart making. Chant the letters in Dorinda's name. Write it, cut it up, and do the letter arranging. Be sure to note the two *d*'s and to talk about first and last letters. As you put *Dorinda* on the bulletin board, compare it to both *David* and *Caroline.* This is a perfect time to notice that both *David* and *Dorinda* begin with the same letter and the same sound. Finish the lesson by having the children write *Dorinda* and draw pictures for Dorinda to take home.

Day four   *Mike* comes out. Do all the usual activities. When you put *Mike* on the bulletin board, help the children realize that David has lost the dubious distinction of having the shortest name. (Bo may now look down at the name card on his desk and call out that his name is even shorter. You will point out that he is right but that Mike's name is the shortest one on the bulletin board right now. What is really fascinating about this activity is how the children compare their own names to the ones on the board even before their names get there. That is exactly the kind of word/letter awareness you are trying to develop!)

When you have a one syllable name with which there are many rhymes (*Pat, Tran, Flo, Sue,* etc.), seize the opportunity to help the children listen for words that rhyme with that name. Say pairs of words—some of which rhyme with Mike—Mike/ball, Mike/bike, Mike/hike, Mike/cook, Mike/like. If the pairs rhyme, everyone should point at Mike and shout, "MIKE." If not, they should shake their heads and frown.

Day five   *Cynthia* comes out. Do the various activities and then take advantage of the fact that the names, *Caroline* and *Cynthia* both begin with the letter *c* but with different sounds. Have Caroline and Cynthia stand on opposite sides of you. Write their names above them on the chalkboard. Have the children say *Caroline* and *Cynthia* several times, drawing out the first sound. Help them understand that some letters can have more than one sound and that the names *Caroline* and *Cynthia* demonstrate this fact. Tell the class that you are going to say some words, all of which begin with the letter *c*. Some of these words sound like *Caroline* at the beginning and some of them sound like *Cynthia*. Say some words and have the children say them with you—*cat, celery, candy, cookies, city, cereal, cut.* For each word, have them point to Caroline or Cynthia to show which sound they hear. Once they have decided, write each word under *Caroline* or *Cynthia.*

Day six—day last   Continue to have a special child each day. For each child, do the standard interviewing, charting, chanting, letter-arranging, writing, and drawing activities. Then, take advantage of the names you have to help children develop an understanding about how letters and sounds work. Here are some extra activities many teachers do with the names:

Write the letters of the alphabet across the board. Count to see how many names contain each letter. Make tally marks or a bar graph and decide which letters are included in the most names and which letters are in the fewest names. Are there any letters that no one in the whole class has in his or her name?

Pass out laminated letter cards—one letter to a card, lowercase on one side, uppercase on the other. Call out a name from the bulletin board and lead the children to chant the letters in the name. Then, let the children who have those letters come up and display the letters and lead the class in a chant, cheerleader style. "David—D-a-v-i-d—David—Yeh! David!

When you have finished all the names, you may want to do similar activities with other concrete words. Many teachers have the children learn the color words using similar activities. When studying animals, add an animal name to an animal board each day. Activities with the children's names and other concrete words can be done even when many children in the class do not know their letter names yet. Young children enjoy chanting, writing, and comparing the words. They learn letter names by associating them with the important-to-them words they are learning.

Being the Words

This activity can be done with any predictable book that the children have read many times or with a chant, song, or poem that has been written and displayed on a chart or poster. In this activity, children are given words to make sentences. They do this by matching their word to the words in the predictable book or on the chart. Two pages of a predictable book or two lines of a poem/chant are matched, then the next two, and so on. To prepare for this activity, write all the words on sentence strips and cut them to match the size of the word. (Do not make duplicate words unless they are needed to make the sentences on the two pages of the book or two lines of the poem/chant that is going to be displayed simultaneously. Make separate cards for any words that are sometimes shown with a capital letter and sometimes with a small letter. Make separate cards for each punctuation mark needed. Laminate these cards so that you can use them for Being the Words and word-sorting activities.)

Begin the activity by passing out all the cards containing the words and punctuation marks. Let the children look at their words and point out the distinction between words and punctuation marks. Tell the children that they are going to *be* their words and will come up to make the sentences. Ask the children to help read the sentences with you. Point to each word as you reread the sentences and have the children look to see if their word matches any of the words they see in the book. Explain that you don't need to say anything when you get to the period, but that it lets you know that the sentence is over. Have all the children who have a word or punctuation mark in this sentence come up and get in the right order to make the sentence. Help the children arrange themselves in the appropriate left-to-right order, get the periods at the end of the sentences, and hold the words right-side up. When everyone is in order, have the children who are not in the sentence read the sentence as you move behind each child who is a word.

"Being the Words" is one of the favorite activities of most children. They ask to do it again and again. Through this activity, children learn what words are, that words make up sentences, and that punctuation signals the end of the sentence but is not read. They also practice the left-to-right order of print and realize that the order of words makes a difference in what is read. Many children also learn new words during this activity. You will observe this as you hand out the words for *Brown Bear, Brown Bear* to do the activity a second or third time and hear children say such things as, "Oh, boy, I'm the bear!" Your most sophisticated children will even learn the abstract repeated words, *what, do, you, see, at,* and *me!*

Many teachers put the book and the laminated words in a center. Children delight in turning the pages of the book and laying out the words on the floor to make the sentences.

Counting Words

For this activity, all children should have ten counters in a paper cup. (Anything that is manipulative is fine. Some teachers use edibles such as raisins, grapes, or small crackers and let the children eat their counters at the end of the lesson. This makes clean-up quick and easy!) Begin by counting some familiar objects in the room such as, windows, doors, trash cans, etc., having all children place one of their counters on their desks for each object.

Tell children that you can also count words by putting down a counter for each word you say. Explain that you will say a sentence in the normal way and then repeat the sentence, pausing after each word. The children should put down counters as you say the words in the sentence slowly, then count the counters and decide how many words you said. As usual, children's attention is better if you make sentences about them. (Carol has a big smile. Paul is back at school today. I saw Jawan at church.) Once the children catch on to the activity, let them say some sentences—first in the normal way, then one word at a time. Listen carefully as they say their sentences because they usually need help saying them one word at a time. Not only do children enjoy this activity and learn to separate words in speech, they are also practicing critical counting skills!

Clapping Syllables

The first way that children learn to pull apart words is into syllables. Say each student's name and have everyone clap the "beats" in that name as they say it with you. Help them to see that Tran and Pat are one beat names, Manuel and Patrick, two beats, and so on. Once students begin to understand, clap the beats and have all the students whose names have that number of beats stand up and say their names as they clap the beats with you.

Once children can clap syllables and can decide how many beats a given word has, help them see that one-beat words are usually shorter than three-beat words—that is, they take fewer letters to write. To do this, write some words that children cannot read on sentence strips and cut the strips into words so that short words have short strips and long words have long strips. Have some of the words begin with the same letters, but have the words be different lengths so children will need to think about word length in order to decide which word is which.

For the category of animals, you might write *horse* and *hippopotamus, dog* and *donkey, kid* and *kangaroo,* and *rat, rabbit,* and *rhinoceros.* Tell the children that you are going to say the animal names and that they should clap to show how many beats the word has. (Do not show them the words yet!) Say the first pair—one at a time—horse/hippopotamus. Help children decide that *horse* is a one-beat word and *hippopotamus* takes a lot more claps and is a five-beat word. Now, show them the two words and say, "One of these words is *horse* and the other is *hippopotamus.* Who thinks they can figure out which one is which?" Explain that because *hippopotamus* takes so many beats to say, it probably takes more letters to write.

Blending and Segmenting Games

The ability to segment words into sounds and then blend them back together is one of the most sophisticated phonemic awareness skills—and for many children one of the most difficult. Call students to line up by stretching out their names, emphasizing each letter. As each student lines up, have the class stretch out the name with you.

As a variation, say a sound and let everyone whose name contains this sound anywhere in their name line up. Be sure you have the children respond to the sound and not the letter. If you say "sss," Sam, Jessie, and Cynthia can all line up!

Display familiar pictures. Let children take turns saying the names of the pictures (one sound at a time) and call on another child to identify the picture. In the beginning, limit the pictures to five or six whose names are very different and are short—*truck, frog, cat, pony, tiger.*

Some teachers help children understand the difficult concept of segmenting and blending by having children "talk like ghosts." Each child says a sentence in a slow, drawn-out moaning voice. Everyone else translates what the ghost said!

Phonemic Awareness Resource

Phonemic awareness is a "hot topic" and there are lots of books on ways to develop it. Many of them, unfortunately, suggest activities that are repetitive, boring, and not apt to engage the attention or minds of the children. One book that has lots of different activities—so you can vary how you do it—and very "fun, silly, child-centered" activities is *Phonemic Awareness: Playing with sounds to strengthen beginning reading skills* by Jo Fitzpatrick, Creative Teaching Press, 1997. It is written by a veteran first grade teacher who clearly understands phonemic awareness and the kind of activities that will hold children's attention!

Nursery Rhymes

One of the best indicators of how well children will learn to read is their ability to recite nursery rhymes when they walk into kindergarten! Because this is such a reliable indicator of how well they will learn to read and because rhymes are so naturally appealing to children at this age, kindergarten and first grade classrooms should be filled with rhymes. Children should learn to recite, sing, clap to, act out, and pantomime the rhymes. In some primary classrooms, they develop "raps" for the rhymes.

Once the children can recite lots of rhymes, nursery rhymes can be used to teach the concept of rhyme. The class can be divided into halves—one half says the rhyme but stops when they get to the rhyming part, the other half waits to shout the rhyme at the appropriate moment:

First half: There was an old woman who lived in a shoe. She had so many children, she didn't know what to
Second half: do
First half: She gave them some broth without any bread and spanked them all soundly and put them to
Second half: bed.

Nursery and other rhymes have been a part of our oral heritage for generations. We now know that the rhythm and rhyme inherent in nursery rhymes are important vehicles for the beginning development of phonemic awareness.

Rhyming Books

While on the subject of methods that have stood the test of time, do you remember being read *Hop on Pop? One Fish, Two Fish, Red Fish, Blue Fish? There's a Wocket in my Pocket?* These books also appeal to the silly rhythm/rhyme oriented child who is our kindergartner. From these books, children develop important understandings. You can nudge these understandings on a bit if you help the children notice that many of the words that rhyme are also spelled alike. As you reread one of these favorite books, let the children listen for the rhyming words and make lists of these. Read the words together. Add other words that are spelled alike and rhyme and make more rhymes with those. Make up "silly words" that rhyme too, and decide what they might mean. Try to illustrate them! If you can have a "wocket" in your pocket, you can have a "hocket" in your pocket. What would a *hocket* be? What could you do with it?

Tongue Twisters

Children love tongue twisters and they are wonderful reminders for the sounds of beginning letters. Use children's names and let them help you create the tongue twisters. Have students say them as fast as they can and as slowly as they can. When students have said them enough times to have them memorized, write them on posters or in a class book.

Two Wonderful Tongue Twister Books

The Biggest Tongue Twister Book in the World (Gyles Brandeth, Sterling, 1978).
Alphabet Annie Announces an All-American Album (Susan Purviance & Marcia O'Shell, Houghton Mifflin, 1988).

Use Favorite Words with Pure Initial Sounds as Key Words

Letter sounds can be learned by rote or by association. Learning the common sound for *b* by trying to remember it or by trying to remember that the word *bears* begins with it when you can't even read the word *bears* requires rote learning. But if you have read and reread and been the words from *Brown Bear, Brown Bear,* you can probably read the word bear. Once you can read the word *bear* and realize that the common sound for *b* is heard at the beginning of *bears,* you no longer have to remember the sound only. You can now associate the sound of *b* with something already known—the word, *bear.* Associative learning is the easiest, quickest, and most long-lasting.

Children from print-rich environments know some concrete words when they come to school. As they are taught letter sounds, they probably associate these with the words they know, thus, making the learning of these sounds easier and longer lasting. We can provide the opportunity for associative learning for children who did not know words when they came to school by capitalizing on the words they are learning from their predictable books and poem/chant charts. Names of children in the class are also concrete words that make it easy for children to remember letter/sound associations.

When teaching the first letter/sound relationships, begin with two letters that are very different in look and sound and that are made in different places of the mouth—*b* and *l*, for example. Show the children the two words, *bear* and *Larry*, which will serve as key words for these letters. Have the children pronounce the two key words and notice the position of their tongues and teeth as they do. Have one child stand in the front of the room and hold the word *bear*. Have Larry hold a card with his name on it. Say several concrete words—*bike, lemon, box, book, ladder, lady, boy* that begin like *bear* or *Larry* and have the children say them after you. Have them notice where their tongues and teeth are as they say the words. Let the children point to the child holding *bear* or *Larry* to indicate how the word begins.

Begin a key-word bulletin board on which you put the letters *b* and *l* and the key words, *bear* and *Larry*. Repeat the activity just described using other *b* and *l* words until most of the children begin to understand the difference in the letter sound. Then add a third letter and a key word—perhaps *m—mouse*. Have them listen for and repeat words beginning with all three letters—*b, l, m*. Be sure to point out that the words they already know will help them remember the sound.

The Alphabet Song and Alphabet Books

"The Alphabet Song" has been sung by generations of children. Children enjoy it and it seems to give them a sense of all the letters and a framework in which to put new letters as they learn them. Many children come to school already being able to sing "The Alphabet Song." Let them sing and teach it to everyone else. Once the children can sing the song, you may want to point to alphabet cards (usually found above the chalkboard) as they sing. Children enjoy "being the alphabet" as they line up to go somewhere. Simply pass your laminated alphabet cards—one to each child, leftovers to the teacher—and let the children sing the song slowly as each child lines up. Be sure to hand out the cards randomly so that no one gets to be the *A* and lead the line or has to be the *Z* and bring up the rear every day!

There are wonderful alphabet books available. You can read these books aloud over and over. Kindergarten children can select these books to "read" during their self-selected reading. Teacher aides, or parent or grandparent volunteers can "lap read" these in the reading corner, and so on. Your class can create their own alphabet book modeled after their own favorite alphabet book.

Letter Actions

Teach children actions for the consonants. Write the letter on one side of a large index card and the action on the other. The first time you teach each letter, make a big deal of it. Get out the rhythm sticks and the marching music when you march for *M*. Go out on the playground and do jumping jacks for *J*. Play hopscotch for *H* and hop like bunnies.

Once the children have learned actions for several letters, there are many activities you can do in the classroom without any props. Have all the children stand by their desks and wait until you show them a letter. They should do that action until you hide the letter behind your back. When they have all stopped and you have their attention again, show them another letter and

Wonderful Alphabet Books

There are some wonderful alphabet books that not only teach the letters, but also help children develop concepts. Here are just a few of our favorites. There are many more.

26 Letters and 99 Cents (Tana Hoban, Greenwillow, 1987).
A My Name is Alice (Jane Bayer, Dial Books, 1984).
A to Z Sticker Book (Jan Pienkowski, Random House, 1995).
A You're Adorable (Martha Alexander, Candlewick Press, 1991).
Accidental Zucchini: An Unexpected Alphabet (Max Glover, Harcourt Brace, 1993).
All Aboard ABC (Doug Magier, Philomel, 1993).
Alphabet City (Stephen Johnson, Viking Press, 1995).
Alphabetics (Suse Macdonald, Bradbury Press, 1986).
Animal ABC (Susan Hood, Troll, 1995).
Anno's Alphabet (Mitsumas Anno, Crowell Publications, 1975).
Ashanti to Zulu: African Traditions (Margaret Musgrove, Dial Books, 1976).
By the Sea: An Alphabet Book (Ann Blades, Kids Can Press, 1985).
Dr. Seuss's ABC (Theodore Geisel, Random House, 1963).
Easy as Pie (Marcia & Michael Folsom, Clarion, 1985).
Eating the Alphabet: Fruits and Vegetables from A–Z (Lois Short, HBJ, 1989).
From Acorn to Zoo (Satoshi Kitamura, Scholastic, 1992).
Hosie's Alphabet (Hosea Tobias, Lisa Baskin, Viking Press, 1972).
It Begins with an A (Stephanie Calmenson, Hyperion, 1993).
K is for Kiss Goodnight: A Bedtime Alphabet (Jill Sardegan, Doubleday, 1994).
NBA Action from A–Z (James, Preller, Scholastic, 1997).
On Market Street (Arnold Lobel, Greenwillow Books, 1981).
Q is for Duck (Mary Elting & Michael Folsom, Clarion, 1980).
Sleepy ABC (Margaret Wise Brown, Harper, 1994).
The ABC Bunny (Wanda Gag, Coward-McCann, 1933).
The Alphabet Tale (Jan Garten, Random House, 1964).
The Sesame Street ABC Book of Words (Harry McNaught, Random House/Children's Television Workshop, 1988).
The Z Was Zapped (Chris Van Allsburg, Houghton Mifflin, 1987).
Where is Everybody? (Eve Merrimam, Simon & Schuster, 1989, *Big Book* by Scott Foresman, 1996).

have them do that action. Continue this with as many letters as you have time to fill. Be sure to make comments such as, "Yes, I see everyone marching because *M* is our marching letter."

In another activity, you pass out the letters (for which children have learned the actions) to individual children. Each child gets up and performs the action required and calls on someone to guess which letter he or she was given.

In "Follow the Letter Leader," the leader picks a letter card and does that action. Everyone else follows the leader doing the same action. The leader then picks another card and the game continues.

Teachers have different favorites for letter-actions and you will have your own favorites. Try to pick actions with which everyone is familiar and that are only called by one name. Here is a list of actions we like. The action for *s* is our particular favorite. You can use it to end the game. Children say, "it is not an action at all" but remember that "*s* is the sitting letter."

bounce	kick	talk
catch	laugh	vacuum
dance	march	walk
fall	nod	yawn
gallop	paint	zip
hop	run	
jump	sit	

Seven Signs of Emergent Literacy

Observe the children as they engage in reading, writing, and the activities described in this section and you will notice:

1. They "pretend read" favorite books and poems/songs/chants.
2. They "drite" and can read what they wrote even if no one else can.
3. They can "track print"—that is, show you what to read and point to the words using left-right/top-bottom conventions.
4. They know critical jargon, can point to just one word, the first word in the sentence, one letter, the first letter in the word, the longest word, etc.
5. They recognize some concrete words—their names and names of other children, favorite words from books, poems, and chants.
6. They recognize if words rhyme and can make up rhymes.
7. They can name many letters and can tell you words that begin with the common initial sounds.

Children develop these critical understandings as they engage in the shared reading and writing described in previous chapters as well as from the activities described in this chapter.

FLUENCY WITH HIGH-FREQUENCY WORDS

For as long as anyone can remember, struggling readers have had difficulty with words like *was, saw, of, for, from, they, that, what, with, will*. Many of these words have no meaning, are not logically spelled, and look a lot like each other. One strategy we have found to be effective for teaching the high-frequency words is "Doing a Word Wall." Doing a Word Wall is not the same thing as having a word wall. Having a word wall might mean putting all these words up somewhere in the room and telling students to use them. In our experience, struggling readers can't use them because they don't know them and don't know which is which! "Doing a Word Wall" means (1) being selective and "stingy" about what words go up there, limiting the words to those really common words that children need a lot in writing; (2) adding them gradually—five a week; (3) making them very accessible by putting them where everyone can see them, writing them in big black letters and using a variety of colors so that the constantly confused words (*for, from, that, them, they, this*, etc.) are on different colors; (4) practicing the words by chanting and writing them because struggling readers are not usually good visual learners and can't just look at and remember words; (5) doing a variety of review activities to provide enough practice so that the words are read and spelled instantly and automatically; and (6) making sure that Word-Wall Words are spelled correctly in any writing the students do. Teachers who "DO" word walls (rather than just have word walls) report that ALL of their children can learn these critical words.

Doing a Word Wall

Select five words each week and add them to a wall or bulletin board in the room. The selection of the words varies from classroom to classroom, but the selection principle is the same. Include words students will need often in their reading and writing, and words that are easily confused with other words. First grade teachers who are using a basal usually select some high-frequency words that are taught in that basal. Others select high-frequency words from big books or other trade books that children are reading.

The word wall grows as the year goes on. The words on the word wall are written on different colored construction paper scraps with a thick black permanent marker. Words are placed on the wall alphabetically by first letter and the first words added are very different from one another. When confusing words are added, put them on different colored paper from the words they are usually confused with.

Beginning with third grade, teachers like to start their word wall by putting up words that are commonly misspelled such as:

they	was	come	of	from
were	where	said	because	again
could	does	pretty	people	have

As children write, look for high-frequency, commonly misspelled words and add these to the wall as well.

Most teachers add five new words each week and do at least one daily activity in which the children find, write, and chant the spelling of the words. The activity takes longer on the day that words are added because you will want to take time to make sure that students associate meanings with the words. You also will want to point out how the words are different from words that they are often confused with. Here are a variety of ways to get at least one daily practice with the word wall words:

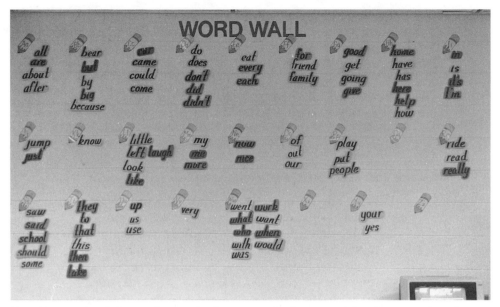

Here is a word wall from a first grade classroom. Cutting around the shapes and putting the words on different colored pieces of paper helps the children distinguish the easily confusable ones and makes an interesting, eye-catching display.

Clap, Chant, and Write

Have students number a sheet of paper from one to five. Call out the five words, putting each word in a sentence. As you call out each word, have a child find and point to that word and have all the children clap and chant its spelling before writing it. When all five words have been written, point to the words and have a volunteer spell each word as students check/fix their own papers.

On the day that you add words, call out the five new words. During the rest of the week, however, any five words from the wall can be called out. Words that children need more practice with should be called out almost every day.

Review Rhyme with the Word Wall

Students clap, chant, and write, but they also find the word that rhymes with a word you give. Give them both a first letter and a rhyming clue such as:

Number one begins with a *t* and rhymes with *walk*.
Number two begins with an *m* and rhymes with *by*.
Number three begins with an *f* and rhymes with *run*.
Number four begins with an *l* and rhymes with *bike*.
Number five begins with a *g* and rhymes with *stood*.

To check the answers, you say the rhyming word and let students say the word they wrote and chant its spelling. "Number one rhymes with *walk*, what did you write?" Children respond, "talk—t-a-l-k."

Review Cross Checking with the Word Wall

To review cross checking, tell students that they will have to decide which wall word makes sense and begins correctly. For each word, write the first letter of the word on the board. Then say a sentence leaving out a word that begins with that letter. Students will decide which word makes sense in your sentence and write that word. Here are some examples.

1. Write *t* on the board. Say, "The first word begins with a *t* and fits in the sentence—*Paula likes to _____ on the telephone.*"
2. Write *r* on the board. Say, "Number two begins with an *r* and fits in the sentence—*Midge had to _____ fast to win the race.*"
3. Write *w* on the board. Say, "Number three begins with a *w* and fits in the sentence—*Carlos went to China _____ his father.*"

To check the answers, read the sentences again and have students tell you what word they wrote and chant its spelling.

Be a Mind Reader

"Be a Mind Reader" is a favorite word wall activity. In this game, the teacher thinks of a word on the wall and then gives five clues about that word. Choose a word and write it on a piece of scratch paper, but do not let the students see what word you have written. Have students number a paper 1–5 and tell them that you are going to see who can read your mind and figure out which of the words on the board you are thinking of and have written on your scratch paper. Tell them you will give them five clues. By the fifth clue, everyone should guess your word, but if they read your mind they might get it before the fifth clue. For your first clue, always give the same clue, "It's one of the words on the wall." Students should write next to number *1*, the word they think it might be. Each succeeding clue should narrow down what the word might be until by clue five, there is only one possible word. As you give clues, students write the word next to each number on their paper that they believe is correct. If succeeding clues confirm the word a student has written next to one number, then that student writes the same word next to the following number. Clues may include any features of the word you want students to notice. (It has more than two letters. It has less than four letters. It has an *e*. It does not have a *t*.) After clue five, show students the word you wrote on scratch paper and say, "I know you all have the word next to number five, but who has it next to number 4? 3? 2? 1? Some students will have read your mind and will be as pleased as punch with themselves!

120 High-Frequency Words Often Found on Primary Word Walls

(*Words help with decoding and spelling lots of rhyming words.)

about	*did	*how	our	they're
after	do	I	*out	*thing
again	don't	*in	over	this
*all	*down	is	people	to
*am	*eat	*it	*play	too
*and	favorite	*like	pretty	two
are	for	little	*ride	*up
*at	friend	*look	said	us
be	from	*made	*saw	very
because	*fun	*make	*school	want
before	get	many	*see	was
*best	girl	me	she	we
*big	give	*more	sister	*went
*black	go	*my	some	were
*boy	good	*new	*talk	what
brother	*had	*nice	teacher	*when
*but	has	*night	*tell	where
*can	have	no	*that	who
can't	he	*not	the	*why
*car	her	of	their	*will
children	here	off	them	with
come	him	*old	*then	won't
could	his	on	there	you
*day	house	other	they	your

1. It's one of the words on the wall.
2. It has four letters.
3. It begins with *th*.
4. The vowel is an *e*.
5. It finishes the sentence: I gave my books to _____.

Reading, Writing, and Word Walls

Once you have a word wall growing in your room, there will be no doubt that your students will use it as they are reading and writing. You will see their eyes quickly glance to the exact spot where a word that they want to

90 Words Commonly Found on Intermediate Word Walls

(Clues including pictures and opposite words are attached to homophones.)

about	except	probably	very
again	excited	really	want
almost	favorite	right (wrong)	was
also	first	said	wear (shirt)
always	friends	school	weather (rain)
another	getting	something	we're (we are)
anyone	have	sometimes	went
are	hole (donut)	terrible	were
beautiful	I'm	that's	what
because	into	their	when
before	it's (it is)	then	where
buy (sell)	its	there (here)	whether
by	knew	they	who
can't	know	they're (they are)	whole
could	laugh	thought	with
didn't	let's	threw (caught)	won
doesn't	myself	through	won't
don't	new (old)	to	wouldn't
enough	no (yes)	too (Too late!)	write
especially	off	trouble	your
everybody	one (1)	two (2)	you're (you are)
everyone	our	until	
everything	people	usually	

write is displayed. Even when children are reading, they will sometimes glance over to the word wall to help them remember a particularly troublesome word.

Word walls provide children with an immediately accessible dictionary for the most troublesome words. Because the words are added gradually, stay in the same spot forever, are alphabetical by first letter, are visually distinctive by different colors of paper, and because of the daily practice of finding, writing, and chanting these words, most children learn to read and spell almost all of the words. Because the words you selected are words they need constantly in their reading and writing, their recognition of these words becomes automatic and their attention can be devoted to the less frequent words and to constructing meaning as they read and write.

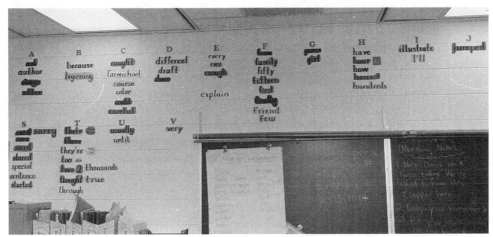

Here is a part of a third grade word wall. Notice the clues next to the homophones (they're—they are, two—2, hour—clock sketch).

CROSS CHECKING

The ability to use some letters in a word along with the sentence or story context is an important decoding strategy. You must do two things simultaneously—think about what would make sense and think about letters and sounds. We have found two ways to help children develop automatic cross-checking abilities. The first is a daily cross-checking activity we call "Guess the Covered Word." The second is the way teachers respond during oral reading.

Guess the Covered Word

Many words can be figured out by thinking about what would make sense in a sentence and seeing if the consonants in the word match what you are thinking of. You must learn to do two things simultaneously—think about what would make sense, and think about letters and sounds. Struggling readers often prefer to do one or the other, but not both. Thus, they may guess something that is sensible but ignore the letter sounds they know or guess something that is close to the sounds but makes no sense in the sentence! Doing a weekly "Guess the Covered Word" activity helps students combine these strategies effectively.

Before class begins, write four to five sentences on the board that start with your students' names, follow a similar word pattern, and end with words that vary in their initial sounds and word length. For the first lessons use only words with single consonants.

Rasheed likes to play **soccer**.
Kate likes to play **softball**.
Rob likes to play **basketball**.
Juan likes to play **hockey**.

Cover the last word in each sentence with sticky notes, tearing or adjusting them to the length of each word.

Begin the activity by reading the first sentence and asking students to guess the covered word. Write three or four guesses on the board next to the sentence. Uncover the first letter. Erase guesses that don't begin with that letter. Have students continue offering guesses that make sense and begin with the correct letter. Write their responses on the board. Keep the students focused on both meaning and beginning letters. When the first letter is revealed, some students will guess anything that begins with that letter. For example, if the first letter is an s, they may guess "sand." Respond with something like, "*sand* does begin with an *s*, but I can't write *sand* because people don't play *sand*." Finally, uncover the whole word and see if any guesses were correct. Repeat the procedure on the remaining sentences.

Once students understand how "Guess the Covered Words" works, include some sentences in which the covered word begins with the digraphs, *sh, ch, th,* and *wh.* Explain that the rules of this game require you to show them all the letters up to the first vowel. Then show them some sentences that contain the digraphs *sh, ch, th,* and *wh* as well as single consonants. Include examples for both sounds of *c.* Vary your sentence patterns and where in the sentence the covered word is.

Corinda likes to eat **cherries**.
Watermelon is Chad's favorite fruit.
Jessica likes strawberries on her **cereal**.
Bo likes strawberry **shortcake**.
Melinda bakes pies for **Thanksgiving**.
I don't know **which** pie I like best.

"Guess the Covered Word" works for teaching or reviewing blends, groups of letters in which you can hear the sounds blended together such as *br, pl,* and *str.* As with digraphs, vary the sentence pattern and where in the sentence the covered word is.

Justin likes to swim in the **summer**.
Curtis plays baseball in the **spring**.
Skiing is Jennifer's favorite sport in the winter.
Jennifer likes to **skate** too.
Val likes to play all kinds of **sports**.

Be sure that when you uncover the beginning letters, you uncover everything up to the vowel. If you have uncovered an *s* and someone guessed the word, *snow,* tell them that that was good thinking for the *s.* Then, have everyone say *snow* slowly and hear the *n.* "My rule is that I have to show you everything up to the vowel so if the word were snow, I would have to show you not just the *s* but the *n* too."

Sometimes, struggling readers get the idea that the only time you use reading strategies is during reading time! It is important to show them how cross checking can help them figure out words when they are reading all kinds of things. You might write a paragraph, such as this, related to your science topic, mammals. Cover the words in the usual way and have the whole sentence read before going back to guess without any letters and then with all the letters up to the vowel (covered words are bold).

> Mammals are warm blooded animals. Their body **temperature** stays the same regardless of the weather. All mammals at some time in their **lives** have hair. For **whales**, they have hair only before they are born. Mammals nurse their babies and give them more **protection** than other animals. Mammals also have a larger **brain** than any other group of animals.

One more way to vary "Guess the Covered Word" is to cover some words in a big book. Use the same procedures of guessing without any letters and then with all the letters up to the vowel. Help children verbalize that one thing you can do to decode words is to read the whole sentence and then think what would make sense, be about the right length, and have *all* the correct letters up to the vowel.

Responding to Oral Reading

Most of the reading children do should be silent reading with a focus on understanding and enjoying what they read. It is also helpful and fun for children to have time to read aloud. Young children like to read aloud and as they are reading, teachers have a chance to see if they are using their strategies and to coach them in the appropriate use.

When children read aloud, they always produce a few misreadings. It is these misreadings that allow teachers a "window on the mind" of the reader. It is in responding to these misreadings that teachers have a chance to coach children into strategic reading. Here are some suggestions for making oral reading an enjoyable and a profitable endeavor.

Have children read silently before reading orally   Making sure that silent reading for comprehension precedes oral reading will ensure that students do not lose track of the fact that reading is understanding and reacting to the meaning of the printed words. Young children who are just beginning to read should also read material to themselves before reading it orally. When beginning readers read, however, it is seldom silent. They don't yet know how to imagine the words in their minds and their reading to themselves can be described as "mumble" or "whisper" reading.

Oral reading should be from material that is fairly easy   Material that students read orally should be easy so that they will make no more than three to five errors per hundred words read. If the average sentence length is seven words, this would be no more than one error every three sentences. It is very important that children do not make too many errors because their ability to cross check drops dramatically when they are making so many errors that they can't make sense of what they are reading.

Children should never correct the reader's error   Allowing students to interrupt and correct the misreadings inhibits the reader's ability to self-correct and forces the reader to try for "word-perfect reading." The same is true when the teacher interrupts and corrects the reader. While it might seem that striving for word-perfect reading would be a worthy goal, it is not, due to the way our eyes move when we read.

When we read, our eyes move across the line of print in little jumps. The eyes then stop and look at the words. The average reader can see about twelve letters at a time—one large word, two medium words, or three small words. When your eyes stop, they can only see the letters they have stopped on. The following letters are not visible until the eyes move forward and stop once again. Once your eyes have moved forward, you can't see the words you saw during the last stop. As we read orally, our eyes move ahead of our voice. This is how we can read with expression because the intonation and emphasis we give to a particular word can only be determined when we have seen the words that follow it. The space between where your eyes are and where your voice is, is called your eye-voice span. Fluent readers, reading easy material, have an eye-voice span of five to six words.

Good readers read with expression because their voice is trailing their eyes. When they say a particular word, their eyes are no longer on that word, but rather, several words down the line. This explains a phenomenon that all good readers use. They make little nonmeaning-changing errors when they read orally. They read "can't" when the actual printed words were *can not*. They read "car" when the actual printed word was *automobile*. Nonmeaning-changing errors are a sign of good reading! They indicate that the eyes are out there ahead of the voice using the later words in the sentence to confirm the meaning, pronunciation, and expression given to the previous word. The reader who says, "car," for *automobile* must have correctly recognized or decoded *automobile* or he or she could not have substituted the synonym, *car*. When the reader says, "car" the word *automobile* can no longer be seen because the eyes have moved on.

Good readers make small nonmeaning-changing errors because their eyes are not focused on the words they are saying. If other children are allowed to follow along while the oral reader reads, they will interrupt the reader to point out these errors. If children were allowed to correct nonmeaning-changing errors, they would learn to keep their eyes on the very word they are saying when reading orally! This fosters word-by-word reading. Too much oral reading, with each error corrected by other children or the teacher, will result in children not developing the eye-voice span all fluent readers have. Constant interruptions by the teacher or other children also work against developing appropriate cross-checking strategies and spontaneous self-corrections.

Eliminating interruptions by other children is not easy (short of gagging them). Since gagging all the listeners would surely be misinterpreted by parents and is probably unsanitary, a simpler solution is to have all the children who are not reading put their fingers in their books and close them! When one child is reading, the others should not be "following along" with the words. Rather, they should be listening to the reader read and "following the meaning."

Ignore errors that don't change meaning   Of course, since you recognize small, nonmeaning-changing errors as a sign of good eye-voice span, you will grit your teeth and ignore them!

When the reader makes a meaning-changing error, wait!   As Archie Bunker often told Edith, "Stifle yourself!" Control the urge to stop and correct the reader immediately. Rather, wait until the reader finishes the sentence or paragraph. What follows the error is often the information the reader needs in order to self-correct. Students who self-correct errors based on subsequent words read should be praised because they are demonstrating their use of cross checking while reading. Students who are interrupted immediately never learn to self-correct. Instead, they wait for someone else to correct them. Without self-correcting and self-monitoring, children will never become good readers.

If waiting doesn't work, give sustaining feedback   If the reader continues beyond the end of the sentence in which they made a meaning-changing error, the teacher should stop the reader by saying something like:

> "Wait a minute. That didn't make sense. You read, then the magician stubbled and fell. What does that mean?"

The teacher now has reinforced a major understanding that all readers must use if they are to decode words well. The word must have the right letters and must make sense. The letters in "stubbled" are very close to the letters in *stumbled* but "stubbled" does not make sense. The teacher should then pause and see if the reader can find a way to fix it. If so, the teacher should say,

> "Yes, *stumbled* makes sense. Good. Continue reading."

If not, the teacher should say something like,

> "Look at the letters in the word you called *stubbled*. What word do you know that looks almost like "stubbled" but is something people often do before they fall?"

If this does not help the teacher might just pronounce the word. Later, it may be useful to return to that page, review the misreading, and point out the *m* before the *b*. Or by suggesting a known rhyming word such as *crumbled* or *tumbled*.

Oral reading provides the "teachable moment"—a time for teachers to help students use the sense of what they are reading and the letter-sound relationships they know. When teachers respond to an error by waiting until a meaningful juncture is reached and responding first with a, "Did that make sense?" question, children focus more on self-monitoring for meaning and they begin to correct their own errors. The rest of the reading group hears how the teacher responds to the error. As they listen, they learn how they should use "sense" and decoding skills as they are reading. Feedback that encourages readers to self-correct and monitor their reading sends a "You can do it" message.

When a child misreads—

1. Wait until the end of the sentence.
2. Ask, "Does that make sense? Does it sound right?"
3. Have student reread.
4. If student still misreads, pronounce the word.
5. Have the student reread.
6. After the story is done, return to page and review the strategy used versus the strategy needed.

DECODING AND SPELLING ONE- AND TWO-SYLLABLE WORDS

English is an alphabetic language. Once you get past the most frequent words, there is a great deal of predictability in the letter-sound patterns. This predictability is not based on a one-letter, one-sound relationship, however, it is based on the pattern of letters that follow the vowel. The vowel and following letters have been given a variety of labels. Some teachers call them word families, others call them phonograms. Linguists refer to them as rimes. While the terminology is not important, we prefer to call them spelling patterns because we want children to learn that there is a pattern to how words are spelled and pronounced.

There are many activities that help children become sensitive to the patterns in words. We will describe two of our favorites: "Using Words You Know," and "Making Words."

Using Words You Know

There are hundreds of spelling patterns commonly found in one-syllable words. Rhyming word charts help children understand that words with the same vowels and ending letters usually rhyme and show them how many words they can read and write by thinking of a rhyming word. This is all critical preparation for what you must do when you see a word that you haven't seen before. Imagine that a young reader encounters the word *blob*. In order to use spelling patterns to decode this word, he or she must:

1. Realize this is an unknown word and look carefully at each letter.
2. Ask himself something like, "Do I know any other words spelled like this?
3. Search through the store of known words in his head looking for ones spelled with an *o-b* at the end.
4. Find some words, perhaps *Bob* and *job*.
5. Pronounce *blob* like *Bob* and *job*.
6. Reread the sentence to cross check pronunciation and meaning.

As you can see, this is a fairly complex mental strategy and some children who have all the prerequisites in place—words they can spell with the same spelling pattern, an understanding that words with the same spelling pattern usually rhyme, and the automatic habit of cross checking—don't know how to orchestrate all this. The following lesson series is designed to help children "put it all together."

Lesson one   Pick three words your students know that have many rhyming words that they aren't apt to know. For the first lesson, pick words in which the spelling pattern is quite different. You might begin, for example, with *job, nine,* and *map.* Using an overhead projector or sentence strip, write a sentence in which you use a word that rhymes with *job, nine,* or *map.* By placing paper over it on the overhead or by folding the sentence strip, cover all words except the word you want students to decode.

Place a sheet of chart paper on your board, divide it into three columns, and head each with *job, nine,* or *map.* Have your students do the same on a sheet of paper. Tell students that you will show them a word that rhymes with either *job, nine,* or *map.* When you show them the word, have them write it in the column under the rhyming word, then have them use the rhyming word to decode the new word. Have them verbalize the strategy they are using by saying something like, "If n-i-n-e is *nine,* s-p-i-n-e must be *spine.*" Record the words in the correct column of your chart once students have told you where to put it. Finally, reveal the sentence and have students explain how the word they decoded makes sense in the sentence.

Conclude the lesson by having students read the known words, *job, nine,* and *map* and the rhyming words, *blob/mob, spine/pine,* and *clap/snap.* Help them verbalize that when you come to a word you don't recognize, you should look at all the letters in it and then see if you know any other words that are spelled like that word and that might rhyme. Save the chart you made to use in the next lesson.

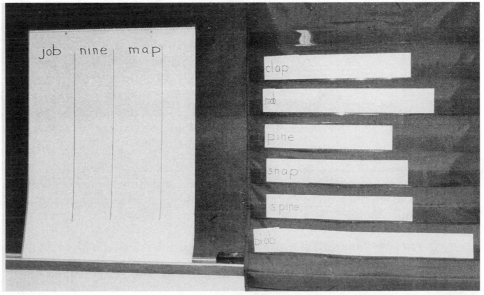

This photo shows how the lesson looks at the beginning. The sentence strips are folded to reveal only the underlined words at first. The children write the sentence strip word under the word it rhymes with on their paper and then the teacher writes it on the chart. After using the known word on the chart to decode the unfamiliar word, the rest of the sentence is revealed and the children cross check their pronunciation with the meaning derived from the other words in the sentence.

Lesson two   Tape the chart from the first lesson back to the board and have the known words and the rhyming words reviewed. Tape another chart next to it and write one more known word—*tell*—on this chart. Have students divide a sheet of paper into four columns and head each with the known words, *job, nine, map,* and *tell.* Do five or six sentences with words that rhyme with all four known words. Follow the procedure from lesson one and have students write the new word under the rhyming word; use the rhyming word to pronounce the new word. (If t-e-l-l is *tell,* s-h-e-l-l must be *shell.*) Then, reveal the sentence and have students explain how the meaning lets them cross check the pronunciation they came up with.

Conclude the lesson by having all the rhyming words read and by helping children verbalize how they use the words they know to figure out words that they don't know, and then reread the sentence to check themselves. Save the chart for lessons three and four.

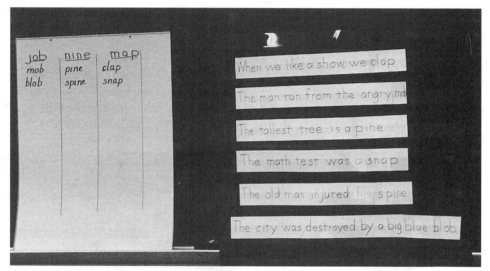

Here are the sentence strip and chart at the end of the second day's lesson.

Lesson three   Add a fifth known word to the chart—perhaps *jump.* Have students label columns with all five words and show sentences that contain words that rhyme with the five known words—perhaps *stump, grump, dine, strap, swell,* and *dump.*

Lesson four   Add a sixth known word—perhaps *make.* Have students label columns with all six words and show sentences that contain words that rhyme—perhaps *flake, shake, rob, plump, line,* and *bell.*

Lessons five–eight   Do the whole procedure again, starting with three known words for lesson five and building until students are comparing the six new words in lesson eight. You may want to use *made, ball, need, ride, frog,* and *but* and have students decode words such as *shut, nut, cut, jog, log, hog, spade, fade, grade, shade, trade, small, stall, mall, fall, wide, slide, bride, hide, seed, bleed, speed, weed,* and *feed.*

Lessons for independence   Now it is time to have students search their own heads for words they know that will help them decode new words. Do not give them any known words to match. Present them with words that can be decoded given many known words. After you show each word, have students write that word on their paper and under that word, have them write any words they know that have the same spelling pattern. Ask volunteers what words they wrote that have the same spelling pattern and list all the possibilities on the

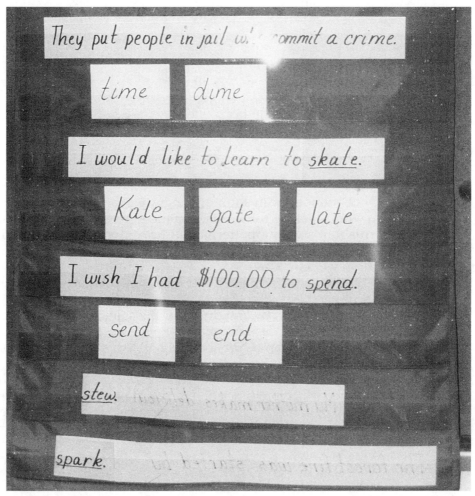

In this lesson to promote independence in decoding, the children must think of a word they know that has the same spelling pattern as the sentence strip word. The children volunteer their words that have the same spelling pattern and the teacher writes them on index cards and places them beneath the word that they are trying to figure out. Just as in the other lessons, the children decode the word without being able to see the rest of the sentence and then the teacher unfolds the sentence strip, revealing the rest of the sentence; the children cross check their pronunciation with meaning. The photo shows the lesson with three of the words decoded and two more—*stew* and *spark*—remaining.

board. As always, when they have arrived at a pronunciation, reveal the rest of the sentence so that they can cross check sound and meaning.

Most Common Phonograms (Spelling Patterns)

Here are the 37 most useful phonograms, or spelling patterns that are found in hundreds of words children read and write: (Wylie & Durrell, 1970)

ack	ap	est	ing	ot
ail	ash	ice	ink	uck
ain	at	ick	ip	ug
ake	ate	ide	it	ump
ale	aw	ight	ock	unk
ame	ay	ill	oke	
an	eat	in	op	
ank	ell	ine	ore	

Once students can look at a new word and search through their known words looking for words with the same spelling patterns, they need to learn about spelling patterns that have two common pronunciations. They also need to realize that cross checking will let them know which pronunciation works.

Write the words *know* and *show* to head one column and the words *how* and *now* to head another column. Help students to notice that the spelling pattern *ow* can have the sound in *know* and *show* or the sound in *how* and *now*. Write the words *food* and *good* to head two more columns and help students notice that the *ood* spelling pattern can be pronounced both ways. Have students head their papers just as you have headed the board.

Tell students that you will show them a word that ends in *ow* or *ood*. They should decide which pronunciation the word probably has and write it in the appropriate column. After each word is written, reveal the sentence and have the students see if their pronunciation makes sense.

A big black bird is a *crow.*
An animal that gives milk is a *cow.*
When it is cold, it may *snow.*
Some houses are made of *wood.*
The teacher was in a good *mood.*

You may want to do another lesson in which you use words that have two different pronunciations. Head the board and have the students head their papers with the words *now/show* and *bread/bead*. Show them sentences such as the following and help them to see that you can't tell which pronunciation to use until you read the rest of the sentence.

The dancer came out and took a *bow*.
He shot the arrow from his *bow*.
My favorite team was in the *lead*.
The part of the pencil that writes is the *lead*.

Students should learn that, "The bad news is that in English, there is not a perfect match between spelling patterns and pronunciations. The good news is that using what you know about spelling patterns and checking to see that what you read makes sense will almost always work!"

The Dove Dove

The Dove Dove (Marvin Terban, Clarion, 1985) is a delightful book with excellent examples of words that are spelled the same but pronounced differently.

Making Words

Making Words (Cunningham & Cunningham, 1992) is an activity in which children are given some letters and use these letters to make words.

Materials Needed for Making Words Lesson

Holders made from file folder cut in thirds—leaving the fold in the middle. Fold up the bottom edge about an inch to create a pocket. Crease well and staple on both ends.
Letter cards for the students that will fit in holder—vowels in different color; capitals on back.
Large letter cards and pocket chart.
Index cards with words to be made written on them.

To plan a Making Words lesson, we begin with the "secret" word—a word that can be made from all the letters. The word for this lesson is *winter*. Using the letters in winter, we choose 10–15 words that will give us some easy and harder words and several sets of rhymes. We then decide on the order in which words will be made, beginning with short words and building to larger words. We write these words on index cards to use in the sorting/transferring parts of the lesson. As all the children make the words in their holders, we choose one child to come and make it in the pocket chart. As the lesson begins, the letters **e i n r t w** are in the pocket chart. The children have the same letters and a holder. The teacher leads them to make words by saying:

"Take two letters and make **in.**"
"Add a letter to make the three-letter word, **tin.** Some cans are made of tin.
    Let's all say **tin.**"

"Now change just one letter and tin can become **ten.** You have ten fingers and ten toes. Say **ten.**"

"Move the letters in **ten** around and turn your **ten** into a **net.**"

"Now change just one letter and **net** can become **wet.**"

"Let's make one more three letter word **win.** Everyone say **win.**"

"Now, we are going to make some four letter words. Add one letter to **win** and you will have **twin.** My friend has a twin sister. Stretch out the word **twin** and listen to the sounds you hear yourself saying."

"Take all your letters out and start over and make another four letter word—**went.**"

"Now change just one letter and **went** can become **rent.** Let's all say **rent.**"

"The next word is a four letter word but you only hear three letters. Make **tire.** See if you can figure out what letter you don't hear but you need it to spell **tire.** Let's all say **tire.**"

"Now change just one letter and **tire** can become **wire.**"

"Now, let's make a five-letter word. Use five letters to spell **twine.** Twine is a heavy string we use to tie things with. Everyone say **twine.**"

"Has anyone figured out the secret word? I will come around to see if anyone has the secret word."

A child who has figured out **winter** makes it in the pocket chart and then everyone makes **winter** in their holders to finish the first part of the lesson.

Once all the words are made, we lead the students to sort for patterns. For the sorting part of the lesson, we put the words on index cards in the pocket chart. The first sort in this lesson is for beginning sounds. We pull out the word **win** and have them find the other words that begin with **w–wet, went, wire, winter.** Next, we take the word **tin** and have them find the other words that begin with **t–ten, twin, tire, twine.** Finally, we separate the **t** words into **tin, ten,** and **tire** and **twin** and **twine** and have them notice that **twin** and **twine** begin with **tw** and that if you stretch the words out, you can hear both letters.

Next we help them sort the words into rhymes:

in	net	rent	tire
tin	wet	went	wire
win			
twin			

When the rhyming words are sorted, we remind the children that rhyming words can help them read and spell words. We then write two new rhyming words on cards and have them place these words under the rhyming words and use the rhymes to decode them:

fire   spent

Finally, we say two rhyming words and help them see how the rhyming words help them spell them:

tent   thin

The children have holders and letters and are ready to begin the lesson. Big letter cards are displayed in the chart.

One vowel lessons   The first several lessons we do have only one vowel and make fewer words:

> Letters: a b l s t
> Make: as at lab tab sat bat bats stab last blast
> Sort for: l b
>   -ab -at -ast
>
> Transfer Words: cab fast past rat
>
> Letters: i g n s w
> Make: in sin win wins sing wing wings swing
>   (2 secret words!)
> Sort for: s w
>   -in -ing
>
> Transfer Words: fin ring pin ping
>
> Letters: i f g s t
> Make: if is it sit fit fits fist sift gift gifts
> Sort for: s f
>   -it -ift
>
> Transfer Words: lit sit lift shift

The teacher finds a child who has the word correctly made and sends him up to make it with the big letters.

Here are the words the children made including the secret word which can be made with all the letters.

Letters: o g n r s t

Make: so no go got rot not rot rots sort song snort
strong

Sort for: g n r s
-o -ot -ort -ong

Transfer Words: clot sport long slot

Here are the words sorted at the end of the lesson. The teacher helps the students use these rhyming words to read two new words and spell two new words with the same rhyming pattern.

Letters: i g n p r s
  Make: in sin pin pig rig rip sip snip sing ring rings
        spring
Sort for: s p r
          -in -ing -ig -ip
Transfer Words: strip string twin twig

We often tie lessons in with what we are reading or with something we are studying. Here are some December lessons:

Letters: e e n p r s t
  Make: net pet pets pest nest rest rent sent spent
        enter pester present (and serpent)
Sort for: n p r
          -et -est -ent
Transfer Words: wet west chest vent

Letters: a e c d l n s
Make: as an can Dan and sand land clan clean dance dances cleans candles
Sort for: c cl
-an -and
Transfer Words: band stand bran hand

Letters: i o c g k n s t
Make: is it in ink sink sing song king tick sick sock stock sting stink stocking
Sort for: s st
-ink -ing -ick -ock
Transfer Words: pink swing shock chick

Lessons in which the last words are sports-related are always motivating:

Letters: a o o b f l l t
Make: at bat fat all ball fall tall tool fool boat flat float football
Sort for: -at -all -ool -oat
Transfer Words: stall stool chat goat

Letters: a c h m p s
Make: am ham Pam Sam sap cap map lap chap mash cash camp champ champs
Sort for: -am -ap -ash -amp
Transfer Words: stash strap cramp clam

Letters: a a e b b l l s
Make: all lab slab blab ball bell sell seal sale bale able sable baseball
Sort for: -all -ab -ale -ell -able
Transfer Words: cable spell flab whale

Some making big words lessons   When working with older students and with more than eight letters, we print the letters on strips and duplicate them. Children cut the strips into letters and use them to make words.

Letters on strip: e e e i c d n p s t
Make: nice need deep seep seen dent sent cent scent spend steep dense tense scene nicest insect decent descent deepest neediest inspected centipedes
Sort for: est (ending)
ent eep ense
seen-scene sent-cent-scent
Transfer Words: spent creep creepiest steepest

Letters on strip: e e o u y l m m n n p t
Make: my ply toy yet pet met melt pelt pony only type
nylon penny money empty enemy lumpy plenty
employ moment monument employment
unemployment
Sort for: ment y (two pronunciations)
oy et elt
word relatives; employ, employment, unemployment
Transfer Words: enjoy enjoyment payment shipment

Letters on strip: e e i y m r s s t
Make: I eye try sty stem mess miss mist misty messy
tries sties miser misery sister resist series
system messier mysteries
Sort for: y (two pronunciations)
y changes to i
I-eye
Transfer Words: cry cries dry driest

Steps in Planning a Making Words Lesson

1. Decide what the "secret word" is that can be made with all the letters. In choosing this word, consider child interest, the curriculum tie-ins you can make, and the letter-sound patterns you can draw children's attention to through the sorting at the end.
2. Make a list of other words that can be made from these letters.
3. From all the words you could make, pick 12–15 words using these criteria:

   - Words that you can sort for the pattern you want to emphasize.
   - Little words and big words so that the lesson is a multilevel lesson (making the little words helps your lower-achieving students; making the big words challenges your highest-achieving students).
   - Words that can be made with the same letters in different places (barn/bran) so children are reminded that when spelling words, the ordering of the letters is crucial.
   - A proper name or two to remind them that we use capital letters.
   - Words that most students have in their listening vocabularies.

4. Write all the words on index cards and order them from smallest to biggest.
5. Once you have the two-letter, three-letter, etc. words together, order them so you can emphasize letter patterns and how changing the position of the letters or changing/adding just one letter results in a different word.
6. Store the cards in an envelope. Write the words in order on the envelope, the patterns you will sort for, and the transfer words.

Steps in Teaching a Making Words Lesson

1. Place the large letter cards needed in a pocket chart or along the chalk tray.
2. Have children pass out letters or pick up the letters needed.
3. Hold up and name the letters on the large letter cards and have the children hold up their matching small letter cards.
4. Write the numeral 2 (or 3 if there are no two-letter words in this lesson) on the board. Tell them to take two letters and make the first word. Have them say the word after you stretching out the word to hear all the sounds.
5. Have a child who has the first word made correctly make the same word with the large letter cards on the chalk tray or pocket chart. Do not wait for everyone to make the word before sending a child to make it with the big letters. Encourage anyone who didn't make the word correctly at first to fix the word when they see it made correctly.
6. Continue to make words, giving students clues such as, "Change the first letter only" or "Move the same letters around and you can make a different word" or "Take all your letters out and make another word." Send a child who has the word made correctly to make the word with the large letter cards. Cue them when they are to use more letters by erasing and changing the number on the board to indicate the number of letters needed.
7. Before telling them the last word, say "Now, it's time for the secret word—the word we can make with all of our letters. I am coming around to see if anyone has the secret word made in your holder." If someone has figured it out, send that child to make the big word. If not, tell them the word and let everyone make it.
8. Once all the words have been made, take the index cards on which you wrote the words and place them one at a time (in the same order that children made them) along the chalkledge or in the pocket chart. Have children say and spell the words with you as you do this. Have the children sort these words for patterns—including beginning sounds and rhymes.
9. To encourage transfer to reading and writing, show students how rhyming words can help them decode and spell other words. Write two words on index cards and have students put these two new words with the rhyming words and use the rhyming words to decode them. Finally, say two words that rhyme and have students spell these words by deciding which words they rhyme with.

STRATEGIES FOR BIG WORDS

Big words present special decoding problems. Most of the words we read are one- and two-syllable words but when polysyllabic words occur, they are often the words that carry most of the content. Decoding and spelling polysyllabic words is based on patterns, but these patterns are more sophisticated and require that students understand how words change in their spelling, pronunciation, and meaning, as suffixes and prefixes are added. The *g* in *sign* seems quite illogical until you realize that *sign* is related to *signal, signature,* and other words. Finding the *compose/composition* and *compete/competition* relationship will help students understand why the second syllable of *composition* and *competition* sound alike but are spelled differently.

In order to decode and spell big words, children must (1) have a mental store of big words that contain the spelling patterns common to big words; (2) chunk big words into pronounceable segments by comparing the parts of new big words to the big words they already know; and (3) recognize and use common prefixes and suffixes. The activities in this section are designed to help children build a store of big words and use these big words to decode and spell other big words.

Big Word Boards

Reserve one of the bulletin boards in your room for use as a big word board. As you teach science and social studies units or read literature selections, identify 15–25 big words that are key to understanding. Write these on large index cards with a black, thick permanent marker. Do not overwhelm your students by presenting all the words at once. Rather, add three or four each day as you introduce these words. As you put the words on the board, have the students chant the spelling (cheerleader style) with you. Then, have them close their eyes and chant the spelling again. Next, have them write a sentence that uses as many of the words as they can and still have a sensible sentence.

Once the words are displayed on the board, draw students' attention to these words as they occur in lectures, films, experiments, or discussions. As students write about what they are learning, encourage them to use the big words and to refer to the board for the correct spelling. Help students develop a positive attitude toward the learning of these big words by pointing out that every discipline has some critical big words; using these words separates the pros from the amateurs.

Here are the words that appeared on a big word board while students were studying about Antarctica:

Antarctica	geologic	regulation
exploration	exploitation	conservation
conservationists	minerals	petroleum
controversial	development	resources
environmentalists	environment	continent
vacationers	policies	confrontation
geologists	inhospitable	international

As you can see, there are numerous big words students will need as they read and write about Antarctica. Notice also how many of the common polysyllabic patterns are illustrated by just this one set of words. Students who can read and write *exploration, exploitation, regulation, conservation,* and *confrontation* now have several known big words that end in the reliable, but totally unexplainable, letter pattern t-i-o-n, which we pronounce "shun!" The words *geologists, conservationists,* and *environmentalists* contain the suffix, *ists,* which usually transforms a word from "the thing" to "the people who work on or worry about the thing." Including two important forms of the same base word—*conservation/conservationists, environment/environmentalists, geologic/geologists* allows students to see how the endings of words often change what part of the sentence they can be used in. If your students are not very sophisticated word users, you can greatly extend the control they have over language by pointing out how words change and by pointing out the similarities and differences in pronunciation, use, and spelling.

Modeling How to Decode Big Words

When you model, you show someone how to do something. In real life, we use modeling constantly to teach skills. We would not think of explaining how to ride a bike. Rather, we demonstrate and talk about what we are doing as the learner watches and listens to our explanation. Vocabulary introduction is a good place to model how you figure out the pronunciation of a word for students. Modeling is more than just telling them pronunciation, it is modeling the thinking that goes on when you meet up with a big word.

The word should be shown in a sentence context so that students are reminded that words must have the correct letters in the correct places and must make sense. Here is an example of how you might model for students one way to decode the word, *international*. Write on the board or overhead:

> The thinning of the ozone layer is an *international* problem.
> "Today, we are going to look at a big word that is really just a little word with a prefix added to the beginning and a suffix added to the end."

Underline <u>nation</u>.

> "Who can tell me this word? Yes, that is the word <u>nation</u>. Now, let's look at the prefix that comes before <u>nation</u>."

Underline <u>inter</u>.

> "This prefix is <u>inter</u>. You probably know <u>inter</u> from words such as, <u>interrupt</u> and <u>internal</u>. Now, let's look at what follows <u>inter</u> and <u>nation</u>."

Underline <u>al</u>.

> "You know <u>al</u> from many words such as, <u>unusual</u> and <u>critical</u>."

Write *unusual* and *critical* and underline the <u>al</u>.

> "Listen as I pronounce this part of the word."

Underline and pronounce <u>national</u>.

> "Notice how the pronunciation of <u>nation</u> changes when we put <u>a-l</u> on it. Now let's put all the parts together and pronounce the word—*inter nation al.* Let's read the sentence and make sure *international* makes sense."

Have the sentence read and confirm that ozone thinning is indeed a problem for many nations to solve.

> "You can figure out the pronunciation of many big words if you look for common prefixes such as <u>inter</u>, common root words such as <u>nation</u>, and common suffixes such as <u>al</u>.

In addition to helping you figure out the pronunciation of a word, prefixes and suffixes sometimes help you know what the word means or where in a sentence we can use the word. The word <u>nation</u> names a thing. When we describe a nation, we add the suffix <u>al</u> and have <u>national</u>. The prefix <u>inter</u> often means "between or among." Something that is <u>international</u> is between many nations. The Olympics are the best example of an <u>international</u> sporting event."

This sample lesson for introducing the word *international* demonstrates how a teacher can help students see and use morphemes, meaningful parts of words, to decode polysyllabic words. Notice that the teacher points out words that students might know and that have the same parts. In addition, meaning clues provided by the morphemes are provided whenever appropriate.

A similar procedure could be used to model how you would decode a word that didn't contain suffixes or prefixes. For the word *resources,* for example, the teacher would draw students' attention to the familiar first syllable *re* and then point out the known word *sources.* For *geologic,* the teacher might write and underline the *geo* in the known word *geography* and then point out the known word *logic. Policies* might be compared to *politics* and *agencies.*

Modeling is simply thinking aloud about how you might go about figuring out an unfamiliar word. It takes just a few extra minutes to point out the morphemes in *international* and to show how *policies* is like *politics* and *agencies,* but taking these extra few minutes is quickly paid back as students begin to develop some independence in figuring out those big words that carry so much of the content.

The Nifty-Thrifty-Fifty

English is the most morphologically complex language. Linguists estimate that for every word you know, you can figure out how to decode, spell, and build meaning for six or seven other words if you recognize and use the morphemic patterns in words. Activities in this section will teach students how to spell a Nifty-Thrifty-Fifty store of words to decode, spell, and build meaning for thousands of other words. These 50 words include examples for all the common prefixes and suffixes as well as common spelling changes. Because these 50 words help with so many other words we have named them the "Nifty-Thrifty-Fifty."

The Nifty-Fifty-Thrifty words should be introduced gradually and students should practice chanting and writing them until their spelling and decoding become automatic. The procedures for working with these words and their important parts are:

1. Display the words, arranged by first letter, someplace in the room. Add four or five each week. You may want to use a bulletin board or hang a banner above a bulletin board and attach the words to it. The words need to be big and bold so that they are seen easily from wherever the students are writing. Using different colors makes them more visible and attractive. Many teachers use large colored index cards or write them with different colors of thick, bold permanent markers.

2. Explain to students that in English, many big words are just smaller words with prefixes and suffixes added to the word. Good spellers do not memorize the spelling of every new word they come across. Rather, they notice the patterns in words and these patterns include prefixes, suffixes, and spelling changes that occur when these are added.

The Nifty-Thrifty-Fifty

(From Cunningham & Hall, 1998)

NIFTY-THRIFTY-FIFTY	TRANSFERABLE CHUNKS	
antifreeze	anti	
beautiful		ful (y-i)
classify		ify
communities	com	es (y-i)
community	com	y
composer	com	er
continuous	con	ous (drop e)
conversation	con	tion
deodorize	de	ize
different		ent
discovery	dis	y
dishonest	dis	
electricity	e	ity
employee	em	ee
encouragement	en	ment
expensive	ex	ive
forecast	fore	
forgotten		en (double t)
governor		or
happiness		ness (y-i)
hopeless		less
illegal	il	
impossible	im	ible
impression	im	sion
independence	in	ence
international	inter	al
invasion	in	sion
irresponsible	ir	ible
midnight	mid	
misunderstand	mis	
musician		ian
nonliving	non	ing (drop e)
overpower	over	
performance	per	ance
prehistoric	pre	ic
prettier		er (y-i)
rearrange	re	
replacement	re	ment
richest		est
semifinal	semi	

NIFTY-THRIFTY-FIFTY	TRANSFERABLE CHUNKS	
signature		ture
submarine	sub	
supermarkets	super	s
swimming		ing (double m)
transportation	trans	tion
underweight	under	
unfinished	un	ed
unfriendly	un	ly
unpleasant	un	ant (drop e)
valuable		able (drop e)

3. Tell students that one way to practice words is to say the letters in them aloud in a rhythmic, chanting fashion. Tell students that while this might seem silly, it really isn't because the brain responds to sound and rhythm. (That is one of the reasons you can sing along with the words of a familiar song even though you couldn't say the words without singing the song, and also why jingles and raps are easy to remember.) Point to each word and have students chant it (cheerleader style) with you. After "cheering" for each word, help students analyze the word, talking about meaning and determining the root, prefix, suffix, and noting any spelling changes. Here is an example of the kind of word introduction students find most helpful:

composer—A composer is a person who composes something. Many other words such as *writer, reporter,* and *teacher* are made up of a root word and the suffix *er* meaning a person or thing that does something. When *er* is added to a word that already has an *e,* the original *e* is dropped.

discovery—A discovery is something you discover. The prefix *dis* often changes a word to an opposite form. To cover something can mean to hide it. When you discover it, it is no longer hidden. *Discovery* is the root word *cover* with the added prefix *dis* and suffix *y.* There are no spelling changes.

encouragement—When you encourage someone, you give them encouragement. Many other words such as *argue, argument; replace, replacement* follow this same pattern. The root word for *encourage* is *courage.* So, *encouragement* is made up of the prefix *en,* the root word *courage,* and the suffix *ment.*

hopeless—Students should easily see the root word *hope* and the suffix *less.* Other similar words are *painless* and *homeless.*

impossible—The root word *possible* with the suffix *im.* In many words, including *impatient* and *immature* the suffix *im* changes the word to an opposite.

musician—A musician is a person who makes music. A beautician helps make you beautiful and a magician makes magic. *Musician* has the root word *music* with the suffix *ian* that sometimes indicates the person who does something. There are no spelling changes but the pronunciation changes. Have students say the words *music* and *musician, magic,* and *magician* and notice how the pronunciation changes.

4. Once you have noticed the composition for each word, helped students see other words that work in a similar way, and cheered for each word, have students write each word. Writing the word with careful attention to each letter and the sequence of each letter helps students use another mode to practice the word. (Do not however assign students to copy words five times each. They just do this "mechanically" and often do not focus on the letters.) Students enjoy writing the words more and focus better on the word if you make it a riddle or game. You can do this simply by giving clues to the word you want them to write such as:

1. Number 1 is the opposite of discouragement.
2. Number 2 is the opposite of hopeful.
3. For number 3, write the word that tells what you are if you play the guitar.
4. For number 4, write what you are if you play the guitar but you also make up the songs you play.
5. Number 5 is the opposite of possible.
6. For number 6, write the word that has *cover* for the root word.

After writing the words, have students check their own papers once more chanting the letters aloud underlining each as they say it.

5. When you have a few minutes of "sponge" time, practice the words by chanting or writing. As you are cheering or writing each word, ask students to identify the root, prefix, and suffix and talk about how these affect the meaning of the root word. Also have them point out any spelling changes.

6. Once students can automatically, quickly, and correctly spell the words and explain to you how they are composed, it is time to help them see how these words can help them decode and spell other words. Remind students that good spellers do not memorize the spelling of each word. Rather they use words they know and combine roots, suffixes, and prefixes to figure out how to spell lots of other words. Have the students spell words that are contained in the words and words you can make by combining parts of the words.

Have each word used in a sentence and talk about the meaning relationships when appropriate. Note spelling changes as needed. From just the eight words: *composer, discovery, encouragement, hopeless, impossible, musician, richest,* and *unfriendly,* students should be able to decode, spell, and discuss meanings for:

compose	pose	discover	cover	encourage
courage	hope	possible	music	rich
friend	friendly	dispose	discourage	discouragement
enrich	enrichment	uncover	richly	hopelessly

7. Continue adding words gradually, going though the above procedures with all of the words. Do not add words too quickly, and provide lots of practice

with these words and the other words that can be decoded and spelled by combining parts of these words. Since this store of words will provide patterns for so many other words, you want your students to "overlearn" these words so that they are called up instantly and automatically when students meet similar words in their reading or need to spell similar words while writing.

Nifty-Fifty-Thrifty Transfer Words

Here are just some of the words they should be able to decode, spell, and discuss meanings for by using parts of all fifty words:

conform	relive	declassify	powerlessly
conformity	repose	decompose	powerlessness
inform	reclassify	deform	superpower
informer	revalue	deformity	finalize
informant	recover	prearrange	finalizing
information	rediscover	resign	finalization
misinform	electrical	resignation	weighty
uninformed	displease	designation	weightier
formation	discontinue	significant	weightiest
formal	disposal	significance	weightless
transform	musical	freezer	undervalue
transformation	continual	freezing	friendlier
performer	employer	freezable	friendliest
responsibility	employment	subfreezing	friendliness
responsive	unemployment	underclass	unfriendliness
responsiveness	unemployed	overexpose	unpleasantness
honesty	employable	underexpose	historical
dishonesty	unemployable	superimpose	historically
honestly	difference	undercover	expressive
legally	consignment	forecaster	impressive
illegally	nationality	forecasting	repressive
responsibly	nationalities	forecastable	invasive
irresponsibly	internationalize	miscast	noninvasive
arranging	interdependence	antidepressant	invasiveness
rearranging	depress	overture	hopefully
placing	depression	empower	hopelessly
replacing	depressive	empowerment	predispose
misplacing	deport	powerful	predisposition
report	deportation	powerfully	deodorant
reporter	deportee	powerfulness	beautician
refinish	devalue	powerless	electrician

"The Wheel"

The popular game show, "Wheel of Fortune," is based on the idea that having meaning and some letters will allow you to figure out many words. On "Wheel of Fortune," meaning is provided by the category to which the word belongs. A variation of this game can be used to introduce big words and teach students to use meaning and all the letters they know. Here is how to play "The Wheel."

Remind students that many words can be figured out (even if we can't decode all the parts) as long as we think about what makes sense and keep the parts that we do know in the right places. Ask students who have watched "Wheel of Fortune" to explain how it is played. Then explain how your version of "The Wheel" will be different:

1. Contestants guess all letters without considering if they are consonants or vowels.
2. They must have all letters filled in before they can say the word.
3. The word must fit in a sentence rather than in a category.
4. They will win paper clips instead of great prizes!
5. Vanna will not be there to turn letters!

Write a sentence on the board and draw blanks for each letter of an important word. Here is an example:

If you were to travel to Antarctica, you would be struck by its almost unbelievable _ _ _ _ _ _ _ _ _.

Have a student begin by asking, "Is there a . . . ?" If the student guesses a correct letter, fill that letter in. Give that student one paper clip for each time that letter occurs. Let the student continue to guess letters until he or she gets a "No!" When a student asks about a letter that is not there, write the letter above the puzzle and go on to the next student.

Make sure that all letters are filled in before anyone is allowed to guess. (This really shows them the importance of spelling and attending to common spelling patterns!) Give the person who guesses the word correctly five bonus paper clips! As with other games, if someone says the answer out of turn, immediately award the bonus paper clips to the person whose turn it was. The student having the most paper clips at the end is the winner!

For our example, a student might ask if there is an *r*? ("Sorry, no *r*!") The next student asks for an *s*. One *s* is filled in.

If you were to travel to Antarctica, you would be struck by its almost unbelievable _ _ s _ _ _ _ _ _.

The student is given one paper clip and continues to ask questions. "Is there a *t*?" "Yes, one *t*!"

If you were to travel to Antarctica, you would be struck by its almost unbelievable _ _ s _ _ _ t _ _ _.

The student asks for an *o*. Two *o*'s are filled in and the student receives two more paper clips.

> If you were to travel to Antarctica, you would be struck by its almost unbelievable _ _ s o _ _ t _ o _.

Next the student asks for an *i* and then for an *n*.

> If you were to travel to Antarctica, you would be struck by its almost unbelievable _ _ s o _ _ t i o n.

After much thought, the student asks for an *m*. Unfortunately, there is no *m*, so play passes to the next student who asks for an *e*, an *a*, a *d*, and an *l* and correctly spells out—*d e s o l a t i o n!* (The teacher points out that desolation is also the emotion felt by the previous student who came so close to winning!) Play continues with another big word introduced in a sentence context.

Students who are introduced to vocabulary by playing "The Wheel" pay close attention to the letter patterns in big words. They also get in the habit of making sure that the word they figure out, based on having some of the letters, fits the meaning of the sentence in which it occurs.

Computer Versions of The Wheel

There are software versions of "Wheel of Fortune" and Hangman available that you may want to use. *Phraze Kraze* ($10, B. Pettit, E. 4212 10th St., Spokane, WA 99202) is our favorite for the Macintosh since it has Vanna, the wheel, and all!

Summary

Reading and writing are meaning-constructing activities but they are both dependent on words. All good readers and writers have a store of high-frequency words that they read and spell instantly and automatically. Good readers and writers can also decode and spell most regular words. Most of the words we read are little words. The big words, however, are often the critical words—the ones that convey the information we need to learn. Many struggling readers have no strategies for decoding big words and have very few big words in their store of words that they can instantly recognize and effortlessly spell. The last section of this chapter is focused on helping children build a store of big words that they can automatically read and write, and on giving them strategies for figuring out new big words. There is another part of the big-word story, which is developing meaning for big words. This meaning is best developed and retrieved when the words to be learned are all related to one topic. In the next chapter, we will describe how you can help all children increase the size of their meaning vocabularies as you help them increase their knowledge of important topics.

REFERENCES

Adams, M. J. (1990). *Beginning to read: Thinking and learning about print.* Cambridge, MA: M.I.T. Press.

Cunningham, P. M. (1995). *Phonics they use: Words for reading and writing* (2nd ed.). New York: HarperCollins.

Cunningham, P. M., & Hall, D. P. (1998). *Month-by-Month Phonics for Upper Grade: A Second Chance for Struggling Readers and Students Learning English.* Greensboro, NC: Carson-DeLosa.

Cunningham. P. M., & Cunningham, J. W. (1992). Making words: Enhancing the invented spelling-decoding connection. *The Reading Teacher, 46,* 106–107.

Wylie, R. E., & Durrell, D. D. (1970). Teaching vowels through phonograms. *Elementary English, 47,* 787–791.

6

SCIENCE AND SOCIAL STUDIES MATTER TO STRUGGLING READERS

When Jimmy was in kindergarten, he wrote about a cow and then drew a picture of it. . . . Large for his age, Jimmy was a shy child and a bit reluctant to speak, although he was well liked by the other children. His social interactions were characterized less by conversation than by actions and gestures. . . . His journal entry on the first day of first grade included an initial consonant for barn, silo, cat, pet, hamster, and grass. By the following May, one of his journal entries was about the number of cows on his family's farm.

"I like cows. We have 80."

In the reader's workshop, Jimmy often spent time studying the farm pages in Richard Scary's *Best Word Book Ever* (1963). In individual conferences, he pointed to a label word such as "corncrib," read it, and then added information from his own experience. In writer's workshop, the first piece he published was entitled "Chores."

I was sleeping. I had breakfast. I milked cows. I fed calves. I went home.

On a class trip to the library to check out books, he walked over to my side so that our arms touched, nudged me, and still staring straight ahead, asked in his deep raspy voice, "Where's the cow books?"

(From Christine Duthie's (1996) *True stories: Nonfiction literacy in the primary classroom*, p. 1.)

As the previous excerpt indicates, Jimmy and most other children are primarily interested in their world. Schools must take the responsibility for helping children learn about their world and the broader world. This has always been a responsibility of the schools, but one that elementary schools have not taken very seriously. When you think about what we teach children in schools, you can divide almost everything into knowledge and skills. The abilities to read, spell, write, do math, use the computer, sing a song, play the clarinet, throw a ball, speak a foreign language, etc. are all skills—things you can do. The understanding that there are seven continents, that each state has two senators, that the Civil War was fought in the 1860s, that mammals are warm-blooded animals, and that Martin Luther King led the civil rights movement are all knowledge—things that you know. For many years, our elementary schools have focused on skills and largely ignored knowledge. In many schools with large numbers of struggling readers, teachers are instructed to "teach the basics." The basics usually referred to are the three r's—reading, 'riting, and 'rithmetic. The knowledge part of the curriculum—usually found in the subjects of science and social studies—are too often ignored in the primary grades of many schools that teach a high proportion of at-risk children.

The emphasis on skill subjects and the exclusion of the knowledge subjects often results in a short-term gain and a long-term deficit. In school after school, in which the primary emphasis in grades K-3 is on skills, children perform adequately on standardized tests through the second or third grade and then show steady declines from fourth grade on. Teachers from fourth grade on are supposed to and try to teach the knowledge subjects such as science and social studies. They often find, however, that even their average students can't read the textbooks or "can read them but don't understand what they are reading." Children who can read the words but cannot understand what they are reading are not really reading.

Basal reader series have typically followed the marketplace. Those developed during the "back-to-basics" era focused primarily on skill development and paid little attention to content. "Whole language" basals included more good children's literature with lots of award-winning modern realistic fiction, but little informational reading, such as biography, history, and scientific material. As this book is being written, "Phonics" is the hot topic and the basals that will be in your classrooms will have lots more space and time devoted to phonics and probably even less time for informational selections and strategy lessons on reading informational text.

Teachers who are committed to helping struggling readers achieve high levels of literacy must not ignore the prior knowledge/reading comprehension relationship. Children in the primary grades must spend a portion of each day engaging in activities in which increasing their world knowledge is the primary goal. Like most complex problems, there is no simple way to achieve this goal in the limited time available. There is, however, an often-tried simple solution that won't work. Having children "memorize" lists of vocabulary words or isolated facts and then testing them on these generally will not increase their world knowledge. (Perhaps you remember being forced to memorize the elements and abbreviations on the periodic chart in Chemistry or the definitions for some uncommon, unrelated words, such as, *abase, abate, abet, ablate, ablaut,* or *abjure* in preparation for the SAT or some other test.)

Learning theorists believe that our brain has two distinct learning systems—the rote system and the associative system (Caine and Caine, 1991). Disconnected facts are stored in the rote system. Storing them here requires much repetition and, once they are stored, they are still quite difficult to retrieve. Most of what we know is stored in the associative system, which is just what its name implies. The facts, terms, etc. in the associative system are all associated with each other in a vast, complex network. When we find one, we find all the others. When you read or hear the word, *brontosaurus,* for example, you not only recognize it as a type of dinosaur, but you think of all the other dinosaur words and facts you know—words like *prehistoric, tyrannosaurus rex,* and *pterodactyl* come to mind immediately. In addition to facts and terms, your associative memory stores places, events, feelings, and emotions. The word *brontosaurus* may "remind" you of a trip to a dinosaur exhibit or of a wonderful dinosaur book you used to have (Whatever happened to that book, anyway?). You may smile as you remember your first crush on a boy or girl who was a "dinosaur nut!"

Our goal in helping children expand their world knowledge must be to help them learn a lot about a number of different topics and to focus on individual words that are part of this topic knowledge. One of the most difficult decisions faced by teachers is which knowledge to focus on. There is so much that children need to know, and in order to teach something well we must invest both time and energy. Most states have established knowledge goals for the elementary grades. These goals can usually be found in the science and social studies curriculums. In the remainder of this chapter, we will suggest a variety of ways that successful schools and teachers make room in their crowded curriculum for in-depth science and social studies learning.

MAKE INFORMATIONAL RESOURCES THE CENTERPIECE OF YOUR INSTRUCTION

Throughout this book, we have emphasized using a wide variety of reading materials. Putting informational books and other materials in the center—rather than in the periphery—of your instruction will go a long way toward achieving dual goals: providing lots of opportunities for children to learn about their world and the world beyond their everyday experiences, and increasing the engagement and motivation of children who love learning about "real things." You can begin to work toward the goal of putting informational resources at the center of your instruction by:

- Reading to children from informational books.
- Providing the largest possible range and variety of informational books and magazines as part of the classroom library.
- Planning unit and author studies around the writers of informational books for children such as Gail Gibbons, Dorothy Hinshaw Patent, Jean George, Alexandra Parsons, and numerous others.
- Providing print-rich classrooms including newspaper clippings, magazine articles, brochures, and content-related poetry.
- Providing research materials including an updated set of children's encyclopedias, almanacs, and internet sites if networking is available.
- Using informational big books for shared reading—even for upper grades in which some wonderful books contain visuals such as graphs, charts, maps, etc. that everyone can see.

You can learn a lot from reading. Many children like to read about "real" things and real people.

Why Information Books?

Answer questions
Ask questions
Encourage critical thinking
Stimulate interest and curiosity
Create a sense of wonder
Develop understanding of people, places, and things
Provide additional models and inspiration for writing
Provide rich vocabulary
Stimulate the making of connections
Enlarge store of background knowledge

Contain wonderful and varied visuals:

    photographs   drawings   maps   graphs   diagrams

Introduce new authors and illustrators
Provide easy reading without the stigma of "baby" books
Show a variety of text patterns, design, and layout features
Reduce "fragmented curriculum/day" by creating links to math, science, and social studies
Engage students in multiple ways of knowing/thinking/behaving

    . . . like an historian
    . . . like a scientist
    . . . like a mathematician

Encourage involvement in learning

USE WHAT YOU KNOW

Many teachers lament that students "know" more than they use. But many teachers don't use what they know either! Often in our classroom observations, we watch a teacher in the language-arts block doing wonderful strategy instruction—modeling, demonstrating, posing thought provoking "queries" and using a variety of partner reading, choral reading, and ERT . . . s (Everyone Read

There are lots of wonderful informational books written just for children.

To . . .). Obviously, this is a savvy teacher who knows and uses "best practice" teaching strategies. Often, however, this same savvy teacher resorts to round-robin reading and low-level questions during social studies and science. Why don't teachers, who know how to do good reading and writing instruction, use their knowledge when doing reading and writing activities during science and social studies?

As students most of us experienced reading in science and social studies as "reading around the room," with each and every student reading one paragraph aloud. Most of us don't remember this fondly. We fidgeted and felt uncomfortable as one of our struggling reader classmates stumbled over all of the big words in his assigned paragraph. Some of us counted paragraphs to find the one that we would read, and practiced so that we wouldn't make a dumb mistake in front of the whole class. Once our turn was over, we breathed a sigh of relief and daydreamed our way through the rest of the period.

Transfer is difficult and past experience is a powerful force. Because of our own experience with reading and writing in science and social studies, it is hard for us to envision the classes we now teach in dramatically different ways. But, we can make this change. Knowledge is power and once we decide we want to use what we know, we are not bound by our past. Here are some of the things described in previous chapters that belong in science and social studies instruction:

- KWLs, QTAs, and Listening-Reading Transfer lessons.
- Drawing and acting, which allows students to use their multiple intelligences to think about content.
- Using a variety of reading formats including partner reading, choral reading, echo reading and ERT . . . s instead of "around-the-room" reading.
- Using choose-your-book groups when you can find multiple copies of three or four books related to the topic being studied.
- Using a variety of graphic organizers, including webs, feature matrices, data charts, timelines, double bubbles, and diagrams to organize the information read.
- Using these same graphic organizers to organize the information gained from field trips, videos, simulations, experiments, and all the varied sources of information you provide.
- Using these same graphic organizers to organize information before writing summaries and reports.
- Using shared and group writing formats to write informational text.
- Using focused writing lessons to model how you write reports, summaries, and other expository forms.
- Using paragraph frames to help students learn to write expository text.
- Using computer programs that help students organize ideas and often provide pictures and other graphics for report writing.
- Taking students through the editing and publishing phases during language-arts time with a piece written during science or social studies time.

- Making sure students spell word wall words correctly in all writing—including writing done during science and social studies.
- Using content words in the words block as the "secret word" in a Making-Words lesson.
- Doing "Guess the Covered Word" lessons with a content-oriented paragraph from a big book or one you have written so that students will transfer their cross-checking skills.
- Making Big Word Boards from your science or social studies vocabulary.
- Modeling how to decode science and social studies big words and pointing out helpful roots, prefixes, and suffixes.

PROVIDE AS MUCH REAL EXPERIENCE AS POSSIBLE

Both research and our own experience tell us that we remember best the real things that we do and see. Books, videos, and internet explorations help build concepts, but there is nothing like seeing it, touching it, doing it, hearing it, smelling it. If we are serious about building the knowledge stores of our struggling students, we must constantly ask if there is any way of taking our students to see "the real thing" or bringing "the real thing" into the classroom.

Field Trips

Mention field trips to a group of teachers and watch them cringe! Field trips can be expensive, a pain to plan, and exhausting to take! Realizing this, we still must begin our specific suggestions for expanding world knowledge by encouraging you to consider the possibility of taking your students somewhere outside the four walls of your classroom. Field trips allow students to experience "the real thing." Field trips can be to areas of the playground or places in the neighborhood. Children can walk or take public transportation to the grocery store, the post office, the local mall, a meadow, a pond, or a stream. Trips further afield often require buses, lunches, and so on, but the cost of taking a few of these each year will be paid back to you in motivation. Children who go to a museum, factory, park, or theater and see, firsthand, the things they are studying often form an emotional attachment to the trip and to the things they experienced on the trip. This emotional involvement is then transferred to the topic that they are studying. Many children have a "Who cares?" attitude toward topics they know nothing about. Taking them on trips to experience real things and real people connected with these things goes a long way toward establishing critical emotional engagement.

Even a field trip to the sidewalk outside the school can prove truly fascinating. Before you go, read and reread Jean Craighead George's book, *Once Upon a Sidewalk*. This book details a day in the life of a worker ant and presents an ant's eye-view of life on, under, and around a sidewalk. The book inevitably creates a real curiosity about the common world under our feet and provides an impetus for taking a careful look at what is going on in our natural environment. The book and field trip provide a wealth of descriptive writing opportunities. A sidewalk field trip can be followed by a playground or park field trip in which children measure and mark a square foot of turf and then observe and record plant and insect activity.

Of course, if you are going to go to all the trouble of taking them on a field trip, you should get every ounce of learning and motivation possible from the experience. This means you must "hype" the trip and prepare them for what they will see and what they want to find out. Showing them pictures, slides, or a video beforehand of what they will see is a good way to get them thinking about what they will experience. You may want to do a KWL lesson in which, before going, you have them list what they know and what they want to find out. Upon your return, have them fill in the column listing what they learned. You may also want to give them each a pocket-sized index card and a stubby pencil and have each student be responsible for finding out and writing down the answer to one or two questions to be shared later with the whole class.

In all schools, field trips are less common today than they were two decades ago. Two-parent working families, single-parent families, liability rulings, and "back to basics" have put a damper on taking children into the very world that we want them to learn about. In schools with a large number of "at-risk" children, field trips are often a real rarity. This is unfortunate because these schools are often located in settings that offer a wealth of opportunities nearby for developing world knowledge. These districts are often poor in terms of funding, but are located in an environment that is rich with opportunities. If we are serious about expanding the world knowledge of at-risk children and about fostering their desire to learn about the world beyond their block/neighborhood, we must reconsider taking them into that world.

Bringing Real Things into the Classroom

When you can't take a field trip or take *them* to *it*, the next best thing is to bring *it* to *them*. As you are planning to have your students learn about a particular topic, look around—beg and borrow objects that are even vaguely related to the topic. Some museums have crates of objects related to commonly studied topics. Some school media centers collect and store "things" that many teachers need. In some schools, teachers take responsibility for gathering objects related to a particular topic and then teach these topics at different times so that everyone can use the same objects.

Whenever possible, use objects that are commonly found in the homes or the environment of your students. When you use these in certain activities or show how they are related to something that you are studying, your students will probably associate the objects with that learning and will think about what they are learning when they see those objects in their own environment. When you use common objects, ask students if they have these at home or have seen them someplace else. Then, suggest that the next time they notice these objects, they explain to someone who is with them—parent, brother, cousin, friend, or uncle—how these common objects are related to what they are learning.

For instance, in conjunction with David MacCaulay's book, *How Things Work* (NY: Little Simon, 1984), bring in an old faucet, a large zipper, or maybe

Sometimes you can get real people to bring real things into your classroom. This class is doing a unit on safety and rules and is learning more about both from a visiting police officer.

an iron or a camera that doesn't work. Partially disassemble the object and key the pages of the book that provide diagrams and explanations of how these objects work. Provide an old magnifying glass for closer looks. We can use this same magnifying glass to examine household plants for mites, or to examine plant structures or the soil in the pot. We can even observe and describe the children's pets that might accompany them to class for an hour or a day.

Of course, these observations and descriptions can and should be recorded—through writing, drawing, and labeling. (Steve Moline's previously described *I See What You Mean* is an excellent source of varied and creative ways to help students record.) Students can work collaboratively in groups or as a class to create their own book about "How School Things Work" or "How We Care for Our Pets." If your school is connected to the information highway, you might publish some of the information learned on the web.

Scavenger Hunts

Have you ever been on a scavenger hunt? Everyone has a list of things to find, a limited amount of time in which to find them, and the team that finds the most things wins. You can adapt the scavenger hunt notion to help your children expand their world and word knowledge (Cunningham, Crawley &

Mountain, 1983). Choose a topic that you are about to study or a piece of literature you are about to read. As you think about what the children will be reading and learning, select words for which you would like to develop meaning and for which children could scavenge for pictures and/or objects.

For the topic, *Weather,* for example, a teacher decided that pictures and/or objects could be found to represent:

cirrus clouds	hurricane
cumulus clouds	lightning
stratus clouds	fog
barometer	frost
thermometer	rainbow
cyclone	meteorologist
tornado	wind vane
blizzard	rain gauge

She made a list of these words and distributed the list to teams of children in her class. She then explained that the class was going to have a scavenger hunt. The teams had one week to collect as many objects and/or pictures as they could to represent the words on the list. They could bring one object and one picture for each word and would get two points for an object and one point for a picture. She then let the teams meet for a few minutes and discuss what the words meant and who thought they could find what objects. When the children protested about not being able to bring in a hurricane, she responded, "No, but perhaps you could bring a picture of a hurricane." When children said, "I don't even know what a rain gauge is," she said, "Well, maybe you had better look it up in the dictionary or encyclopedia or ask someone who does know, if you want your team to win the scavenger hunt."

All week, the teacher let the teams meet briefly each day to discuss what they had found and what they still needed. She stressed that they should whisper and keep their finds secret because they didn't want the other teams to figure out where they were finding things. When asked if drawings (of the objects) were allowed, she responded that they were as long as they were well drawn and actually looked like the object being represented. Later, someone asked if you could bring "something like the object, but smaller, like a model of it." She responded that, "If the model or smaller thing really represented the real thing, it would count as an object."

On the designated day, the children came with the "scavenged" objects and pictures. Each team gathered and laid out their finds. Most teams had pictures—drawn, found, or copied—of almost everything. There were also a surprising number of real objects, including a handmade rain gauge and one of those small, glass balls with a scene inside that becomes a "blizzard" when you turn it upside down! The team who had thought of this was particularly pleased with their cleverness and the other teams did have to admit that it was "kind of like a model of a blizzard."

The winning team was rewarded for its efforts. They got to create the weather bulletin board! They put all the words up and then made a collage of the pictures brought in by all of the teams. They labeled the objects and put these on a nearby table. They then put in big letters:

WEATHER BULLETIN BOARD CREATED BY WINNERS OF WEATHER
SCAVENGER HUNT

and signed all their names.

This first scavenger hunt was a "limited" success. The children learned what a scavenger hunt was and discovered that there were ways to make real things and find models of real things. As the year went on, and after several more scavenger hunts, the children became very clever at hunting and creating. Their world and word knowledge increased, as did their enjoyment in searching for and creating real things and pictures.

DESIGNATE SOME DAYS AS INTEGRATED DAYS

The fragmentation of our curriculum into specific subject areas is frustrating to many teachers and makes learning difficult for many children. For decades, experts have asked why we need a separate time and curriculum for reading—particularly in the intermediate grades. To become better readers, children have to read something. Why shouldn't that something be related to some science or social studies topic we want them to learn about?

While integrating the learning across subject areas makes a great deal of sense, there have been many barriers to its implementation. There is often a separate curriculum guide and/or textbook for each subject area. Each subject also has its own set of distinct goals and objectives. Most schools still require grades to be given in the separate subjects. Finally, in some elementary schools, teachers are, unfortunately, departmentalized and children move to different teachers for different subjects.

While these barriers are real and make integration difficult, there are compelling reasons to integrate. The first and most obvious reason is time. When you teach a comprehension lesson using some material about Canada or have children research a particular animal and then write and illustrate a class-produced animal encyclopedia, you "kill two birds with one stone." All elementary teachers know that we are constantly adding to the elementary curriculum and we never take anything away. Integrating the skills of reading and writing with the knowledge-oriented subjects, such as science and social studies, is one way to make better use of the time we have (Walp & Walmsley, 1995).

Relevance and application are equally compelling arguments for integration. Many children don't see any reason for learning to read, write, and compute. When reading, writing, and math are taught as separate skills, children often do not apply them at other times or to other subjects. The difficulty children experience reading in their content-area textbooks can be partially traced to the fact that they have spent most of their time learning how to read stories. Assessment data in math shows that children can solve almost any problem if it is all set up for them. When presented with a story problem that requires them to decide what operations to perform on what numbers, however, their

Integration Ideas

Here are just a few of the topics explored on Integrated Days and some of the wonderful informational books related to those topics:

Dolphins (Grades 2–3)

Dolphins Home. Donna Bailey & Chris Butterworth (Steck-Vaugh).
Different Kinds of Dolphins. Donna Bailey & Chris Butterworth (Steck-Vaugh).
The Sea World Book of Dolphins. S. Leatherwood & R. Reeves (Harcourt, Brace, Jovanovich).
Dolphins! June Behrens (Children's Press).
Dolphins. Norman Barrett (Franklin Watts).
Whale and Dolphin. (Raintree-Steck-Vaughn).
Dolphins. Margaret Davidson (Scholastic) Harder book.

Early America (Grades 2–4)

Sarah Martin's Day: A Day in the Life of a Pilgrim Girl. Kate Waters (Scholastic).
Colonial Crafts: The School. J. H. Corwin (Franklin Watts).
If You Lived in Colonial Times. Ann McGovern & B. Turkle (Scholastic).
The Boston Coffee Party. Doreen Rappaport (Scholastic).
Sam the Minuteman. N. Benchley (HarperCollins).
George Washington: First President. Carol Greene (Children's Press).
The Connecticut Colony. D. B. Fradin (Children's Press) Harder book.

The Civil War Era (Grades 4–5)

Turn Homeward Hannalee. Patricia Beatty (Morrow) Harder book.
Caddie Woodlawn. C. R. Brink (Scholastic).
Across Five Aprils. Irene Hunt (Follett).
Freedom Train: The Story of Harriet Tubman. D. Sterlin (Scholastic).
The Perilous Road. W. O. Steele (Scholastic).
Rifles for Waitie. H. Keith (HarperCollins).
The Civil War Soldier at Atlanta. W. Sanford & C. Green (Children's Press).
Slave Dancer: Paula Fox (Dell) Harder book.
The Boys' War. Jim Murphy (Clarion Books).

Dinosaurs (Grades 1–3)

Digging up Dinosaurs. Aliki (HarperCollins).
Dinosaur Story. Janna Cole (Scholastic).
Dinosaur Time. Peggy Parrish (HarperCollins).
The Littlest Dinosaurs. B. Most (Harcourt, Brace, Jovanovich).
Baby Dinosaurs. P. Dodson & P. Levangis (Scholastic).

Eyewitness Books: Dinosaurs. (Albert Knopf).
Over 65 Million Years Ago: Before the Dinosaurs Died. R. Moody
    (Macmillan).
Life and Death of Dinosaurs. P. Chenel (Children's Press).
*The Dinosaur is the Biggest Animal that Ever Lived and Other Wrong Ideas You
    Thought Were True.* S. Simon (HarperCollins).
Prehistoric Marine Reptiles. J. A. Massare (Franklin Watts).
The Last Dinosaurs. Douglas Dixon (Gareth Stevens).

Life Cycles—Frogs (Grades 1–5)

Life Cycles: The Frog. (Raintree-Steck-Vaughn).
Frogs. B. Watts (Franklin Watts).
Tadpole Diary. (Rigby).
The Tadpole. (Raintree-Steck-Vaughn).
The Frog in the Pond. (Gareth Stevens Books).
Frogs and Toads. J. Dallinger (Bancroft-Sage).
Eyewitness Juniors: Amazing Frogs and Toads. (Albert Knopf).

There are a variety of sources for integrated-curriculum books. Here are a few of the best that are currently available:

A to Zoo Subject Access to Children's Picture Books (3rd ed.). Carolyn W. and
    John A. Lima (R. R. Bowker, 1989).
*Eye Openers! How to Choose and Use Children's Books About Real People, Places
    and Things.* Beverly Kobrin (Penguin, 1988). This book lists activities and
    children's books that can be used to study Hawaii, Australia, Japan, Italy,
    Kenya, and Brazil.
Multicultural Explorations: Joyous Journeys with Books. Mary Ann Heltshe and
    Audrey Burie Kirchner (Teacher Ideas Press, 1991).
Children Exploring Their World: Theme Teaching in Elementary School. Sean
    Walmsley (Heinemann, 1993).
Social Studies Through Children's Literature. Anthony D. Fredricks. (Teacher
    Ideas Press, 1991).
Adventures with Social Studies (through literature). Sharron L. McElmeel.
    (Teacher Ideas Press, 1991).
Books You Can Count On. Rachel Griffiths & Margaret Clyne.
    (Heinemann, 1991).
Have You Read a Good Math Lately?: Children's Books for Mathematical Learning.
    David Whiten & Sandra Wilde. (Heinemann, 1992).
Science Through Children's Literature. Carol M. & John W. Butzow. (Teacher
    Ideas Press, 1989).
True Stories: Nonfiction Literacy in the Primary Classroom. Christine Duthie.
    (Stenhouse, 1996).

mathematics abilities are abysmal. Rarely in life are we confronted with straightforward numbers to multiply or percentages to figure. Children who cannot apply their reading, writing, and math skills to real-world situations are not being educated to succeed beyond the walls of their classrooms.

Realizing that integration across subject areas will save time, make the skills more relevant, and will provide constant opportunities to apply the skills being learned, teachers in some schools have begun setting aside one day each week as an "integrated day." On integrated day, the usual schedule of separate subjects and the use of separate textbooks is abandoned. The *topic* is the focus for that day and all reading, writing, math, art, music, etc. activities are chosen because they help children learn about that topic.

Teachers who teach these "special days" report that both they and the children are much more excited about learning when they have a whole day to pursue a topic and find out a lot about it. Children look forward to this day as a break from the routine of subject-structured days. Teachers enjoy planning for this day, they *find* time for the children to work together on projects and *to do* some creative activities that often get ignored in the busy elementary school day. When we first started doing one integrated day each week, Friday was the day that most teachers chose. After several years of experimenting with the integrated-day notion, most teachers now like to do their integrated day on Monday. They use the whole day on Monday to really get the topic going and to get the children involved with research and creative projects. For the rest of the week, children can continue working on these projects at other times during the school day or at home. Teachers who use Monday as their special-topic initiating day often spend an hour or more on Friday afternoon to let children share what they have done or learned and also to use it for closure of the topic. In classrooms where Monday is the special day, the normally "blue" Monday often becomes everyone's favorite day of the week!

INTEGRATE SCIENCE AND LANGUAGE ARTS

The combination of science and language arts may sound like a strange one. If subjects are combined, language arts is more apt to be put with social studies, and science is often linked with math. There are compelling reasons, however, to think about linking language-arts curriculum with your science curriculum.

The federally funded NRRC—National Reading Research Center—has been carrying out research on ways to improve literacy instruction. One of the main thrusts of the NRRC is student engagement.

> At the NRRC, our over-arching goal is to study how to cultivate self-determining readers who are the architects of their own learning. Our research is unified by an engagement perspective which suggests that productive learners are motivated, strategic, knowledgeable and collaborative. Engaged students participate in literacy activities to gain knowledge, perform tasks and enjoy literary experiences. (Guthrie, McCann, Hynd and Stahl, 1998 p. 1)

The engagement perspective of the NRRC was partly motivated by data that shows that a huge number of students are alliterate—choosing not to read despite good reading ability. Recent NAEP (National Assessment of Educational Progress) data indicate that 25 percent of fourth graders and 50 percent of eighth graders report reading ONCE A MONTH OR LESS for their own interest! Clearly, the literacy problem in this country goes beyond decoding and comprehension. Readers are not just people who can read, they are people who select books that appeal to them and set aside time to read for their own pleasure and information.

NRRC carried out many classroom-based research projects during its five years. Two of them linked language arts and science. The linkage between science and language arts came about because the researchers asked themselves questions such as,

> "What turns elementary kids on?"
> "What are they interested in?"
> "What do they want to learn about?"

The answers to many of these questions lie in the domain we call science. Kids observe things—animals, plants, weather, physical phenomena, stars, etc.—and they have a natural curiosity about what is happening and why. The unusual linking of science and language arts makes sense when you consider that the content and process of science are natural motivators for children's learning.

One language-arts-science linkage research project took place in six third-grade classrooms (Morrow, Pressley, Smith & Smith, 1997). Two of these classrooms were designated as control classes and carried out their language arts and science instruction as they had in past years. Instruction was carried out using basal readers and science textbooks. Language arts was allotted 90 minutes daily for a total of seven and one-half hours each week. Science was given three 45-minute periods each week for a total of two hours and 15 minutes. Two other classrooms, designated as literature classrooms, continued teaching science in the traditional way for the same two hours and 15 minutes weekly, but divided the language arts tie between the basal reader and literature. Teachers read to the children daily, engaged the children in a variety of writing, dramatizing, and retelling activity related to books read and provided time and a variety of books for independent readings.

The other two classes, designated science/literature classrooms also divided their language-arts time between basal reader instruction and literature, but their science time was also divided between textbook reading and literature. Five science books were read and responded to for each science unit throughout the year. Students were given time to read science informational books and encouraged to write about what they were reading.

At the end of the year, a large amount of data was collected including standardized test results, writing samples, book title recognition measures, and attitude measures gathered through teacher and student interviews. Students in the science/literature classrooms scored significantly higher on all literacy measures and on two of the three science measures. Perhaps, more importantly, students in both the literature and science/literature classes read more than students in the basal/textbook only classrooms, and students in the science/literature classrooms read science on their own more often than children in the literature classrooms.

A final encouraging outcome relates to student attitudes toward science. The majority of students in the two science/literature classrooms reported that they liked science, while the majority of students in the other four classrooms reported that they didn't like science because it was "boring!"

The other classroom-based research study that integrated language arts and science was CORI (Concept-Oriented Reading Instruction). The CORI framework was first tried out in one fifth-grade classroom and in subsequent years was extended to a variety of upper-elementary and middle grades in many different sites.

In CORI classrooms, teachers spend two hours daily in an integrated science and language arts block. During this time the science is "real" hands-on science—textbooks are used rarely and only as resources. The language arts focuses primarily on the reading of "real" books—both fictional and informational (No basal readers allowed!) and on writing in personal logs to record what they are thinking and learning and about various products—posters, books, letters to parents, etc. they are using to communicate what they are learning.

In addition, teachers provide some other blocks of time during the week to accomplish language-arts goals that don't fit well with science content. Most teachers schedule two hours for "Writer's Workshop" writing in which children explore their own topics and ideas, unconstrained by the science topic. Most teachers also have a separate spelling time in which they use some topic-related words and some pattern words. Many of the teachers read aloud books related to the topic, but teachers also read grade-level favorites that are unrelated. This description will focus on the two-hour science language-arts block, but keep in mind that these teachers actually spend more than two hours a day when you add in the hours given to Writer's Workshop, teacher-read-aloud, and spelling.

Each CORI classroom studies three science topics, one life science, one physical science, and one earth science. In third grade, for example, they studied the adaptation of animals to their environment and focused specifically on birds. They also did units on the solar system and weather. For each unit, students go through four stages. In each stage, important literacy strategies are taught.

The first stage is called Observe and Personalize. During this stage, students observe phenomena such as clouds or crickets. They collect things such as the crickets or water samples. They carry out experiments. They activate prior knowledge and generate questions such as:

"Where do crickets go in the winter?"

The second stage is called Search and Retrieve. Students use a variety of books, computer data bases, and other sources. They learn to locate information using the table of contents and index. They take notes and outline information.

In the third stage, Comprehend and Integrate, they use information from a variety of sources to synthesize information. They analyze, summarize, make inferences, and draw conclusions.

The final stage, called Communicate to Others, involves the students in writing, making videos, drawing maps, and producing a variety of things that allow them to share what they have learned.

Much of the learning done in CORI classrooms is done in teams composed of three to five students. Teachers do whole-class strategy instruction as needed and then support teams as they work though the various stages.

Research with the CORI model has been carried out in a variety of different settings across several years. The results, while complex, support the idea that achievement and motivation are increased when science and language arts are linked. For detailed results and more about the instructional model, we highly recommend that you read "Growth of literacy engagement: Changes in motivations and strategies during concept-oriented reading instruction" (Guthrie, Van Meter, McCann, Wigfield, Bennett, Poundstone, Rice, Faibisch, Hunt & Mitchell, 1996).

Motivation matters when it comes to literacy achievement. As children go through school, their motivation for school and reading decreases. The less they like to do it, the less they do of it. How much children read is the best predictor of how well they read. If we want all our children to read and write as well as they possibly can, we must find ways to combat the problem of decreasing motivation. We can capitalize on children's natural affinity for science by integrating some of our reading and writing instruction with science topics. Their science knowledge will increase as will their motivation to read. Having more science knowledge and spending more time reading will result in better readers.

ORGANIZE YOUR "SPECIAL TEACHERS" TO SUPPORT SCIENCE AND SOCIAL STUDIES

All over the country, schools are rethinking how special teachers are being used to support children with learning problems or who find learning to read difficult. One possibility that is being tried in some schools involves the special teachers supporting classroom teachers in the areas of science and social studies. This support takes a number of different forms. In some schools, the remedial reading or resource teacher is scheduled into the classroom during science or social studies and the classroom teacher and special teacher team up to work with all the students. The special teacher might use the knowledge of books and other materials to find more interesting and readable books. If nothing but the textbook is available, the special teacher might rewrite important portions of the text, making them simpler and clearer. Special teachers might teach reading-strategy lessons focused on building prior knowledge and vocabulary and help children learn to deal with expository text structure. They might model how to read graphs, maps, and other visuals and help students learn to write reports and summaries.

Another possibility that is being tried involves the special teacher working with only those students designated as having learning or reading problems, but still focusing on science or social studies content. Whether the special

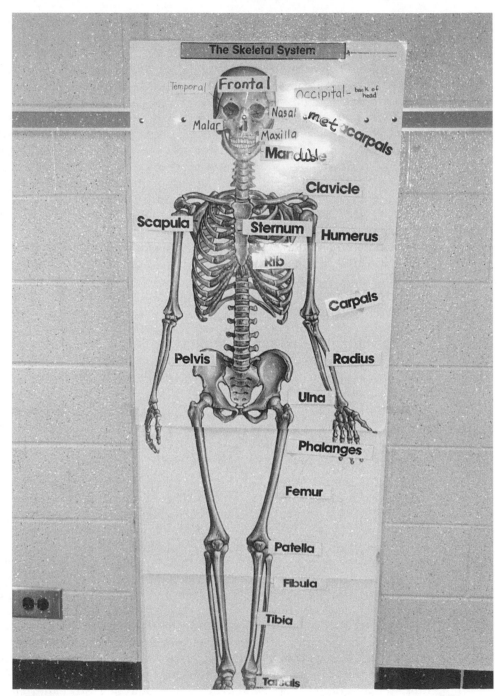

Children are fascinated by science. Integrating science and language arts increases motivation and gives them real things to read about and write about.

teacher works in the classroom or in a room down the hall, the remedial time is scheduled during science or social studies and the special teacher provides instruction in reading and writing covering the same content being covered in the classroom. Again, special teachers will find or rewrite simpler, clearer text, develop prior knowledge and content vocabulary, and help students learn how to read and write informational text.

Learning to read is a complex process. Children who are struggling with reading need help with all aspects of reading and they need more time and practice to learn effective reading strategies. When the special instruction they need is provided during science and social studies time instead of during language-arts time, they get an extra "dose" of literacy instruction. When the content of that instruction is a part of the classroom science or social studies curriculum, they increase—rather than fall further behind in—their knowledge stores.

TRANSFORM EVERY STUDENT INTO AN "EXPERT"

All of the activities described in the chapter so far have been based on having the teacher select the topics around which to develop knowledge. The last activity is centered on the various interests of each child. Many children have a hobby or a passion for some topic about which they will willingly dig and devour information. As they learn about this topic, they not only increase their knowledge of this topic, but of their general knowledge as well. Children who collect baseball cards, and can give you the stats for all of their favorite players, learn a lot about baseball, but they also expand their general knowledge. Any baseball enthusiast knows the meaning of the general words—*average, rare, trade, manager, major,* and *minor.* In addition, baseball card collectors learn about geography and economics. Professional baseball teams are located throughout North America. Students can locate these cities and mark them with a replica of a team banner. Students can develop some basic economic knowledge while learning about the prices offered for baseball cards. Listing price trends, basis for pricing, and tallying prices of cards owned by members of the class are all activities that foster basic economic knowledge.

First Grade Experts

Christine Duthie's wonderful book *True stories* has lots of ideas for creating classroom experts. Here are some of the topics first graders became experts in:

dancing	camping	in-line skating	bikes	kittens
cars	cats	scary movies	ponds	beaches
baseball	frogs	jump rope songs	space	horses
policeman	basketball	skateboards	asthma	babies
spiders	recycling	making stuff out of wood		

Children who become fascinated with a topic learn, of course, about that topic. In addition, they learn the meaning of some words used in that specific topic that could have a wider, more general use. They also learn how to find and evaluate information about that topic—a skill we call *research.* Perhaps the most important thing they learn, however, is that learning and gaining knowledge (when you care about the topic) is an intrinsically motivating and satisfying pursuit. Because there are so many academic and attitudinal benefits obtained by children who become interested in and pursue one topic, we believe that all elementary children should be encouraged to become experts at something! The strategy we use to help children become experts is called "You Be the Expert."

To get children interested in becoming experts, it is important to help children see that there are all kinds of topics that people can become experts in. Invite some people into your class to share what they are experts in. Make sure that children understand that the area that you are an expert in is not necessarily the same area as what you do for a living. Perhaps you, the teacher, have something you know a lot about and keep up with. Begin with this. Do you collect antiques? Watch birds? Grow roses? Track hurricanes? Bring some of the things—books, magazines, and so on—that relate to your expert knowledge; share this knowledge and enthusiasm with your children. Then invite a friend, neighbor, relative, other teacher, or staff member to come and share what they are an expert on. Talk with the children about their hobbies and interests and have a time each week when they can bring in things that they know a lot about to share with the class. You may be amazed at what your children know and are interested in.

Two-Language Children as Experts

It is not difficult to find a classroom that includes a Jamaican child, a Hmong child from Cambodia, a Mexican child, or a Russian-Jewish child. Each of these immigrant children could easily still be acquiring English as their second language and yet each is an expert on the kind of cultural and world knowledge that the other children are wholly unaware of. Too often, these children are viewed as having substantial deficits in world knowledge because their expertise does not match the curriculum in our schools. We would like to think of these children as experts—experts whose specialized knowledge can be tapped to broaden the world knowledge of others in the classroom. We might have them provide us with knowledge of the geography or the climate of their native land or with training in speaking their native language. We might have them develop our knowledge of the history of their cultural group. We might work to make sure that our classroom has books that reflect their culture and that we incorporate their knowledge into our discussions.

Once children understand that people become experts by devoting some time and energy to learning about a specific topic, and once they learn that there are an infinite number of topics about which a person can become an expert, let each child choose a topic about which he or she can "Be the Expert." Allot some time each week for your experts to share the new things they have learned. Encourage the children to bring sources of information and to show where they found certain facts. Help them find a variety of ways (scrapbooks, notebooks, file folders, etc.) to keep up with what they are learning. As children are sharing, encourage other children to ask questions. If the experts can't answer the questions, point out that an expert is always adding more facts and knowledge and suggest that your experts try to find out the answers before the next "Expert Share."

SUMMARY

Helping children expand their knowledge stores should be a major goal of every teacher. This goal is particularly important when teaching children whose families may not be able to provide them with "enrichment" experiences. Because knowledge expansion is an enormous and never ending goal, it is never completely finished or "mastered" and is not easily measured. When considering how to promote literacy for struggling readers, it is easy to focus on the small, visible components of reading and writing and lose track of the knowledge/reading/writing/thinking connection. In order to read and write about a variety of topics, you must have a lot of specific and general world and word knowledge. Successful schools for at-risk children achieve a balance between the need to teach skills and the need to expand world knowledge. These schools understand that children can learn to read and read to learn simultaneously, and that the most powerful classroom lessons reflect both goals. This chapter has offered a variety of ways teachers get organized and use their precious time to "do it all!"

REFERENCES

Caine, R. N., & Caine, G. (1991). *Teaching and the Human Brain*. Alexandria, VA: Association for Supervision and Curriculum Development.

Cunningham, P. M., Crawley, S., & Mountain, L. (1983). Vocabulary scavenger hunts: A scheme for schema development. *Reading Horizons, 24*, 45–50.

Guthrie, J. T., Van Meter, O., McCann, A. D., Wigfield, A., Bennett, I., Poundstone, C. C., Rice, M. E., Faibisch, F. M., Hunt, B., & Mitchell, A. M. (1996). Growth of literacy engagement: Changes in motivations and strategies during concept-oriented reading instruction. *Reading Research Quarterly, 31*, 306–332.

Guthrie, J. T., McCann, A. D., Hynd, C., and Stahl, S. (1998). Classroom contexts promoting literacy engagement. In J. Flood, S.B. Heath, & D. Lapp (eds.) *A handbook for literacy educators: Research on teaching the communicative visual arts.* Newark, DE: International Reading Association.

Morrow, L. M., Pressley, M., Smith, J. K., & Smith, M. (1997). The effect of a literature-based program integrated into literacy and science instruction with children from diverse backgrounds. *Reading Research Quarterly, 32*, 54–75.

Walp, T., & Walmsley, S. A. (1995). Integrating literature and composing into the language arts curriculum. *No Quick Fix, 90*, 251–274.

7

Extra Support for Students Who Need it Most

Throughout this book we have described ways that classroom teachers provide support for children who find learning to read a challenge. Taking into account the new criteria for what children must do to reach the basic proficiency standard, we have emphasized instruction in which children learn to think as they read. Many children who are currently "just a little below level" can achieve basic and even proficient levels of reading achievement if their elementary literacy instruction includes: lots of reading and writing (as described in Chapter 2); guided reading activities in which they learn to think about, compare, and evaluate what they read (as described in Chapter 3); writing lessons in which they learn to write thoughtful responses to what they are learning and reading about (as described in Chapter 4); activities designed to produce fluent decoders and spellers—including big words (as described in Chapter 5); and an emphasis on applying reading and writing strategies as they learn science and social studies content (as described in Chapter 6).

In this chapter, we will describe some ways that classroom teachers, often working with others—special teachers, older-student tutors, volunteers, and so on—provide extra help for those students they are most concerned about. If you are doing all you can within the framework of your balanced literacy program and there are still children whose literacy needs you know you are not meeting, consider these possibilities:

Form an After-Lunch Bunch

An after-lunch bunch is a small group that gets together for 10–15 minutes after lunch (or at another time if you want to come up with another name for it!) and reads easy books "just for fun." For example, in one first-grade classroom in January, the teacher was doing guided reading in primer and late preprimer level materials. When the children were partner reading, they could all read the primer with their partners' help. The teacher knew, from observing the partners during partner reading, however, that four of the first graders were missing many words and were not really at instructional level in these books.

The teacher decided that these children needed some additional reading with easy early preprimer level materials. Thus, the after-lunch bunch was formed. Membership in the after-lunch bunch changed daily, but the teacher made sure that the four children, whose needs had instigated the formation of this group, were in the group often but not every day. Every child was included in the after-lunch bunch every week, but the best readers were only included once each week. Thus the membership changed daily, but the group always included a majority of children who needed some easier reading and other children who were good reading models. No child ever suspected that this was "a bottom group" (and in fact, it wasn't!).

Each day, when the children returned from lunch, they would check the list posted at the back table to see if they were in the after-lunch bunch that day. The six children who found their name there gathered eagerly at the back table "to read some fun books with the teacher." The children read for 10–15 minutes, often reading through several easy stories. Sometimes these stories were found in old preprimers, sometimes, they were "skinny books" made from old preprimer stories. Sometimes, when the teacher had been able to find several copies for them to share, they read "real" easy books. During this after-lunch bunch, there was no teaching of comprehension strategies as there was during guided reading. The teacher did however coach them on how to figure out words, and meaning was always emphasized.

The after-lunch bunch idea can be used at different grade levels and with a variety of materials. Teachers find it most useful when they have just a few children, who are not on instructional level with the materials the class is using, for guided reading. If children share books, you can do an after-lunch bunch with only three or four copies of the easy material you have selected. It is critical for the children to see the after-lunch bunch as a chance to "just read and enjoy" some fun things and that the membership varies so that there are always some good reading models and no child is in the same group every day.

Scheduling Easy Reading Time

After-lunch reading can also be after-school reading (or even before-school reading if school opens later). We have seen programs similar to the one described above that involved teachers, parents, and children after-school. In some cases the reading and special education resource teachers work on "flex-time" and begin their school day a bit later than other teachers in order to be available to organize the after-school program and to be available for this extended day program at no additional cost. In one of these schools each teacher schedules a single child to stay after school each day (except Friday) to work with individually for 15–20 minutes. The child then joins the after-school children for some fun easy reading with a small group.

SCHEDULE 30 MINUTES OF "OPEN CENTER TIME" INTO YOUR DAY

We know what you are thinking. You are thinking that you can't get it all done now—much less with 30 minutes less time! We are going to try to convince you that you will get back your 30 minutes in increased productivity during the rest of the day, that students need time to pursue their own interests, and that freeing you up to work with individuals/small groups on whatever the most pressing needs are is a valuable use of your time.

First, let us consider what "open centers" are—and what they are not. Open centers are centers that contain "things" kids like to work with and in which they can pursue their own interests. Open centers usually don't change very much, although a new center is often added that connects to a current theme or unit. Here are some of the things often found in open centers:

> legos® or other building materials
> puzzles
> board games
> computer with games, drawing, and publishing software
> computer linked to the internet
> math manipulatives
> math games
> science manipulatives
> play-doh® or other sculpting material
> chalk, paint, or other drawing material
> markers, paper, stamps, and other writing/drawing materials
> children's magazines
> children's encyclopedia and other reference books
> vcr/monitor showing a Reading Rainbow book or other video

From this list, you should get the idea that open centers contain "open-ended" materials, things children can enjoy and learn from on their own in a way not unlike the way they might do this at home, if they lived in this kind of enriching environment. Open centers do not contain worksheets, assignments, etc. While students do "produce" things in some centers, these are things they choose to make. Students do not feel that they must complete things and turn them in and nothing is graded or checked on.

To get open centers to work, you must have rules and routines and spend whatever time is required making sure everyone understands and follows these. Decide on a way of determining who will go to which center. Since children are following their interests, it is not necessary or even desirable that every child go to every center. In many classrooms, children are designated as days of the week and do a variety of things on their day. On Mondays, the Monday children share in the Authors Chair, conference with the teacher during self-selected reading time, and so on. Use this or some other system to let children choose centers. On Monday, the Monday children choose first and then the Tuesday, Wednesday, Thursday, Friday children choose. But on Tuesday, the

Monday children are the last to choose as the order is Tuesday, Wednesday, Thursday, Friday, Monday. The number of children allowed at each center is determined and once children choose a center, they stay in that center for the remainder of the 30 minutes. Appoint one child in charge of each center for a week. Choose a child who often chooses that center and let center leaders go to their centers and get materials ready a minute before others go to the center. At the end of center time, the center leader sees that all of the center materials are stored and ready for the next day.

Before beginning center time, use this 30 minutes to have some class members role-play what should happen in each center, how center materials are treated, and the quiet voices required if everyone is to work in centers. Stop the role plays regularly and ask the children who are watching what is being done right and what needs to be done differently. Do not begin centers until all children understand—even if they do not perfectly carry out—what must happen in the centers. When you begin open-center time, spend whatever part of the 30 minutes is required getting kids to the centers, making sure they know what they are allowed to do there and that they may not migrate to other centers, and making sure centers are tidy and ready for the next day. If children are not used to caring for materials and working independently, it may take several weeks of your persistent reminders to teach all your children what is expected. Do not hesitate to close a center—sending the members back to their desks—if the whole group at the center was not following procedures. If an individual child is not cooperating, sharing, using a quiet voice, etc., send that child back to his or her seat. Some teachers require that the children sent back to their seats use this seat time to write an explanation of what they were doing and what they should have been doing. They are not allowed to choose a center the next day until a satisfactorily written explanation is produced.

Eventually, if you are determined and persistent, your centers will work almost without you. Leaders will care for materials; children will know which days they get to choose first. The occasional child who must be removed will, after sulking for a few minutes, write the required explanation so that he or she can go to centers tomorrow. Once this happens, you can begin to reap the benefits of this time. Explain to the children that on some days, you will need some of their center time to work with them individually or in small groups. Explain further that because you are taking some of their time today, they will get first choice of the centers tomorrow, regardless of which day of the week they are. Now you have some uninterrupted time to tutor individuals or work with small "after-lunch bunch" groups or do individual running records or catch a child up who has been absent for a week or chat with a child who needs some attitude adjustment as well as some of your undivided attention.

The notion of balance in classrooms is a critical issue. We must balance the instructional approaches we use because children learn in different ways. We must allocate time to different subject areas because there are many important things to learn. One way in which many classrooms are "out-of-balance" is addressed by the concept of open centers. Children who are exploring through manipulating, drawing, playing games, etc. are learning—but they are pursuing their own interests and learning in a way they are best suited for. If you consider Gardener's (1993) important concept of multiple intelligences and you look at what happens across an entire school day, you often don't see many learning opportunities for children whose intelligence is more visual/spatial, musical, or rhythmic. Because the centers contain a variety of things and because children choose their center, the learning possibilities are greatly expanded.

Another way in which open centers create a more balanced classroom day is by freeing up the teacher to do whatever is most needed on that day for particular groups or individuals. When every minute of every day is allocated to a particular subject and the teacher has just that time to teach that subject to everyone, individual needs go unmet. One of the great frustrations of teaching is seeing something that desperately needs to be done and even in many cases knowing what to do about it but not being able to find the few minutes it would take to do it. Classrooms with smooth-running open-center time provide teachers opportunities to do the little things that add up to big differences in a particular child's learning.

Now, if you are convinced that you need some open-center time, where will it come from? In most classrooms, there is a lot of time wasted in transitions. Teachers who are looking for 30 minutes should clock how long it takes to settle down after lunch and how much time they spend waiting for "everyone to get ready." In some classrooms, 15 minutes is spent taking attendance each day and children spend 15 minutes getting ready to go home! To find that thirty minutes, try carving three to five minutes off transitions, attendance taking, getting ready to go home, etc. and see if it can't be done. If your school day ends at 3:15, imagine that it was ending at 2:45. You don't want to leave any subject out, but could you "tighten it up a bit" and find 30 minutes? There is 30 minutes of slack in most school days and this 30 minutes could provide you and your students with a more balanced, less frustrating day.

FIND AND TRAIN A TUTOR FOR YOUR MOST NEEDY CHILD

In many classrooms, it is easy to be overwhelmed by the scope of the literacy problems our children have and by how much needs to be done. If we have lots of struggling readers, we may realize that we can't do everything and so we end up doing nothing. Think now about the one child you have who is most behind in reading and writing and is not receiving any individual help. Perhaps this child is just learning to speak English or has not attended school regularly. For whatever reason, this child's reading and writing level is well below that of the other children.

Most children who are far behind in reading and writing can make considerable progress if they have a strong classroom program and some one-on-one tutoring. Before thinking about where you might find this tutor, you must decide what you would train the tutor to do. The most important component of any successful tutoring program is through the repeated readings of materials at the child's instructional level. So, your first task is to find some materials that are "just right." As described previously, there is disagreement about what exactly constitutes instructional level, but materials in which the child misses no more than five words per hundred and that are interesting to the student would be ideal. Fortunately, you have a wealth of easy materials to choose from. The best list of easy-to-read books can be found in Marianne Lanino Pilla's *The Best High/Low Books for Reluctant Readers* (1990). In this book, she describes 374 books that she has found to be accessible and appealing to reluctant readers. Of course, new books are being published at a phenomenal rate so you should be constantly on the lookout for easy books that appeal to your students.

Easy But Interesting Books

Any list of high/low books is out-of-date before it is published, but to give you some idea of the variety available and to entice you to find some books that will appeal to your kids, here is a sampling of what is out there:

Eek: Stories to Make You Shriek! (Grosset and Dunlap). Easy-reader chapter books in which children experience scary, spooky—but not violent—adventures.

Eye Witness Books (Dorling Kindersly). Science and social studies topics—rocks, birds, machines, etc. in an attractive, highly visual format.

Bridgestone Early Reader Science (Capstone). Reading levels, 1–3. Our favorite is the transportation set—featuring bulldozers, fire trucks, freight trains, and tractors.

Capstone High-Low Nonfiction (Capstone). Dozens of theme sets on reading levels 3–4. Our favorites include the set on lizards and the one on racing that includes hot rods and stock cars.

The Reading Scene (Continental Press). Each book contains four (7-page) stories. Mysteries, biographies (including those of Bruce Springsteen and Bill Cosby), and young adolescent problems are the major topics covered.

Galaxy 5 (Fearon, David S. Lake Publishers). This science fiction series of six books (60 pages each) follows the adventures of the crew of the spaceship Voyager as it establishes a colony of humans on a far-off planet.

Laura Brewster Books (Fearon, David S. Lake Publishers). This mystery series of six books (60 pages each) finds a jeans-clad Laura Brewster roaming the world and solving mysteries for her insurance company employer.

Sportellers (Fearon, David S. Lake Publishers). This series of eight (60-page) books gives a fictionalized account of how stars in various sports train and grow.

Tom and Ricky Mystery Series (High Noon Books). This series of ten (45-page) books and several other series also published by High Noon, have reading levels of first and second grade and are particularly helpful in providing easy reading material to very poor readers for whom English is a second language.

Great Lives (Scholastic). This is one of several themed collections available. The series focuses on biographies of famous Americans and offers links to social studies topics.

Concept Science (Modern Curriculum Press). This series includes 44 titles such as, "Earthworms are animals" and "Our changing earth." The books are available in Spanish.

World of Dinosaurs (Steck-Vaughn-Raintree). This series includes ten books and offers short, easy reading opportunities about a most popular topic.

In addition to high/low series of books, there are many other books with a particular appeal to struggling readers. Many teachers find that their students like to read books that relate to TV shows, such as the *Deep Space Nine* and *Voyageur* books. Many struggling readers enjoy books about real things, such as David Macaulay's books, *Pyramids* and *Cathedral,* or the Time-Life, *How Things Work, Ripley's Believe It or Not,* and *The Baseball Encyclopedia.* Cartoon characters such as Garfield and Heathcliff are enormously popular with some intermediate-aged children. Comic books have long been a mainstay of preteen reading and actually require sophisticated reading skills to follow what is happening.

So, your first task is to find some books that will interest your student and that the student will be able to read with some help from the tutor. If your student is a "nonreader" or such a beginning reader that you cannot find anything, you will have to create the materials. This is not as hard as it sounds. Simply sit down with your struggling reader and write an introductory paragraph of five or six sentences about him.

> Carlton is nine years old. He goes to Washington School. He is in the fourth grade. Mrs. Cunningham is his teacher. He likes Washington School. He likes Mrs. Cunningham too.

This paragraph will become the reading material he will read with the tutor for the next several days until he can read it fluently and knows most of the words in it. When he demonstrates to you that he can do this, ask him what else he would like the book to tell about him and have him watch while you write the second page:

> Carlton has six brothers and sisters. Their names are Robert, David, Manuel, Thomas, Patrice, and Jackie. They live on Willow Road. His father works at the Ford place. His mother works at Ken's Quik-Mart. His cousin, Travis, lives with them too.

The procedure continues with the teacher creating the pages of Carlton's book and the tutor reading and rereading them with Carlton until he can fluently read each page and most of the words. Future pages will tell about any pets

Carlton has, places he has gone, friends and what they do together, foods he likes to eat, jobs he does at home, things he doesn't like, etc. Once Carlton can fluently read this beginning book, he will have a good bank of known high-frequency words and it should be possible to begin tutoring him in one of the easiest high/low books.

Once the material that the child is going to read has been chosen or created, tutoring procedures follow a predictable pattern.

1. The child rereads pages for several days. After reading each page, the child puts check marks on index cards containing previously missed words that he or she read correctly today. Words with three checks are "retired."

2. The tutor and child preview a new book or several new pages of a book, naming things, talking about what is happening in the pictures, and reading any headings or labels.

3. The child reads one page without help from the tutor, figuring out words in whatever way he or she can.

4. The tutor points out good strategies the reader used: sounding out an unfamiliar word, using picture clues, going back and correcting at the end of a sentence, etc.

5. The tutor then points out any words that the child did not read correctly and helps the child figure them out by showing the child how the picture, the letters in the word, and the sense of the sentence help with that word.

6. The tutor writes the words missed on index cards along with the page number on which they were missed.

7. The same procedure is repeated with each page. Pictures, headings, and labels are discussed. The page is read by the child unaided. The tutor points out good strategies the reader used and then gives help with missed words. The missed words are written on index cards with the page number.

8. When several pages have been read and three to six missed words are written on cards, the tutor and child return to the first page read that day. The missed words are displayed in front of the child but they are not pronounced by the tutor or the child. When the child has finished the page, he puts a check next to any word correctly read in the text this time. The tutor and the child talk about words that were not correctly read and how they can be figured out. The child continues to reread pages with the index card words for that page visible as he reads, checking those correctly read when the page is finished and getting help with those incorrectly read.

9. The word cards are put in an envelope and clipped to the book and are ready for the next day's reading.

10. Together, the tutor and the child write in a notebook a sentence or two summarizing what was read today. The child and the tutor first agree on what to write. Then the child writes, getting help from the tutor with

spelling as needed. The tutor and child decide on one word each day to add to the child's portable word wall folder. This folder has the alphabet letters and spaces for words needed. By having the folder open while writing, the child can quickly find a word he or she remembers deciding that he or she needs to learn to spell.

<u>A</u> are also about	<u>B</u> before	<u>C</u> can't could	<u>D</u> don't	<u>E</u> enough	<u>F</u> first favorite
<u>G</u> getting	<u>H</u> have	<u>I</u> I'm into	<u>J</u>	<u>K</u> know knew	<u>L</u> let's
<u>M</u> myself	<u>N</u> new	<u>O</u> one our	<u>P</u> people	<u>Q</u>	<u>R</u> really
<u>S</u> said school	<u>T</u> then there threw to	<u>U</u> until	<u>V</u> very	<u>W</u> want was wear whether	<u>X</u> <u>YZ</u> your you're

For Carlton's book, this procedure should be varied somewhat. Because Carlton knows almost no words, each sentence should be written on a sentence strip, read, and then cut into words. Carlton should reassemble the words to match each sentence in the paragraph. Eventually, he should make the whole paragraph by matching and assembling the cut-apart words. Carlton should write a sentence at the end of each day, perhaps choosing his favorite sentence from the paragraph and then trying to write it without looking with spelling help from the tutor. He and the tutor would decide on a word each day to add to his spelling folder and Carlton would learn to find and use these words to help him write his sentence each day.

As you can tell, the trickiest part of this tutoring is finding the right book. If you find a book in which the child is missing a word every 20 words or so, the reading will be fluent enough so that the child can figure out words and self-correct. The number of missed words you write on index cards will be small enough so that the child will be able to learn these words and accumulate the three checks necessary to "retire" them. Once you have the tutoring set up, you will need to monitor the progress of the child. When children are accumulating few index card words, it is time to move them to slightly harder books.

Reading Recovery Leveled Books

Reading Recovery uses a 1–16 point scale to indicate the difficulty of books from very easy to about mid-second-grade level. Many publishers include the Reading Recovery levels on their books. Using these levels to help determine what book you might move children to can be very helpful. *Guided Reading* (Fountais & Pinnell, 1997) lists levels for hundreds of books.

Now, how will you find this tutor? Consider these possibilities:

1. Do you know a parent who drops off or picks up at school every day and could stay 30 minutes or come 30 minutes early? Many parents are on a tight schedule, but most schools have some parents with the flexibility to spend 30 minutes tutoring a child if they know they are needed and have a specific, workable tutoring system such as that just described.

2. Is there a capable lunchroom worker or bus driver with 30 minutes a day to spare? Some part-time workers would love to have the opportunity to make a difference in the life of a child. Some schools even have money to pay this person a little extra each week for the extra hours worked.

3. Is there a high school nearby that begins or ends earlier or later than your school? Many high schools encourage (or even require!) volunteer service by their students. Perhaps there is a future teacher who would love to have the experience tutoring your child could offer.

4. Does your school have older students, one of whom might be your tutor? Ask a teacher friend who teaches older children if there is a student who could afford the half-hour it would take each day to tutor your child. The schedule could be staggered so that the tutor didn't miss the same thing each day or the tutor could come when other students are going to band, chorus, etc.

5. Do you have a student who could be the tutor? If you are an intermediate teacher and you have a sophisticated, nurturing budding teacher in your classroom, you may already have the help you need. Most intermediate-aged children are not sophisticated or dedicated enough to do this, but there is often one in every class.

6. If you can't get one person to come for 30 minutes every day, could you get four people to come for two hours one day each week? One school

found four retired people willing to give up one afternoon each week to tutor children. Two teachers worked together to find and train these tutors. On their day each week, each tutor worked individually with four children, two from each class. Each tutor knew the procedures and each wrote a note in the child's notebook for the next day's tutor, telling how far they had gotten and pointing out any "good things" the child had done that day. On Friday, the classroom teachers took turns meeting with each child being tutored while the other teacher read to both classes. During this Friday time, they monitored the progress of each child and decided when to move each child to higher-level books. They also wrote a note in the child's notebook letting the tutors know how much progress each child was making and how appreciative they were of the help.

A Model for Volunteer Tutors

The University of Virginia sponsors a volunteer tutoring program. The program is organized by reading specialists and graduate students. Their job is to determine reading levels for children and take running records on books read. They put critical words on cards in pockets in the back of books. When a child has read that book and learned the words, these word cards are added to the child's shoebox word bank. The tutor makes a duplicate set of word cards to replace those in the pocket. Each child's shoebox word bank has an alphabet strip and sound boxes taped on the outside. For more details, see Invernezzi, Juel & Rosemay, 1997.

PARTNER OLDER STRUGGLING READERS TO TUTOR YOUNGER STRUGGLING READERS

This idea is based on a tutoring program set up at Webster Magnet school in Minnesota (Taylor, Hansen, Swanson, and Watts, 1998). Fourth graders who were reading on beginning third-grade level tutored second graders, most of whom were reading on primer level. The second graders were all participating in an early intervention program in their classroom in which they read books on their level. The fourth graders spent 45 minutes on Monday and Tuesday with the reading coordinator or with their classroom teacher preparing for their 25-minute tutoring session on Wednesday and Thursday. On Monday, the fourth graders selected a picture book to read to their second grader and practiced reading the book. They also practiced word-recognition prompts that they would use when their second grader was reading to them. On Tuesday, they practiced again and developed extension activities to develop comprehension strategies including story maps and character sketches. They came up with several good discussion questions based on the picture book they were planning to read.

On Wednesday and Thursday, the fourth graders met with their tutees. During this session, they listened to their second grader read the book currently being read in their classroom's early-intervention program. While listening, they helped their second graders identify words by giving them hints such as: "Look at the picture." "It starts with *pr*" and "Sound in and out in chunks. What would this part be (covering all but the first syllable)?" Next, they read from the picture book they had chosen, built meaning vocabulary from the book, lead a discussion based on their discussion questions, and did the comprehension extension activity.

On Friday, the fourth graders had debriefing sessions with their teacher in which they discussed how their tutees reacted to the book, how well their word recognition prompts were working, the success of their discussion and comprehension activities, as well as problems encountered and progress noticed. They also wrote a letter to project coordinators detailing the successes and problems of that week. They received a response to their letter on Monday.

Data reported on this project shows that both the second- and fourth-grade struggling readers made measurable progress. This is not surprising because this program combines all of the elements essential for reading growth. Second graders were getting daily guided-reading instruction in materials at their level in their classrooms. In addition, during the tutoring session, they were reading material at their level to someone who knew how to help them with word recognition. They were also increasing their knowledge stores and comprehension strategies as they listened to their fourth-grade tutor read the picture book to them and as they engaged in the discussion and comprehension activities. Fourth graders got lots of practice using the material on their instructional level, reading the picture book, and learning word recognition and comprehension strategies, as they prepared and carried out the tutoring with their second grader.

Getting this to work would take some organization and if you have a reading coordinator/specialist at your school, it would be good to get him or her involved. Given the results reported and the "just plain sensible" nature of the cross-age tutoring program, you are almost guaranteed to "get your money's worth" out of the time required to set up such a program.

COORDINATE WITH REMEDIAL READING AND RESOURCE ROOM TEACHERS

Many struggling readers participate in remedial or resource room instruction in addition to classroom reading instruction. Such programs can provide much-needed support for the children, but they can also result in a confusing and unhelpful conglomeration of reading lessons and activities. Special programs are most effective when they provide supportive instruction that is designed to ease the difficulties that participating children are having in their classrooms.

To accomplish this, however, means that remedial and special education teachers must be familiar with the classroom reading program. New federal regulations for remedial and special education programs promote cooperative planning of instruction between classroom teachers and specialist teachers. In addition, the support instruction must be designed to improve classroom performance. The goal of these regulations is to accelerate children's reading development in order to move them back into the classroom with no further need for assistance.

Struggling readers who participate in remedial or resource room instructional support programs are the very children who need the kind of reading instruction that is coherently planned and richly integrated. We have seen a variety of ways in which classroom teachers work with support teachers to develop such programs.

In one school, the support teachers come into the classrooms to work with participating children. They support the children's progress through both the basal and the tradebooks that are used in the core-reading/language-arts program. The special teachers may have the children reread a story and work on fluency and self-monitoring behaviors. At times, they reteach a strategy lesson from the basal or model summary writing for a *Weekly Reader* article. These teachers work with both small groups and individuals depending on the classroom and the students. With support teachers in the room working at supporting progress through the core curriculum, less time is needed to meet and plan instructional roles.

In another school, the support teachers work in the classroom occasionally but more often work on extending classroom reading lessons in another room. In this case, the coordination is achieved through the use of a traveling notebook that the teachers have children carry back and forth each day. Both teachers jot down comments about what they are working on and the problems or successes the children had that day. The notebook allows the support program teacher to monitor core curriculum lessons and to develop lessons that extend or support this learning.

In another school, the support teachers work only with the tradebooks that children are reading in the classrooms. The support teachers focus on extending comprehension of the stories being read in the classroom by working with children to develop scripts from books and stories, and to develop performances of these. Another example of classroom/special teacher coordination is found in one school where the sixth graders who attend the remedial program read tradebooks linked to their social studies curriculum. With the support of the specialist, these struggling readers read historical fiction and biographies; this adds greatly to their background knowledge and allows them to be active participants in social studies class discussions. A similar link could also be made between reading and science.

What is common among the very best remedial and special education programs is that children spend most of their time actually reading and writing in a way that supports classroom success. The support children receive from the specialist teacher provides immediate returns in improved reading and writing during classroom instruction.

Evaluate the Support You Are Providing Your "Two-Language Children"

A decade ago, in many parts of the country, teachers didn't have children in their classrooms whose first language was not English. This is no longer the case. All over the country, in urban and rural areas, children come to school speaking little or no English. These children usually take longer to become literate. This is not surprising because they must learn another language at the same time that they are expected to learn to read, write, and increase their content knowledge. There is no agreement about "the best way" to help these children achieve literacy. Bilingual programs provide some instruction (including reading and writing) in the first language of the child as he or she is learning English. Bilingual programs, as their name suggests, have as their goal that the child will become literate in both languages. In ESL programs, there is more emphasis on the child's acquiring English and providing support for the child as English is acquired. Many teachers have strong opinions about the ESL versus Bilingual issue but they often have no choice but to provide the best literacy instruction they can for their "two-language" children.

Many of the strategies described in this and other chapters of the book that help struggling readers in general also help two-language children. The following list contains instructional practices generally agreed to support the literacy of all children having difficulty, including two-language children. You are probably already doing most of these and may indeed be doing more than you realize.

1. *Cooperative groupings.* Christian Faltis, in his excellent book, *Joinfostering: Adapting teaching strategies for the multilingual classroom,* has many practical tips for making small-group work more productive for two-language children. These include: keeping group size at three or four so that two-language children feel a need to participate; encouraging everyone to participate using such devices as talking chips in which each person puts down a chip after speaking and no one is allowed to add a second chip until everyone has put one down; paraphrasing passport in which each person must paraphrase the previously given idea before giving a new idea; and three-step interviewing in which pairs of children interview each other about a question and then share the results of the interviews with the group of four; making sure that group members all face each other so that they can hear each other clearly; making sure that group tasks promote positive interdependence in which students cannot successfully complete the task without the active participation of all members of the group; making sure that there is individual accountability by activities such as paraphrase passport, three-step interviews, and numbered heads, an activity in which each member of the group has the number, 1, 2, 3, or 4. As each task or question is posed to the group, the whole group discusses and agrees on a response that is then given by whatever numbered head the teacher calls out.

2. *Partner activities.* "Two heads are better than one!" Whether it is partner reading or writing or a "Think-Pair-Share" activity children learn from each other. This is particularly true for two-language children who are often hesitant to talk in a group. Your child, who is learning English, will benefit more from the partnership if you consider carefully who to partner him or her with. Look for a child who is nurturing, clever in explaining things, and alert to nonverbal signals. If you have another child who speaks the same language as the child you are supporting, but who is more proficient in English, you may want to partner these children together if your concern is with content learning, because that child's bilingualism may allow things to be explained. But, if your concern is primarily language development, you may want to rely on a nurturing partner who does not speak the first language of the child being supported.

3. *Graphic organizers for reading and writing.* Webs, timelines, double bubbles (Venn diagrams), and story maps show relationships without using all of the connecting words that are often confusing for children learning English. Using these devices before reading helps two-language children focus on important words and makes the purpose for reading clearer. When used as organizing frameworks before writing, they help fledgling English writers create more coherent texts.

4. *Picture walks and other attention to visuals.* "A picture is worth a thousand words" for children learning a new language. Use picture walks before reading and let your students name what they see in the picture and then try to find a word on the page to match the spoken word. Help all your students—but especially your children learning English—to become excellent interpreters of diagrams, maps, graphs, and other visual displays that require minimal word reading. Finally, instead of always requiring a written or spoken response, have your children respond to their reading using visuals—pictures, diagrams, graphs, etc. An excellent source for lots of ways to use visuals and to have children learn to create visuals is Steve Moline's *I see what you mean: children at work with visual information.*

5. *Real things.* Real things are always motivating to children and for children learning a new language, they are crucial. Point to things in your room as you give directions. Bring in things that connect with what your students are going to read during guided reading. Make sure that your science, social studies, and math activities are as centered in manipulatives as possible.

6. *Predictable text.* Predictable text, in which sentence patterns repeat and pictures support the words, help two-language children get a jump-start in reading and expand the oral sentence patterns they can use in speaking.

7. *Reading to children.* It would be hard to overstate the benefits of reading to children from a variety of different books. If you have two-language children in your classroom, be alert for idioms, multimeaning words, homophones, and other language peculiarities that make sense to you but are always difficult when learning a new language. Read the book for enjoyment and/or information and then return to those difficult language structures and use the full context of the book, pictures, etc. to clarify the meaning of the word or phrase.

8. *Providing time for self-selected reading and conferencing.* Self-selected reading time is critical for children learning a new language. They need to be encouraged to read and reread books and they need help in choosing books with pictures and predictable text. When you conference with them, let them show and tell you what they liked and then ask them to find some parts that were confusing to them so that you can help them understand. You may want to give your two-language child a pack of little sticky notes to stick on confusing places, so that they can quickly find the things they did not understand. You may also want to let them choose a friend to read with them during self-selected reading time, so that they can get lots of language about the book they have chosen.

9. *Prereading activities that build prior knowledge and set purposes and postreading activities that follow up purposes and help students monitor comprehension.* These help all readers but are critical for children trying to read and comprehend in a language that they are learning at the same time.

10. *A print-rich classroom.* Rooms with a word wall, a theme board containing both words and pictures, environmental print, labels, and signs that promote reading, writing, and language development.

11. *Every-pupil response activities.* Activities such as Making Words and others in which all children—rather than just one child—respond promote student engagement and are less threatening than activities in which one child is "called on and signalled out." Teachers with two-language children can also make use of a variety of every pupil's response techniques, including using yes/no cards, numbers of fingers held up, and a variety of gestures to help students stay involved and to show what they know as they develop their oral language facility.

SUMMARY

There are two levels of "struggling" readers in most classrooms. Some children have a literacy level that is close to grade level but need to become more thoughtful readers and writers, and often need more experience with text found in science and social studies and with the big words that comprise these informational texts. Most of these struggling readers can achieve basic and even proficient levels of reading and writing if their elementary years are rich in the type of instruction described in the previous chapters of this book. This chapter has described a variety of ways teachers can organize and "mobilize" to meet the needs of children whose literacy levels are way below the level of others in the class. Teachers who have several children for whom the material read in guided reading is not at instructional level can hold short "after-lunch-bunch type" easy-reading sessions, in which everyone is included on some days, but the children who really need this extra reading are asked to join the group more often. Teachers might find the time to meet with this easy-reading group and to meet other individual needs by scheduling 30 minutes of open centers sometime in the day. In addition to freeing up the teacher to meet whatever needs are most pressing that day, the open-center time allows children to pursue their own interests in a variety of ways. Children who find learning to read particularly difficult often benefit from a period of regular tutoring in addition to all the classroom instruction. If carefully structured, tutoring can be provided by a variety of people, including older struggling readers. The most effective teachers are informed about what is happening to their children when they are with special teachers and work with those teachers to provide a "nonfragmented," "noncontradictory" instructional program. Finally, many two-language children need additional support in learning to read and write. Eleven "tried-and-true" classroom practices that enhance the learning of all children, including two-language children, were described.

REFERENCES

Faltis, C. J. (1993). *Joinfostering: Adapting teaching strategies for the multilingual classroom.* New York: Merrill.

Fountais, I. C., & Pinnell, G. S. (1996). *Guided Reading.* Portsmouth, NH: Heinemann.

Gardner, H. (1993). *Multiple Intelligences: The theory in practice.* New York: Basic Books.

Invernizzi, M., Juel, C., & Rosemay, C. A. (1997). A community volunteer tutorial that works. *The Reading Teacher, 50,* 304–311.

Moline, S. (1995). *I see what you mean: children at work with visual information.* York, ME: Stenhouse.

Taylor, B. M., Hanson, B., Swanson, K., & Watts, S. (1997). Helping struggling readers: Linking small-group intervention with cross-age tutoring. *The Reading Teacher, 51,* 196–208.

CLASSROOMS WHERE THEY ALL READ AND WRITE

In the next three chapters, we will take you to some classrooms where the principles, strategies, and activities described in previous chapters are put into practice. The classrooms described are not single classrooms, but composites of the best organization and instruction we have seen in a variety of classrooms. We will describe "typical" days and weeks, knowing full well that there is really no such thing as a "normal" day in the real world of public schools. The classrooms described in this chapter are not meant to be models that you can replicate in your classroom. No two classrooms are alike; each teacher must determine the best schedule, mix, etc. based on a particular group of children, the teaching environment, and the teacher's style. Our goal in these chapters is that, by getting a chance to see how some teachers put together the parts of this giant puzzle of literacy instruction, you will get ideas for the particular shape that your classroom might take so that all your children become readers and writers.

8

A DAY IN A LITERATE HOME SIMULATION KINDERGARTEN

In previous chapters, you learned that many children have had 1,000 or more hours of "informal" literacy encounters before coming to school. From these encounters, they develop critical understanding about the nature of reading and writing and the "I can" attitudes toward their inevitable inclusion into the literate community.

1. They know that when you read or write, there is some story or information that you are trying to understand or communicate.
2. They know reading and writing are two important things that everyone who is bigger than them can do and that they too must learn to do because they want to be big.
3. They know from the overwhelming adult approval and pleasure at their fledgling attempts at pretend reading, at reading some signs and labels, and at writing, that they are succeeding at mastering this mysterious code.

Our major literacy goal in kindergarten should be to simulate the reading and writing encounters many children have had that lead them to develop these critical understandings and attitudes. It is important to think of at-risk kindergartners primarily as children who have had few experiences with print, stories, and books. Thinking of these children as "inexperienced" creates a different view of their instructional needs than thinking of them as "developmentally delayed," "language impaired," "slow," "unready," or any of the other labels commonly given to children who enter school inexperienced in literacy activities. The critical nature of providing these children with a print-rich, story-rich, book-rich classroom becomes clear when we take this view. Here is how one day might look in a literate home simulation kindergarten:

8:00–9:00 Choice Centers

The children arrive at different times, depending on buses, rides, etc. They come to the classroom immediately and, once in the classroom, come to one of the many centers in the room. During this first hour, they can choose to go to any center as long as there is space at that center. Each center has a limited number of tickets that are laminated and strung with yarn. The children choose a ticket, put the ticket on, and then go to that center. They can stay at each center as long as they like, but must return that center's ticket and get another one before moving to another center.

The teacher spent a lot of time and effort at the beginning of the year helping the children learn what they could and could not do at each center, how to clean up the center before they left, and so on. This initial effort paid off; now there are seldom problems with behavior and routines during center time.

During center time, the teacher circulates throughout the room, greeting children and helping them get the day off to a good start. As always, she has her file-folder labels on a clipboard and, when she notices accomplishments, problems, or other things that she wants to remember, she records this by putting the child's initials, date, and the comment she wants to make on one of the labels. At the end of the day, she will peel these off and attach them to each child's anecdotal record folder. Today she jots down notes about the child "reading" a little book in the library corner to a stuffed animal, noting that his voice sounds like a reading voice and that he is doing a good job of telling a story that matches the pictures. She also notes that another child is drawing at the writing table and "reads" her drawing when asked by the teacher. Also at the table is a child who has created strings of letters in rows and "reads" her "writing." The notes describe the different levels of conceptual development that each child exhibits about writing.

The teacher tries to talk to each child during the morning center time and spends a few extra minutes with the children she has identified as being most needy. For her children whose English is limited either because English is not their first language or because they have had few real conversations with adults, she makes sure to engage them in some conversation about what they are doing at the center. She points to things in the pictures they have painted or to their block construction and fosters their talk with her by asking what they are doing. She asks them about the little books that they are "reading" and about the writing they produce. Because these conversations are one-on-one and are related to something they actually are doing, the children are more willing to talk than they are in a small-group or whole-class setting. She also notices that the children talk with each other more during center time. In fact, knowing that listening and speaking are major goals of kindergarten, she encourages this child to child talk as she visits the various centers and engages the children in conversations in which she gets them to talk to one another about what they are doing.

9:00–10:00 Big Group

When the teacher goes to the rocking chair and sits down, the children realize that center time is over. They quickly clean up what they have been working on and come sit on the floor in front of her. As the teacher waits for everyone, she leads the children in some of their favorite songs, chants, and fingerplays. When the whole group assembles, she picks up her newspaper and says, "I found something last night to add to our animal board." She then shows them a picture of a baby tiger born at the zoo and reads the first part of the accompanying article. After a brief discussion, she cuts the picture and the article from the newspaper and adds it to a board that is already full of information, pictures, and words about animals. Several other children have brought animal pictures/articles that they have found. As they tell about each one—where they found it, who read it to them, and so on—it too is added to the collage. She then takes some index cards and writes labels on them—*pit bull, zoo, python, Siamese cat*—and attaches these labels next to the pictures/articles. This animal board bears little resemblance to the neat, bordered bulletin boards sometimes found in classrooms. It is cluttered with a motley collection of animal-related articles, pictures, and words that the teacher and children have been on the lookout for since they began their animal unit. It is clear from the responses of the children, however, that they are proud of "their" animal board and that they are learning that magazines and newspapers are a real-world source of information to which they have access.

Next, the teacher takes out a big book of *Brown Bear* by Bill Martin. It is clear from the children's responses that they have read this book several times before. The teacher points to each word as the children read in chorus with her:

"Brown bear, brown bear, What do you see?"

Before turning the page, she asks the children if they remember what the next animal is going to be. Most children know that the red bird is next. She turns the page and the children are delighted to see that they are correct. Led by the teacher, who continues to point to the words, they all read:

"I see a red bird looking at me.
Red bird, red bird, what do you see?"

The teacher encourages the children to try to remember which animal is coming next. As they get toward the middle of the book, they get confused about some animals but still enjoy turning each page and seeing who is there.

Once the book has been read and enjoyed once more, the teacher passes out two or three words to each child. The words have been written on sentence strips and cut so that the size of the strip each child is given matches the size of the word that is written on it. "Being the Words" is a favorite activity in this classroom. They have been the words before to make the sentences in other predictable books and in chants and poems, but this is the first time they have gotten to be the words for *Brown Bear.* The children eagerly look at the words they are given and then look up at the still-displayed *Brown Bear* book. Some children recognize a few words, particularly the concrete ones. The child holding the word *bear* says, "Oh, boy! I get to be the bear!" Other children recognize the color words *red, yellow, green,* etc. Children who get commas, periods, and question marks clearly recognize these as punctuation marks used in sentences.

The teacher then opens the book back to the first page and the children eagerly read,

"Brown bear, brown bear, what do you see?"

As they read, they look at the words/punctuation marks they are holding to see if they are any of the words in this sentence. Some children immediately recognize their words. Others need help from the teacher or from a child sitting near them. The children then come up next to the book in order to get themselves lined up to make the sentences. There is some confusion about the two words *bear* and the two words *brown*. The teacher helps them see that the *Brown* with the capital *B* must start the sentence. (The child who has the *brown* with the small *b* doesn't look too happy about this!) She also leads them to see that the two words *bear* are exactly the same and can be in either position. This is also true of the two commas.

Once the words are all in place, the children who are not being the words for this sentence read the sentence as the teacher moves behind each child holding a card. The teacher praises them for pausing briefly at the commas but not saying anything. She also reminds them that the question mark is very important even though you don't say "question mark" because it tells you the sentence is finished, and that the sentence is a question. The children seem to understand these punctuation marks, having been them in other "Being the Words" activities.

These children sit down and the teacher displays the next page. The teacher points to the words as the children read,

"I see a red bird looking at me."

As they read, they look at their words to see if they are any of these words. Again, the children who are the words in this sentence get themselves in the correct left-right sequence (with a little help from their friends), while the other children read the sentence.

The children continue to be the words for a few more pages. The next several pages are matched and sequenced much more quickly as the children begin to realize where their words come in the pattern. The children are much quicker to understand that the *red* with a capital *R* must begin the sentence, but that the two words *bird* can be in either place as they make the sentence:

"Red bird, red bird, what do you see?"

After making seven pages in the book, the teacher collects the word cards, assuring the children who are complaining about not getting to be the word yet that they will be the words for the other pages later in the week.

The teacher then leads the children in a quick "get the wiggles out" movement activity in which she has them move like the animals in the *Brown Bear* book. After this brief but essential break, the children settle back down while the teacher picks up a marker and gets ready to write. She "thinks aloud" about what she might write and the children watch eagerly, encouraging her to "draw something!" (The teacher tries to model different levels of writing on different days. Some days, she writes a whole paragraph. Other days, she just writes a sentence and then illustrates it. On some days, she draws a picture and labels it. Yet on other days, she writes a list. As she writes, she invent-spells some words, saying the words aloud very slowly and putting down some letters to represent the sounds. In this way, she demonstrates for the children all the different levels of writing and shows them that all these ways of writing are accepted.)

On this day she writes two sentences:

Mr. Hinkle will vizit us after lunch.

He will bring his pet turtl.

She doesn't read the words aloud as she writes them, except for saying the words very slowly when she is using invented spelling to model this for the children. The children all watch very closely and try to read what she is writing. Many of them recognize the words *Mr., lunch,* and *pet.* She then draws a simple picture to illustrate the sentence and labels Mr. Hinkle and the turtle. Even though (or perhaps, because) she is not very artistic, the children love to watch her draw. Once her drawing is complete, she reads what she has written, pointing to each word as she does. The children are amazed to hear that Mr. Hinkle—who teaches fourth grade—has a pet turtle. They also point to her stick-figure drawing of him and remark that they can't wait for Mr. Hinkle to see his picture! The teacher assures them she will hide it before he arrives!

The time allotted for whole-class language arts is almost up for the day. The teacher points to several charts with animal poems and finger plays written on them and as the teacher points to the words, the children sing/chant/say them with her.

10:00–10:30 Recess/Snack

As the children line up to go outside, the teacher picks a child and asks the child what letter she or he wants the children to be as they go outside. The child thinks and decides that they should all be M's today. The teacher lets that child lead the line and all the children march to the playground because *march* is the action they have learned for the letter *m.* (Earlier in the year, they learned an action for each consonant letter. Now, they review this every day by going to the playground using one of the actions. On days when they have to stay inside during recess, they play games in which they review all their letter actions.)

When they return to the classroom, they find some peanuts on each of their desks. They look up at the "food board" and notice that the teacher has attached a picture from the peanut jar to the space under the letter *p.* As they munch on their peanuts and whatever else they might have brought for snack time, they review the other foods they have up on their food board. So far, only five letters have food pictures attached to them:

b—bananas, d—donuts, m—milk, j—juice, p—peanuts

The children are curious about what foods will go with the other letters. They make the sounds of the letters and try to predict what they might find for a snack one day. One child says he hopes there are hamburgers for the *h* but another child protests,

"She won't bring us hamburgers for snacks!"

The teacher picks up on their conversation and helps them think about what the possibilities are for the various foods. She suggests that, as they eat lunch today and when they eat meals and snacks at home, they should look at the packages and think about what letters these food names begin with.

10:30–11:30 Assigned Centers

During this time, the children go to centers once more but, unlike the morning hour when they choose the centers and activities, now they are assigned to centers and all of the children rotate through all the activities. Today, the teacher has four centers set up and children are to spend 15 minutes in each. Before they go to the centers, she directs their attention to each center and makes sure they know what they are going to do.

In the math center today, she has put a pile of the laminated words used in the "Being the Words" activity for *Brown Bear*. There are also eight baskets designated 1–8. The children's job in the math center today is to take the words from *Brown Bear*, count the letters in each word, and then put it in the appropriate basket. She points out the baskets that are designated 1–8 and helps the children see that some words will only have one letter and that the longest words will have eight letters. She reminds the children that, at the math center, they work with their partner and take turns counting and then checking each other. She has a math partnership come up to demonstrate how one child would pick up a word, count the letters, and point to the basket that the word would go in. The partner's job is to "play teacher" and respond with encouragement, "Right!" or to give help, "Let's count those letters again." With each word to be counted, the partners switch roles. The one who counted first becomes the teacher for the second word, and so on. The children have been working with partners in the math center, alternating the teacher/student role for several weeks now. They understand the procedures and even though they have not counted letters in words before, they have counted all kinds of concrete objects. She reminds the children that they will spend 15 minutes in the math center and won't have time to count the letters in all the words. "Just count and sort until your math center time is up," she encourages them.

The activity at the next center takes little explanation. The children are making their own take-home books patterned on the *Brown Bear* book. Their book is about the animals you might see in a zoo. Each day they make a page by tracing the printed sentence at the bottom and drawing a picture to illustrate that page. On one side of today's page, they say:

I see a yellow lion looking at me.

Printed on the back is the sentence:

Yellow lion, yellow lion, what do you see?

The teacher picks up one of these dittoed sheets and reads it to the children. She also points to several books that are opened to display various lions and reminds the children that their lion should be yellow, but that it can be as big or as scary or as cuddly as they like. "People who draw the illustrations in books use their imaginations to make their illustrations different from anyone else's," she says.

The third center that children will go to today is the listening center. Here, they will listen to a tape of two books about real animals. The teacher picks up the books and quickly shows them some pictures, reminding them that they have been studying animals and reading books about how real animals live and what they do, and have also been reading silly books about imaginary animals. Today, they will listen to two books about real animals and perhaps learn some facts to add to the animal chart this afternoon. As she says this, their eyes turn to a data chart made by stringing yarn along a bulletin board. Going down the chart are the names and pictures of some animals that are being studied. The columns across are labeled with words such as, *eat, move, live, body covering,* etc. The teacher reminds them that the chart is not yet finished and that there are spaces where they need to add information for the animals that are listed as well as space to add five more animals. The teacher reminds them that when there is just one book, the group leader of the day gets to turn the pages and must try to hold the book so that everyone can see.

Finally, the teacher points to the writing center. The writing center has a variety of things to write and draw on and with. In addition to paper, there are index cards, labels, postcards, and old stationery. The teacher reminds the children that she wants them to write something in addition to drawing something, and that scribble writing and one-letter writing is fine as long as they know what they are writing.

For the next hour, the children rotate in 15-minute blocks through each of the four centers. The children are assigned to groups, each of which contains the whole range of children—from those most experienced with print to those least experienced, and from the most agreeable to the most difficult. Each group has a leader for the day. This child is "in charge" at the center and sees to it that materials are put away and are ready for the next group as they leave each center. As the children work, the teacher circulates with a clipboard and file-folder labels in hand. She stops for a few minutes at each center and makes observations and/or gives help as needed.

While observing in the math center, she notices one child counting the letters in a word, from right to left. She stops and explains to this child that we always have to start the other way when we read words and that it is important to always go a certain way when we look at the letters in a word. She then helps the child count some letters correctly and notes this directional confusion on a label that she will attach to his folder. Having seen one child do this, she is alert to problems that other children might have. As the group rotates into the math center, she notices that several children are counting the letters from right to left. She notes this on labels and makes a note to herself to pull these children together soon and work on left-to-right directionality with them.

As she observes the children in the listening center, she notices that two children are very inattentive to the tape. One of these has a very limited use of English. The other is a very "antsy" child. She worries about their inattentiveness and decides to think about ways to alleviate it; she makes these notes on the labels.

The children doing the yellow lion page of their take-home book are busy tracing and drawing. Again, she notices some children tracing the letters from right to left. She explains that they must go the other way when they read and that they should trace this way to get in the habit. She helps them get reoriented

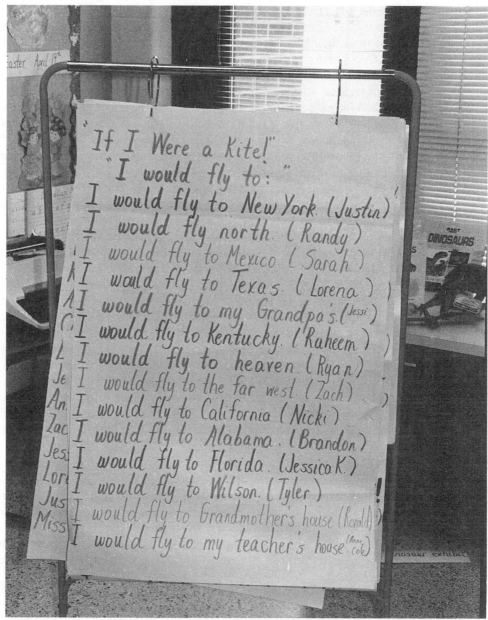

In March, this class studied about, made, and flew kites. In these photos, you see the shared writing chart on which the teacher recorded where the children would choose to fly if they were a kite. You also see some of their own writing toward the end of the year. Notice the different stages of writing and spelling development. Earlier in the year, there were children who scribbled, but by the end of the year, everyone knows that words are represented with letters. Kindergarten children need both shared writing and opportunities to write by themselves in whatever ways they can.

and again jots a note to herself to pull together the children who lack this print orientation. She begins compiling a list of these children. She asks several children to read their page to her and to touch the words as they read; she notes their success at doing this on labels, which she will attach to their folders later.

As she stops in the writing center, she is once more reminded that all children can write, if whatever writing they do is accepted. She picks up a paper that is clearly a list in "scribble writing" and asks, "Read what you wrote to me." The child proceeds to point to each scribble and tells her that these are foods he likes to eat and he then reads his scribbles about the foods. The teacher notes on the child's label that he can read his own scribbles, seems to have top-bottom and left-right orientation, but hasn't written specific letters yet. Another child has made a drawing of himself and his pet and has labeled the drawing with his name and his pet's name. One child is writing sentences that have many correctly spelled words in them and other words that are clearly readable from his invented spelling. Another child is listing animals, copying the words from the newspaper animal board, from the list of animals on the side of the data chart, and from a book on animals he has picked up from the bookshelf next to the writing center.

The teacher reminds herself that children have various "experience" levels. Some children arrived at school understanding that writing is talk written down, but many did not. Some had been writing at home for a long while. Others did not hold their first pencil until starting school. Knowing this and knowing the importance of providing many experiences with written language, she has all the children write every day. She encourages children to write words in any way they can, but some children won't write them unless they know they are writing them right! She realizes that by providing the acceptance and support for a variety of writing levels and the "words available in the room support" for children who have to do it right, she will allow children to write in whatever ways they can!

11:30–12:00 Lunch

Just before the children line up, the teacher reads the lunch menu. Usually, she just reads it to them but, capitalizing on their interest about what letters favorite foods begin with, she generates some little riddles to give them some clues about what the foods are and what the beginning letters of the foods are.

"Today, you are having another food that begins with a *p*. The one you are going to have just has cheese on it. I like it with cheese and with another *p*-word—*pepperoni!*"

The children make happy sounds as they realize their favorite—*pizza*—is on the menu.

"With your pizza, you will have something that is very nutritious and contains lots of vitamins. It has lettuce and other vegetables and begins with an *s*."

Most children guess, "salad."

"For dessert, you will have something that comes in different flavors and colors. Sometimes it is yellow, sometimes brown, sometimes white. Today it is white with chocolate frosting and begins with the letter *c*."

The children guess "cake" and have no trouble guessing that their beverage will be the *m* food from their food board—milk.

12:00–12:30 Reading with, by, and to Children

When the children arrive back from lunch, some children go to their tables, others go to a corner of the room that contains all the predictable big books that they have read this year, others go to the reading corner that, in addition to books, has puppets and stuffed animals. The observer would have trouble knowing which children were supposed to go where, but the children know exactly where to go. Each child has one day to read in the reading corner, another day when they can read the big books, and on the other three days they read at their seats. This procedure has been in place for two weeks now and is working quite well. Having all the children spread out in the room created problems because there just weren't enough good "spreading-out places." This new arrangement seems to have just the right balance of freedom and structure so that the children spend most of their time actually reading (or pretend reading, if that is what they are doing!).

Reading at their tables, the children find trays of books there. The trays contain a variety of books and are rotated so that each table gets a different tray each day. One tray is filled with animal books—the topic they are studying in a combined science/social studies unit. Included in the tray are the two books children listened to at the listening center this morning. Many of these books are too hard for most of the children to read but they love talking about the pictures and do find some animal names they recognize.

A second tray contains books gathered up for the last topic studied—weather. The children enjoy looking at these books, most of which have been read to them. Many children can read the predictable books such as *What Makes the Weather?* and *Our Friend, the Sun* (Troll).

Another tray of books contains "oldies but goodies," which the children request to have read again and again. All children can make some attempt at reading such favorites as *Go Dog Go; Inside, Outside, Upside Down;* and *The Three Little Pigs.*

Another tray contains class books. The books written during shared writing and illustrated by the children are perennial favorites of the children. The first class book contains a photo and a few sentences about each child in the class. This is still one of the most popular books and is reread almost every day by someone. Currently, they are writing and illustrating a class book about animals that will be added to this tray when it is finished.

There are also two trays of library books—one tray contains those checked out from the public library and the other contains those checked out from the school library. The teacher has arranged with both libraries to check out 20–30 books to keep in the classroom for a month. She chooses two or three children to go with her on a special trip to the public library every month to return the old books and pick out new ones for the "Public Library" tray. By the end of the year, all children will have made this special after-school trip. For many children, it is their first trip to the public library, and some of them (and their parents!) are amazed that you can get books to take home "for free." At the end of the year, the whole class makes a trip to this library again and most of the children get library cards. The monthly trips with two or three children to the public library and the library card field trip takes extra time and effort but the teacher feels that introducing these children to a free, unlimited source of reading material early makes the time and effort worthwhile.

Each day, when the children return from lunch, they read books. They can read by themselves or, if they use quiet voices, with a friend who sits near them. The children who go to the book corner often read to the puppets and stuffed animals that reside there.

When the children have read their own books for about 10–15 minutes, the teacher chooses several books or parts of books to read to the class. She chooses from a variety of books, often reading a few pages from an informational book, an "oldie but goodie" favorite (which the children never tire of having reread to them), and a new book. As she reads aloud, the teacher talks about print and artwork, allowing children to "see" how a good reader thinks while reading. She turns the book to face the children and shows them features of the book.

12:30–1:00 Big Group

This half hour usually is devoted either to math or to the topic they are studying for science/social studies. Today, Mr. Hinkle arrives with his turtle and with a book about having turtles as pets. He talks with the children about the turtle and reads them the book. When he leaves, they add turtle information to their data chart on the bulletin board, along with some facts that they learned from listening to the two taped informational animal books in the listening center that morning.

1:00–1:30 P.E.

As they march to P.E. class, the teacher leads them in a "whisper" version of a favorite song, ditty, or rhyme. Today they are marching along to one of the "raps" recorded by the African-American poet Lindamichellebaron (*The Sun Is On*, book and tape available from Harlin Jacques Publishers, 507 Panache Suite, 200 Fulton Ave., Hempstead, NY 11550). This use of rhythm and rhyme serves the children because it is fun and it helps children develop their phonemic awareness.

1:30–2:00

On three afternoons, the children have this half-hour once again to choose activities in the various centers. One day each week, they go to the computer lab. On another day, today, their "Big Buddies" from the fifth grade arrive to read and write with the children. Each fifth grader is assigned one kindergarten buddy. They bring a book that they have practiced reading and read it "lap style" to their kindergarten. They then let the kindergartner choose a book to read to them. (It took some explaining, but the fifth graders have learned that "pretend reading" is a critical beginning step and they accept whatever kind of reading their kindergartner does.) Next, they write whatever their kindergartner would like them to write in that child's "All About Me" book. They have learned to talk with the child about "the interesting things that have happened since I came last week" and to record some of these things in simple sentences. These weekly journals are records of lost teeth, new jackets, birthdays, family moves, births, and deaths. The children love to have someone record what has happened in their lives and, once today's record is made, they pester their big buddies to, "read all about me from the beginning of the year."

2:00 Daily Summary/School-Home Connection

The children prepare to go home. They talk about what they have done today and what they will do tomorrow. They look forward to "Being the Words" again to make some more *Brown Bear* sentences. They also are ready to do another page in the take-home zoo animals book they are making.

The teacher lets each of them choose a little book, an index card, and a pencil to put in a reclosable bag. Each night, their "homework" is to read the book to someone or have someone read it to them, and to write or have someone write something for them on the card. Today, given their interest in how foods are spelled, they are to try to copy some names of foods they like from the boxes and cans that they find at home.

Once the children are gone, the teacher peels the file-folder labels off the backing and attaches them to the appropriate children's folders. She thinks about how each child is developing in his or her literacy and looks again at the list of literacy goals she has for them:

1. They "pretend read" favorite books and poems/songs/chants.
2. They "write" in whatever way they can and can read what they wrote even if no one else can.
3. They "track print," that is, show you what to read and point to the words using left-right/top-bottom conventions.
4. They know critical jargon, can point to just one word, the first word in the sentence, just one letter, the first letter in the word, the longest word, etc.
5. They recognize and can write some concrete words—their names, names of other children, favorite words from books, poems, and chants.
6. They are developing phonemic awareness—including the ability to clap syllables, recognize if words rhyme, make up rhymes, and stretch out words.
7. They can name many letters and tell you words that begin with the common initial sounds.
8. They are learning more about the world that they live in and are more able to talk about what they know.
9. They can listen to stories and informational books and can retell the most important information.
10. They see themselves as readers and writers and as new members of the "literacy club."

She feels that, even though they are at very different places, all of her kindergartners are making progress toward achieving these critical understandings. While some children arrived without print, story, and book experience, her classroom is organized to immerse these children in literacy experiences. These experiences with print, stories, and books form the base for her instructional planning. She thinks about whole-class, small-group, and individual activities she can do tomorrow to further their development.

A Day in a Four-Blocks Primary Classroom

The activities described in the kindergarten chapter are equally appropriate in first grade, particularly at the beginning of the year. Some children spent the summer in print-rich home environments but others have had few such experiences since the day they left kindergarten. Re-immersing all children into print-rich classrooms goes a long way in fostering easy and early reactivation of the concepts and strategies they developed last year. Print-rich classrooms, shared reading and writing, opportunities for every child to read and write daily, rhymes and chants to develop phonemic awareness, and opportunities to expand knowledge through science and social studies units are the cornerstones of successful literacy programs for at-risk first graders. The ten goals listed at the end of the previous chapter are the goals that first grade teachers must evaluate and work toward as they begin the year.

As children demonstrate that they have the emergent literacy knowings under varying degrees of control, first grade teachers must then provide activities that further the development of reading and writing. We organize important primary-grade activities within a framework we call Four Blocks. These blocks—Guided Reading, Self-Selected Reading, Writing and Working with Words—provide numerous and varied opportunities for all children to learn to read and write. Here is what one day in a four blocks primary classroom might look like.

8:30–8:50 Opening

The children enter and prepare for the day. When they have their gear stowed, they gather around the teacher. They share things that have happened to them over the weekend, do some calendar activities and talk about the events planned for the day. Next, the teacher reads a new informational book with lots of pictures of seeds and the plants that grow from them. She tells the children that they will learn much more about seeds and plants as they begin their new science unit. As she finishes reading the book, she places it in the tray labeled, "seeds and plants," which has many other books in it. As she picks up three or four of the other books and shows a few pages of each, she reminds the children that each time they start a new science or social studies unit, she gathers up books from both the school and the public library and puts them in a special tray. The children are all anxious to look at the books, but it is time to get on with other things. They know, however, that this tray of books will be waiting for them during self-selected reading time. Finally, the teacher shows them a seed catalog that she has brought from home, quickly flipping through it and pausing briefly to show a page or two of the illustrations. She then puts the catalog on the tray also.

8:50–9:20 The Working with Words Block

The two hours and 15 minutes designated for reading/language arts in this class are divided into four blocks of 30–40 minutes each. The first block this teacher does is the Words block. Activities in this block are designed to help children achieve two critical goals. In order to read and write independently, children must learn to automatically recognize and spell the high-frequency words that occur in almost everything we read and write. They must also learn to look for patterns in words so that they can decode and spell the less frequent words they have not been taught. To accomplish these two goals, the teacher depends on a daily word wall activity and a second activity designed to help them become better decoders and spellers.

The children are seated at their desks and, since today is Monday, they are eager to see what five new words will be added to the wall today. The teacher looks at Roberto, who just arrived in her classroom last Wednesday, and realizes that he does not really know what the word wall is for. She decides to use this opportunity to remind the children about the importance of the words selected for the word wall.

The teacher begins by directing the children's attention to the bulletin board word wall. She asks the children how many words they think are currently on the word wall and gets some wild guesses. She decides that this is a good math opportunity and leads the children to count the words. There are 95 words. She then asks someone to explain to Roberto how many words are added each Monday and how she decides what words to add.

The children explain that five words are added each week and these are the most important words. When asked to explain what "most important" means, the children explain that, "You use them all the time," "You can't read and write without them," and "A lot of these words aren't spelled the way they should be, so when you want to write one of the word wall words, you look up there to remember how to spell it instead of trying to figure it out."

"Why are the words arranged according to their first letter?" the teacher asks.

"To make it easier to find them. When you need the word, you just think how it begins and then you can find it faster."

"Why are the words different colors?" she asks.

"To make the word wall pretty," one child explains.

"Well, it does make the word wall pretty to have the different colors, but does it help us in any other way?"

"It helps you to remember the words that look almost alike, which word is which—*then* is pink and *them* is green and I can find *them* quicker if I look for the green one under the *t*."

Satisfied that the children understand why learning to read and write these words is so important and how to find them when they need them in writing, she goes on to show the children the five new words that she will add today. She reminds the children of the selections they had read last week during the guided reading time and that she had introduced them to many new words as they read these selections.

"It was hard to choose only five words, but I chose the ones that you see most often in books and that I think you all need when you write. I also chose one word that occurs fairly often but that also begins with a letter for which we don't have any words yet. Some of you have been complaining about not having any words that begin with *q* or *z* and I have told you that not many words begin with those two letters. But, I have been on the lookout for a *q* or *z* word in one of our selections, which you might see in books and need in your writing. Last week, as you were reading, I spotted one."

As she said this, she put the word *question*, written with a black permanent marker on yellow construction paper, on the word wall next to the *q*. "Remember that everyone kept telling the boy not to ask so many *questions* in the story you read. *Question* will be our word wall *q* word. She then wrote *question* on the overhead as the children wrote it on their handwriting paper. She reminded the children of the proper letter formation as she wrote each letter. They seemed pleased to have a *q* word on the word wall and were amazed that it was such a big word. The teacher lead them to count the letters in *question* and pointed out that many of the words we read and write most often are pretty short words.

Taking less time, she added the other high-frequency words to the wall that were introduced last week during guided reading—*about, where, many, this*—and demonstrated correct letter formation and had the children write the words on their half sheet of handwriting paper.

Once they had written them on the front, with the teacher's direction for handwriting, the children turned their paper over on the back and the teacher gave clues to the five words that were just added to the word wall.

The first word I want you to practice is our new *th* word. Who can remember what it is?" The children responded, "this."

The teacher then pointed to *this* and had them clap rhythmically and chant the letters three times—"t-h-i-s, t-h-i-s, t-h-i-s—this!" After clapping and chanting the word, they wrote it on the back of their handwriting paper. The teacher did not demonstrate how to write *this* this time, but she did remind them to "make the letters just as they did on the front." She continued to ask them to identify, clap, and chant in this manner, and to write the other four new words that were just added to the word wall. After they had written all five, she demonstrated how to write them once again and the children checked their own papers.

She finished the word wall activity by reminding the children that on Monday when five new words were added, they practiced only those five new words. "From now on this week, I will pick different words from the wall to practice." (On days when old words are being practiced, the procedure is for the teacher to call out any five words, the children clap and then write them. Next, they check the words for correct letters and handwriting by tracing around the word as the teacher traces around the same word on the board or overhead.)

One child pointed out that if they had 95 before they added today's words, they must have 100 now. Several children looked skeptical about this, so the teacher let them count the words once more; sure enough, they had reached the magic number—100! The children seemed very pleased to have 100 "important" words on their wall and to finally have a word for *q*. The teacher promised to be on the lookout for a *z* word in one of the selections they read so that every letter would have at least one word!

Next, the children went to the second activity in the words block, today they were making words. (On other days, the activity might be Guess the Covered Word, Using Words You Know or an activity with lots of rhyming words.)

The Monday children at each table (who, of course, are the people in charge on Monday!) picked up the letter tray that was on their table and distributed the needed letters to each child. For this particular lesson, each child had five consonants, *c, r, r, s, t,* and two vowels, *a* and *o*. In the pocket chart at the front of the room, the teacher had large cards with the same seven letters. Her cards, like the small letter cards used by the children, had the uppercase letter on one side and lowercase letter on the other side. The consonant letters were written in black and the two vowels were in red.

The teacher began by making sure that each child had all the letters that were needed. "What two vowels will we use to make words today?" she asked. The children held up their red *a* and *o* and responded appropriately. The children then named the consonants they had and were surprised to notice that they had two *r*'s. The teacher told them that sometimes you need two of the same letter to make certain words and that they would need both *r*'s to spell the secret word that ended the lesson.

The teacher then wrote the numeral 2 on the board and said. "The two-letter word I want you to make today is a word that you already know—*at*. She watched as the children quickly put together the letters *a-t* and she checked to see that Roberto was able to follow along. She sent someone who had correctly spelled *at* to the pocket chart to make *at* with the big letters and to put an index card that had the word *at* written on it along the chalkledge.

Next, she erased the 2 and wrote a 3 on the board. "Add just one letter to *at* to make the three-letter word *sat*," she instructed. She chose a child who had arranged his letters correctly at his desk to make *sat* with the big pocket chart letters. The lesson continued with children making words with their individual letter cards, a child going to the pocket chart to make the word, and the teacher putting a card with that word along the chalkledge. (The teacher did not wait for everyone to make the word before sending someone to the pocket chart and some children were still making their word as the word was being made with the pocket chart letters. Before moving to make another word, the teacher reminded the children to fix their word to match the one made with the big letters.) Directed by the teacher, the children changed *sat* to *rat*, *rat* to *rot*, *rot* to *cot*, and *cot* to *cat*. "Now, we are going to work some magic on the word *cat*," the teacher explained, "Don't take any letters out and don't add any either. Just change the places of the letters and you can turn your *cat* into *act*. After we read stories, we like to *act* them out." The teacher had the children say the word *act* slowly, stretching out the sounds to figure out where to move the letters to transform *cat* into *act*.

The teacher erased the *3,* wrote a *4* on the board, and asked them to make *Rosa.* "We read a story earlier this year about a girl named Rosa—who was unhappy about always being too little. Make the name, *Rosa.*" She observed them saying "Rosa" very slowly, emphasizing each sound, and then finding their letters. She was pleased to notice that almost everyone turned the *R* card to display the capital *R.* She had been including at least one name in almost every Making Words Lesson and the children were getting very good at remembering that names needed capital letters. Next, they made *coat* and then *oats.*

The teacher erased the *4* and wrote a *5* and told them that if they added just one letter to *oats,* they could turn *oats* into *coats.* She then had them, without adding any letters or taking any out, transform their *coats* into *coast* by changing where they put some of the letters. She helped them say the words *coats* and *coast* slowly and to listen for how these words sounded. Most children were able to move the *s* and the *t* around to make this change; she noted their growing phonemic awareness. "Now make one more five-letter word by changing just one letter and turn your *coast* into a *roast.*"

As a child was making *roast* at the pocket chart, many of the other children were manipulating all of their letters trying to come up with a word. They knew that each lesson ended with a word that used all of their letters and they always liked to figure it out. The teacher walked around looking for someone with the secret word and just as she was about to declare that "since no one could figure it out, she would make the secret word" she noticed a child who had the word made and sent that child to the pocket chart where he made the word, *carrots.*

After making the words, it is time to sort for patterns and then use those patterns to read and spell a few new words. The teacher had the children read all the words they had made now displayed in the pocket chart.

| at | sat | rat | rot | cot | cat | act | Rosa |
| coat | oats | coats | coast | roast | carrots | | |

She picked up *at* and said, "Who can come and hand me three words that rhyme with *at?*" A child handed her the words *sat, rat,* and *cat.* She then had someone find the word that rhymed with *rot*—*cot,* the word that rhymed with *oats*—*coats,* and the word that rhymed with *coast*—*roast.* The children spelled the rhyming words and decided that these words all had the same letters from the vowel on. The teacher reminded the children that words that have the same spelling pattern usually rhyme and that knowing this is one way many good readers and writers read and spell words.

She then showed them an index card on which the word *lot* was written. "What if you were reading and came to this word and didn't know it? Don't say this word even if you know it, but who can go and put this word with the rhyming words that will help you figure it out. A child placed *lot* under *rot* and *cot* and all the children pronounced all three words and noticed that they had the same spelling pattern and rhymed. The same procedure was followed with another rhyming word, *flat.*

"Thinking of words that rhyme helps you when you are trying to spell a word too. If I were writing and wanted to write *boats,* which of the rhyming words that we made today would help me?" The children decided that *boats* rhymed with *oats* and *coats* and would probably be spelled *b-o-a-t-s.*

"If I were writing about foods I liked and I wanted to spell *toast,* what rhyming words would help me?" The children decided that *toast* rhymed with *roast* and *coast* and would probably be spelled *t-o-a-s-t.*

Finally, she showed them their take-home making-words homework sheet. The letters *a, o, c, r, s, t, t* were in boxes along the top and there were larger boxes for children to write words. "When you show this to someone at your house, do you think they will figure out the secret word or will you have to tell them?" she asked. Most children thought that this would be a "toughie." They always enjoyed their making-words homework sheet. They cut the letters apart, wrote the capitals on the back, and then filled the boxes with the words they could make—including some made in class and others they could think of. Parents and older siblings often got involved and because it made the secret word done in class that day, the children were always smarter than anyone else and enjoyed stumping their often "competitive" families!

a	o	c	r	r	t	s

The letters you need to "Make Words" tonight are at the top of the page. Write capitals on the back. Then, cut the letters apart and see how many words you can make. Write the words in the blanks.

Take Home Sheet for Making Words

9:20–10:00 Guided Reading

In this classroom, the Words Block is followed by the Guided-Reading Block. On some days, they do a shared reading in a big book. The teacher reads the book first and the children join in on subsequent rereadings. On other days, the teacher guides the children's reading in selections from basal readers, literature collections, or tradebooks, of which they have multiple copies. For today's lesson, the teacher has chosen *The Carrot Seed* (Ruth Krauss, Harper, 1945). As often as possible, the teacher tries to find reading material that ties in to the children's science or social studies unit. *The Carrot Seed* is perfect for their current *Seeds and Plants* unit.

The teacher picks up *The Carrot Seed* and points to the title. She asks, "What word do we see here that we made with an *s* added in our Making Words lesson?" The children quickly identify the word *carrot*. The teacher then points to the word *seed*, and asks the children to look at the picture on the cover of the book and to think about what the boy is doing and what word the letters *s-e-e-d* might spell. The children realize that the boy is planting something; using the picture clue and what they know about letters and sounds, they are able to figure out the word *seed* and read the title of the book, *The Carrot Seed*.

Next, the teacher directs the children to look at all the pictures in the story and to think about what is happening.

"You know that we can read lots of words we haven't seen before if we look at the pictures, think about what is happening, and then think about what words we might read to tell what is happening."

She leads the children on a picture walk in which they use the pictures to make predictions and develop some vocabulary. First, they look at the pictures and identify the characters—a little boy, his mother, his father, and his big brother. The children all know the word *mother;* she writes it on the board and underneath it writes *brother.* She underlines the *other* in both *mother* and *brother* and asks the children what they know about words that have the same spelling pattern. The children respond that the words usually rhyme and the teacher leads them to figure out the new word *brother* from their known word *mother.* The teacher follows the same procedure to help them decode the new word *weed* based on the rhyming word *seed.*

Next, the teacher leads them to decide what the boy is doing on certain pages. On the first page, they decide that the boy looks like he is planting the seed. The teacher asks them to say the word *planted* slowly and decide what letters they would use if they were making the word *planted.* The children decide that they hear a *p-l* at the beginning and that it ends in *e-d.* "Look on this page and find a word that might be *planted.* Put your finger on it when you find it." The children quickly find and say the word *planted.*

The children look at other pages and decide that the boy is pulling up weeds and sprinkling the plant with a watering can. The teacher has them say the words and think about what letters they would use to make the words *pull* and *sprinkle.* They then search the text for these words. Throughout this phase of the lesson, the teacher develops useful strategies for children to use as they read. This lesson, using artwork to predict specific text content and attending to sounds in spoken words, represents an attempt to support children's development of the integrated strategy, using both the meaning and sounds of words in combination with one another.

Having guided them to look at the pictures, to talk about what was happening, and to use that knowledge to figure out some unfamiliar words, the teacher then asks them to make some predictions about what they will find out as they read the story with a partner. Finally, she tells them what they will do when they gather back together after reading the story. She shows them six index cards on which she has written the words:

carrot seed	mother
carrot	father
little boy	big brother

She also shows them that she has written the word *everyone* on 17 other index cards.

The children read the words with her and she tells them that after reading, she will shuffle and distribute the cards and they will get to play a part in acting out the story. Everyone will get a part, even if their part is to be part of the *everyone*. Since they don't know which card they will get, they should read the story and think about what they would do for each part, no matter which card they got.

The children then go to read the story with their partners. The teacher had partnered up struggling readers with better readers. The children had learned to take turns reading pages and to help each other when help was needed. The teacher reminded the children to examine the pictures before beginning to read and to help but not to tell each other an unknown word. She then reminded them of the steps they had learned for figuring out words that they didn't recognize immediately:

1. Put your finger on the unknown word and say all the letters.
2. Use the letters and the picture clues.
3. Try to pronounce the word by looking to see if it has a spelling pattern or rhyme that you know.
4. Keep your finger on the word and read the other words in the sentence to see if it makes sense.
5. If it doesn't make sense, go back to the word and think what would have these letters and would make sense.

She also reminded the children that, when their partner was reading a page, they were to "play teacher" and, if their partner was having trouble with a word, they should help go through the steps, instead of just telling what the word is.

The partners went to designated places and read the story. The teacher circulated, with clipboard and labels in hand, and made notes on how fluently the children were reading. She praised the partners who were helping other children use the steps to figure out unfamiliar words by telling them that they could "soon have her job" and that "they were great little teachers!"

It took only about seven minutes for the partners to finish reading. When she noticed that they had finished, she handed each of them an index card, indicating what part they would play in the story reenactment. She then gathered the children around her again and had them retell the story with emphasis on what the main characters would do. The child who had gotten the "seed" card would be put on the floor and lie there, motionless. The "carrot" would be pulled from the ground and wheeled away by the little boy. The mother, the father, the big brother, and the "everyone" would shake their heads and say, "It won't come up!" The little boy would plant, sprinkle, pull weeds, and finally wheel the carrot away proudly.

Space was cleared in the center for a "stage" and *The Carrot Seed* was acted out. This was a low-budget, off-off Broadway production that lacked props, costumes, and rehearsal, but no one seemed to care. The children took their places and the story was retold with the events happening in the correct sequence. The only complaint was from the children who had to be part of the "everyone" and who wanted starring roles instead! The teacher assured them that there were no little parts and that tomorrow they would reread the story and act it out again and more people would get the "big parts"!

10:00–10:15 Break/Snack

The children and the teacher went outside and took one brisk walk around the school, singing a favorite marching rhyme on their way. Once inside, they all had juice and crackers. Many children in this school did not eat very nutritious meals and the ones who needed it most brought no snack at all or brought "junk food." The teacher had prevailed on those parents who could send something to send large cans of juice and boxes of crackers or to donate money so that she could buy juice and crackers at the local warehouse. Many parents donated willingly because they didn't have to send something each day and, when everyone had juice and crackers for a snack, their children couldn't pester them to bring junk! Arranging for the juice and cracker morning snack took some time and preparation, but she knew that some children needed this healthy snack; she also couldn't stand to watch some of them eat while others sat there hungry. During this break, the teacher talked with the children about the kind of seeds and plants that produced much of the food they were eating. She had even thought to bring in some raw carrot slices for everyone to munch on and a whole raw carrot for all to examine.

10:15–11:15 Math and Science or Social Studies Unit

During this hour each morning, the class did math and activities related to their science or social studies unit. On some days, it was impossible to integrate the two so they did one or the other or divided the hour between the two. Today, she integrated a math lesson with the new science seeds and plants unit. She passed out containers filled with various kinds of seeds. She then led the children in a variety of counting, sorting, predicting, classifying, and weighing activities with the seeds. The children worked in groups at their tables, sorting the seeds by putting the ones that were alike together, estimating, counting to see how many of each type of seed they had, and graphing to show which seeds they had more and less of. The teacher gave out simple balance scales and had the children predict which seeds weighed the most and the least. They then weighed the different seeds and determined that it would take "more than they had" of the tiniest seeds to weigh as much as one of the largest seeds. The children were particularly amazed by how tiny carrot seeds were.

When the hour allotted for this hands-on math/science activity was almost over, the teacher showed the children some pages from the seeds and plants book that she had read to start the day. She helped the children identify the seeds and the plants that grew from them. The children were amazed to realize that hickory nuts, acorns, and white beans were all seeds. They remembered seeing seeds like the little ones they had when eating cucumbers and apples. The children then regretfully dumped all their seeds back into the containers and the teacher promised that they would do some more exploring and computing using the seeds tomorrow.

11:15–11:50 Writer's Workshop

Each day after math/science, the children had their writing block. This block always begins with the teacher writing something on the overhead as the children watch. As she writes, she thinks aloud, modeling the way she thinks about writing. It is this think-aloud writing that supports children as they develop as readers and writers. She writes about a variety of topics and in a variety of formats. Today, she decided to capitalize on the children's interest in the new seed and plant unit by writing about some of the things they had found while exploring with the seeds.

She sat down at her overhead, pen in hand. The children settled down on the floor in front of her, eager to see what she would write about today. They watched and listened as she thought aloud about what to write.

"I always have so many things I want to write about on Mondays. I could write about going shopping this weekend and finding my car with a flat tire when I came out of the store! I could write about the funny movie I watched on TV. I could write a list of the different seeds I ordered from the seed catalog this weekend. But, I think I will write about what we did with the seeds this morning because you all seemed to have so much fun with them." She then wrote a description of some of the activities the children had just done.

As she wrote, she modeled for them how she might invent-spell a few words. (Early in the year, she told the children that she used to love to write when she was their age and that she would write all kinds of things. She wrote stories and kept a diary and was always making lists. She pretended that she was a great writer and wrote wonderful books for children to read. She explained that, of course, when she was their age she couldn't spell all the words she needed so she just put in all the letters she could hear so that she could read it back. She told them that she used to "invent-spell" the big words and would show them how she used to do this at the beginning of each writer's workshop.) As she was writing, she would stop and say a word aloud slowly and would write down the letters she could hear. She also looked up at the word wall a few times and said, "I can spell *many* because we just put it on our word wall" and "I will look at *some* on our word wall because *some* is not spelled the way you would think it should be." When she got ready to write the last sentence, she picked up the book and said, "I can use this book to help me spell the names of some of the seeds we had." She also omitted one ending punctuation mark and failed to capitalize one word.

When she finished writing, she said, "Now, I will read it to make sure that it makes sense and that it says what I wanted it to say." She read it aloud as the children watched. As soon as she finished, the children's hands were raised, volunteering to be editors. She gave one boy a different color marker to go to the overhead and lead the class in helping her edit her writing. Each editing convention the children had learned so far was covered and the class checked her draft for these features. When they found a missing feature they volunteered what needed fixing. Possible misspelled words were circled, capitals and punctuation marks were added. The boy who was editing changed and inserted like a pro! So far, they had learned five things to look for. They read the short paragraph and put a check on the bottom as they checked each of the five things:

1. There is a title in the middle.
2. Every sentence makes sense.
3. Every sentence begins with a capital and ends with a punctuation mark.
4. People and place names have capital letters.
5. Words that might be misspelled are circled.

The writing minilesson took approximately 10 minutes, including the editing. The children were then dismissed from the big group to do their own writing. The children were at various stages of the writing process. Five children were at the art table, happily illustrating their books. When asked why they got to make books, they proudly explained that you had to write three pieces first. Then, you had to pick the best of the three and get a friend to be your editor—just like we do for the teacher at the overhead. Then, you get to go to the editing table and the teacher helps you edit it and you copy it in one of these books (holding up a premade half-sheet construction paper covered book that is stapled). One child who was illustrating a book about her best friend proudly turned to the back blank page in her book and said, "That's where she's going to write about me." When asked what the teacher might write, the author responded, "She's gonna say, Nikita is seven years old. She has three brothers and four sisters and this is her fourth book!—something like that!"

Four children were at the editing table with the teacher. She was helping them do a final edit of their pieces in preparation for copying them into books. A pair of children were helping each other edit before proceeding to the editing table. The other children were working away at their desks, in various stages of producing their three pieces so that they too could get to the art table. Children wrote about whatever they chose to. Some days, they continued writing on something they had started the day before. Other days, they started a new piece. This morning, some children wrote about seeds and about what they had done with the seeds. Another child paged through the seed catalog and wrote a list of all the seeds that they wanted to order. Other children wrote about things they had done over the weekend. The teacher's minilesson and her pondering about what to write each morning always got them thinking about what to write. The children often wrote about what the teacher wrote about, although the teacher neither encouraged nor discouraged them from choosing the same topic. Many children could be seen glancing up at the word wall when they realized that the word they were trying to spell was up there. Some children had a book opened to use as a reference for ideas and spelling.

The classroom was a busy working place for about 15 minutes. Then, with a signal from the teacher, the children once again gathered on the floor and the Monday children lined up behind the Author's Chair! (All of the children are designated by a day of the week; on their day, they get to share!) The first child read just two sentences of a piece that was started today. He called on various children who told him that they liked the topic (dinosaurs) and gave him ideas for what he might like to include. One child suggested a good dinosaur book for him to read. The second child read a completed piece. She called on children who told her that they liked the way she had stayed on the topic (her new baby sister) and asked questions ("What's her name?" "Does she cry all night?" "Is this the only sister you've got?") The third and fourth children read some unfinished pieces and received praise and suggestions. Nikita was the final Monday child. She read her book and showed her illustrations and then handed it to the teacher, reminding her to, "Write about me on this page!" The sharing took approximately 9 minutes, for a total of 34 minutes of Writer's Workshop.

11:50–12:20 Lunch

Each day, as the children were lining up, the teacher read the lunch menu to them. Today, she told them that one of the foods they were going to have for lunch was made mostly from seeds. She then read the menu and no one could figure out that peanut butter was the food made mostly from seeds. Many children seemed quite astonished! The teacher decided that a peanut butter cooking activity would be a great tie-in to the unit.

12:20–12:35 After-Lunch Bunch

Each day, as the children came back from lunch, six children joined the teacher at the back table to read some "fun" books. (The other children rested or engaged in some quiet activity at their desks.) The teacher had formed this after-lunch bunch just after Christmas when she realized that many children were not fluently reading the books and stories she was using during the morning guided-reading block. These children read with partners and, in this manner, were able to enjoy, discuss, and act out the stories. She knew, from the observations that she made and wrote on the file-folder labels, that many children were not really at instructional level in these materials. They depended on their partners to help them figure out many words. The teacher knew that, while they were enjoying being included in the activities, they needed to read some easier selections. In order to develop their reading fluency and to learn to figure out unfamiliar words independently, she had to provide them with some reading materials in which they could recognize almost all the words.

She decided to use the 15 minutes after lunch (which had been resting time, but by Christmas had evolved into quiet time because few children wanted to rest after lunch anymore) to provide some easy reading time to meet the needs of children for whom the material read during the guided-reading time was really too hard. Furthermore, she decided that she wanted some "good reading models" in the group that came to be called the after-lunch bunch. Every day, the children came in from lunch and looked to see if they were in the after-lunch bunch. Every child, even the very best reader, found his or her name there at least once a week, but the children whose need for continued easy reading had instigated the formation of the group found their names there three or four (but not five) days a week. By including all of the children (but the struggling readers more often), the teacher was able to provide for the needs of the weaker readers without having the after-lunch bunch viewed as a "bottom group."

Each day, the children who found their names on the after-lunch bunch list joined the teacher and read something together. The teacher used a variety of materials—stories from old basals, multiple copies of easy library books, etc.— but always chose material in which the lowest readers could read almost all the words. Generally, she got the children talking about the book or story by looking at the pictures, talking about what was happening, letting each child read it by himself or herself, and then leading a brief meaning-oriented discussion of the story. She also had the children reread selected parts orally when there was time. Before the children started to read, she reminded them of the strategies they knew for figuring out an unfamiliar word:

1. Put your finger on the unknown word and say all the letters.
2. Use the letters and the picture clues.
3. Try to pronounce the word by looking to see if it has a spelling pattern or rhyme that you know.
4. Keep your finger on the word and read the other words in the sentence to see if it makes sense.
5. If it doesn't make sense, go back to the word and think what would have these letters and would make sense.

If she observed that someone is stumped on a word as the children were reading, she would prompt the child to use these strategies. Sometimes, she would give them a clue such as "Yes, this word is spelled g-r-u-m-p; we have a word on our word wall spelled j-u-m-p." or "Do you see an animal in the picture that might be spelled d-r-a-g-o-n?" Once the child had figured out a word, she would remind them to, "Go back and reread the sentence and see if it sounds correct now." She made notes on her file-folder labels about their fluency and about how well they were using the decoding strategies she had taught them.

The combination of easy reading, in which they knew most of the words along with some reminders and support (when they tried applying the strategies they were learning to the unfamiliar words), seemed to be helping even the poorest readers become independent readers. Having a few good readers in every after-lunch bunch provided models for expressive oral reading and discussion. The short after-lunch bunch reading sessions were generally enjoyable for all the children and for the teacher as well.

12:35–1:35 P.E./Library/Art/Music/Open Centers
During this hour each day, the class was scheduled for their classes with the specialists. They did not have specialists each day for the whole hour; they also used this time to go outside, to the gym, to the library, or to do music and art. On some days, they had Open Center Time for part of this hour. Sometimes, the special teachers would plan an activity that was connected to what the classroom teacher was doing. The music teacher was particularly agreeable about coordinating with classroom teachers. Today, she taught them some new songs about seeds. She had the words to the songs on an overhead and pointed to the words as the children sang along. At the end of the period, she passed out a dittoed sheet on which she had written the words to one of the songs that they had sung several times. "Take this home and teach it to someone at home," she suggested.

1:45–2:15 Self-Selected Reading
Each day, the teacher began this block by reading aloud to the children for 10–15 minutes. After reading to them, she dismissed them to their tables for their own reading time. The teacher had arranged books into several plastic crates and put one crate on each of the five tables. The crates contained a variety of books including some related to the science unit—seeds and plants—"old favorites" such as, *Are You My Mother?*, *One Fish, Two Fish,* and *Robert The Rose Horse.* Some were class books and books the children had written. The trays were rotated each day so that all the children would have lots of books to choose from without leaving their seats, but wouldn't see the same old books every day.

The children eagerly read the books. As they read, the teacher conferenced with the Monday children. Each child brought the teacher a book that he or she had selected and read a few pages from that book. The teacher made anecdotal notes about what the Monday children were reading and about how well they were reading. She noted their use of picture clues, attempts to figure out unknown words, fluency, self-correction, and other reading behaviors. She also asked them what they liked about the book they were reading and sometimes suggested another book that they might like.

2:15–2:30 Daily Summary/School-Home Connection
During this time, the children prepared to go home and the teacher helped them talk about what they had learned today and what they could talk about at home. Because so many of these children came from homes in which English was not the spoken language, she felt it was important to promote as much home/school talk as possible. She helped them recall the seeds they had learned about in the book and what they had done with the seeds. She reminded them that they had eaten peanut butter—made mostly from seeds—at lunch. She made sure that they had their song sheets from music class and

asked them if they thought someone at home would enjoy learning the song. She reminded them of *The Carrot Seed* and had them think about their part in the reenactment. She distributed the making words homework sheets and reminded them to bring them back tomorrow so she could see the other words that could be made from these letters that "she hadn't been smart enough to think of!" Next, they identified the five new words added to the word wall today. "Be sure to tell your family that we finally have a *q* word—*question*—on our word wall and that we are looking for a useful, important word that begins with the letter *z*." She also reminded them to tell about what they had written about during Writer's Workshop and what they were reading during self-selected reading. She reminded the Tuesday children that tomorrow was their day to do everything special and that they should decide which book they wanted to share with her during their conference tomorrow. Finally, she gave them a science homework assignment.

"Look around your house and street and try to find three different kinds of seeds. You might find these seeds in your kitchen. Sometimes, the seeds might be part of a food. Some seeds can be found outdoors. Bring these seeds in if you can. If not, write down their names so you can remember them when we share what you have found first thing tomorrow morning."

After the children left, the teacher attached the labels on which she had written anecdotal comments to each of their folders. She then put a clean sheet of labels on her clipboard. She put the initials of each Tuesday child on several labels so that she would remember to take note of their progress and problems tomorrow. She also put the initials of several other children and a few words—solves math problems? using self-correction strategies? using strategies taught for figuring out unknown words? really reading during self-selected reading?—on several other labels to remind her to observe some problem areas she was concerned about for particular children tomorrow. Then she began to get the materials organized for tomorrow's science lesson—planting beans in cups and watching them sprout. Of course, the children would observe, sketch, and write descriptions of the growth of the bean plants over the next two weeks.

10
A WEEK IN AN INTEGRATED INTERMEDIATE CLASSROOM

Throughout the chapters of this book, we have tried to convey to you that, when working with children who find learning to read difficult, the earlier we start teaching them to read, the better. Children who receive the kind of instruction provided in literate home simulation kindergartens and four-block primary classes are usually reading and writing when they reach the intermediate grades. They do still need good instruction, but have achieved some basic literacy skills, and perhaps more importantly, view themselves as readers and writers. They have—in the current lingo—"the right attitude!"

Unfortunately, children who have experienced many years of frustration and failure have developed, justifiably perhaps, "the wrong attitude!" They say with their eyes, their bodies and, sometimes, boldly with their mouths:

"I won't do it!"
"You can't make me!"
"Reading and writing are dumb and stupid and sissy!"
"I don't care!"
"Who needs it?"

What most of them really mean is:

"I can't do it!"

Throughout this book, when describing activities for intermediate-aged, still-struggling children, we have tried to describe activities that involve real reading and writing and that provide for success on a variety of levels. The principles behind the activities we have described are:

1. All children can learn to read and write—and all of them really want to.
2. Success precedes motivation and once children see that they can be successful, they will participate; thus, teachers must engineer success!
3. Real reading and writing are intrinsically motivating.
4. Traditional seatwork is a waste of time.

5. Children learn from each other.
6. The mastery model is wrong—teachers must teach for and look for improvement, growth, and approximation—not perfection.

The intermediate classroom where struggling readers become readers and writers is not the traditional classroom. You can't just make "a few little changes" and transform the children. Things must change—and these changes are fairly radical.

One thing that must change is the way grades are determined. Grades must be based on effort and not on some notion of grade level and "the tests in the teacher manuals." This is difficult for everyone to accept because we all want to have high expectations for students and maintain standards. But, no one will work if they know that they are going to fail no matter what! If children come to you reading and writing two or three years below grade level, they can't pass grade-level tests and standards. If they know that they are going to fail regardless of effort, they won't try! If they don't try, they can't learn!

Once you decide to grade on effort primarily and you communicate this clearly to the students, your students will be motivated to "hang in there" and to "give it another try." It is not your fault that they come to you functioning far below grade level. It is not your job to get them all to grade level and to fail them if they can't get there. It is your job to teach them and to help them move toward a literate future. You can't do this if you must fail them for their illiterate past.

Another thing that must change is the schedule. In many intermediate classrooms, time is allocated to more than a dozen different subjects during the day. In some cases, even the language arts are broken down into separate areas: reading, writing, spelling, language, and handwriting. Then there is math, health, science, social studies, P.E., music, art, foreign language, guidance, and computers. The instruction cannot help being in small, isolated segments when all of these separate subjects are presented every day. In addition to being choppy and fragmented, this type of scheduling is antithetical to our current understanding of how people learn. The associative theory of learning described in Chapter 6 demonstrates that we learn when we associate the material with other things and events. We do not learn by memorizing facts and practicing small skills. Rather, we learn as we work with information, applying what we are learning to solve problems and to achieve goals. In classrooms in which intermediate-aged children are transformed into readers and writers, teachers do whatever is within their power to help children make connections. They take whatever time is allocated to them and create a schedule that allows for as much integrated learning as possible.

The final big change that must be made relates to how the teacher and the children work with one another. An intermediate classroom that succeeds cannot be one in which the teacher teaches the whole class all the time nor can it be one in which children are assigned to static reading groups based on achievement levels that rotate to meet with the teacher while the other children complete seatwork assignments. Intermediate-grade children span the whole range of reading and writing abilities. Instruction that treats them all the same or that arbitrarily divides them into three groups will not meet their diverse needs. The intermediate classroom in which many struggling readers are learning and growing is one in which various kinds of cooperative learning arrangements are used. Children read, write, edit, and research with partners and in small groups. Teachers who succeed with older struggling readers spend a great deal of time early in the year role-playing and modeling these cooperative ventures and make the "working together" atmosphere a top priority in their classrooms. They have a "we're all in this together" and a "united, we stand, divided we fall!" attitude. They work with children to help them learn how to work with one another.

Those of you who actually teach intermediate-aged, struggling readers are probably thinking, "Easier said than done!" You are right. It is not easy to change your grading system, to develop a less choppy schedule, and get your students working together, but it is essential and it can be done. Teachers in schools all over this country make up their minds, close their doors, and restructure their classrooms so that it is possible for children to become more literate. If children have failed in the past, it will take them a while to get on board and to realize that in your classroom, "Things are different." But, most will realize eventually. They are still children, in spite of their sometimes grown-up facade, and they have the same primary needs that all children, and indeed all humans, have. They want to succeed, to be liked, and to know that they "are somebody."

Given all that there is to accomplish, intermediate teachers can't usually do everything every day in the same way that primary teachers can. In addition, intermediate-aged children need larger blocks of time to pursue reading, writing, and research. Consequently, in the remainder of this section, we will describe a week of instruction in an intermediate classroom. We will assume a six-hour instructional day, but we will assume that one of those hours each day is given over to specials—music, art, computers, P.E., foreign language, etc.— and that another hour is allocated to math. We will further assume that, as in most states, 120 minutes should be allocated to language arts daily, 40 minutes each to science and social studies, and 20 minutes to health. In our classroom, however, the teacher will alternate between teaching a social studies unit and a science unit each week. Health will be combined with science, when possible, and thus, a combined science/health unit might get two weeks. If the curriculum demands it, a week-long health unit would be taught. Most nine-week grading periods would contain four week-long social studies units, four week-long science units, and one week-long health unit. Thus each day, we have 220 minutes available to teach language arts and one topic from science, health, or social studies. This will allow us to meet the guidelines for content subject teaching in most states, while reducing the fragmentation found in classrooms that try to schedule each subject every day. We will make every effort to foster reading and writing development even during content topic time. Developing strategies for mastering the forms of reading and writing that students do during these content topic sessions will prove quite valuable as they move up through the grades.

We would create a schedule that allowed large blocks of uninterrupted time whenever possible. However, because such blocks are not as common in elementary schools now, the sample day we present here strikes us as more typical of what most teachers now face. Even though it doesn't matter when we get the 220 minutes of available time, we will assume the following daily schedule:

8:00–8:30 Children arrive at different times, depending on buses, breakfast, etc.; attendance taken, routines, etc.
8:30–9:15 Language arts/unit time (45 minutes)
9:15–9:45 Some kind of special subject
9:45–9:55 Break
9:55–11:00 Language arts/unit time (65 minutes)
11:00–11:55 Math
11:55–12:25 Lunch
12:25–1:40 Language arts/unit (75 minutes)
1:40–2:10 Some kind of special subject
2:10–2:45 Language arts/unit (35 minutes)

This is not an ideal schedule. There are lots of comings and goings in the day and lots of time lost getting started and getting settled back in. Ideally, we would like to get in all of our 220 minutes in the morning and let the children have their specials, etc. after lunch. We would also like the specials to connect and integrate with the classroom instruction, but unfortunately, these decisions are not generally within the control of the classroom teacher. However, classroom teachers can request that special teachers schedule their children for either morning or afternoon instructional sessions. Without such requests, special programs tend to schedule around their own convenience. Even having all children in attendance all morning (or afternoon) will be an improvement in many classrooms. (See the last chapter—"Beyond the Classroom: Things Worth Fighting For"—for suggestions on affecting the total school schedule.)

Once we know the time frame we are working with, we can decide what will happen. Not all components can be used every day, but all the important ones should be implemented on a regular basis. Here are the time allocation guidelines that a successful teacher of struggling readers might follow:

Every day (No matter what!):

- Teacher reads to the class from a trade book.
- Teacher reads something to the class from a newspaper, magazine, riddle book, joke book, book of poetry, or other "real world" source.
- Children read something they choose from a large and varied selection.
- Children learn more about the topic that they are studying.
- Children do a word wall activity with high-frequency, commonly misspelled words and/or with topic-related big words.

Two or three times a week:

- Children participate in guided reading/thinking activity.
- Children participate in a focused writing lesson.
- Teacher models topic selection and writes a short piece.
- Children write on a topic of their own choice.
- Children work with words—looking for patterns, learning how to chunk and decode big words, etc.

Once a week:

- All children share something they have written.
- All children share something they have read.
- One-third of class revises, edits, and publishes a piece of writing.
- Children read to their little buddies.
- Children do research related to their topic.

This is what one week of instruction might look like using the allocated 220 minutes and making sure that all of the activities we want children to engage in happen as often as we have decided.

8:30–8:45 Teacher Read-Aloud/Real-World Sources
The teacher in this class begins each morning by reading to the class from a variety of real-world sources. On Monday mornings, the teacher usually brings in a newspaper and shares some of the more interesting tidbits with the children. Children are encouraged to bring in interesting things from the weekend paper too. Pieces shared are added to the collage-style newspaper board. On other mornings, the teacher reads from informational books, magazines, joke and riddle books, pamphlets, etc. The message that the children begin with each day is that reading is an essential part of their real world.

8:45–9:15 Working with Words
This half hour each day is devoted to words. The goals are that children (1) learn to spell the high-frequency words that they need in their writing (2) learn to read, spell, and develop meanings for big words that are part of the science, health, or social studies topic they are studying, and (3) learn how to decode and spell unfamiliar words—particularly polysyllabic words.

Monday is usually the day on which a new unit of study begins so the teacher adds 10–12 unit-related big words to a Big Word Board. These words are related to the unit topic for the week. As the teacher puts the words on the board, she helps the children associate meanings for the words. This week's unit is on pollution. The words added to the Big Word Board are:

pollution	environment	recycle
pollutants	environmental	conservation
resources	chemicals	fertilizers
pesticides	combustion	renewable

Each week, the teacher tries to include some words that have the same root—pollution/pollutants, environment/environmental. As she introduces the words to the children, she helps them distinguish the different forms of the words from one another. She helps them understand that *pollution* is the word we use to describe the whole problem and that *pollutants* are some of the things—including *fertilizers*, *chemicals*, and *pesticides*—that cause pollution. Although the word *pollute* is not included on the board (the number of words must be limited if children are really going to focus on them and make them part of their listening/speaking/reading/writing vocabularies), she writes it on the chalkboard and reminds the children that an *e* at the end is often dropped when endings such as *tion* and *ant* are added, and helps them see that "*pollute* is what you do that causes the problem of *pollution*." In a similar way, she helps them understand that the *environment* is the surroundings in which we live and *environmental* is the word we use as a describing word. "We can say that pollution is a problem for our environment or that pollution is an environmental problem." She has the children contribute several sentences describing how pollution is a problem and using the words *environment* and *environmental* to help them develop a sense in their listening vocabulary of when each word is used.

The other words get introduced and the teacher alerts the children to similar morphemes and meanings.

Recycle, renewable, and *resources* all begin with the prefix *re* and have related meanings. "When you *recycle* something, you use it again. *Renewable* resources, such as trees, will grow again." The teacher also writes the word *non-renewable* on the board and helps the children think about what the addition of *non* does to *renewable* and to think of some *nonrenewable* resources.

The words *pollution, combustion,* and *conservation* are discussed. Then the teacher writes the words *pollute, combust,* and *conserve* on the board, drawing their attention to how the word changes as it is used differently in both speaking and writing. Throughout this introduction phase, the teacher talks about the words, defines them, uses them in sentences, and focuses on word structure and other cues.

Once all the words have been introduced and attention has been devoted to their meaning and to similar chunks, the teacher leads them in a clapping/chanting activity similar to the cheering you would hear at a basketball game. The children say each word, clap and chant its spelling, and then say the word again. The teacher leads them to spell the word in a rhythmic way, pausing briefly between the syllables—"pollution—p-o-l__l-u__t-i-o-n—pollution, pollutant—p-o-l__l-u__t-a-n-t—pollutant."

The lesson ends with each student writing the 12 words in a vocabulary notebook. One of their regular Monday night homework assignments is to write a sentence and/or draw a picture giving a personal example for each word.

In addition to helping intermediate children develop a store of big words, many struggling readers still misspell (or don't know how to spell) common words that are needed in their writing. In this classroom, there is a word wall of frequently misspelled words. The teacher began the word wall at the beginning of the year with words that she knew many of the children would misspell. The first five words added to the wall were:

they   were   friend   from   said

The next week, she added five more frequently written but often misspelled words:

are   what   because   could   once

As the year went on, she became alerted to words many children were misspelling in their first-draft writing and added words that evidently the children needed. She also added homophones, putting a picture or word clue next to all but one of the words:

to   two   too   there   their   they're   buy   by   write   right

Now the word wall contained the contractions that students used a great deal:

can't   didn't   won't   wasn't   we're   let's

Five high-frequency words were added to the word wall each Tuesday. After adding the five new words, the teacher calls out the five new words for the week and five review words. The children clap, chant, and write these ten words. The new words the teacher is adding this week are:

new   knew   doesn't   terrible   until

Each Wednesday, Thursday, and Friday, the children write Big Word words and word wall words in a variety of ways. On some days, the teacher simply calls out five words from the Big Word Board and five from the word wall of frequently misspelled words and has the children clap, chant, and write them. On other days, she gives clues to the words or does the "Be a Mind Reader" activity and the children have to guess the word. She also dictates some short sentences that can be made by combining words from the Big Word Board and the word wall. Regardless of what activity she uses to review these words, she always involves the children in some chanting and writing because these activities focus their attention on all of the letters in the words. In addition, when children are writing, she encourages them to use invented spellings or whatever resources they have for spelling words. The teacher insists, however, that the words from the Big Word Board and the word wall be spelled correctly because they are so readily accessible. Students' eyes can be seen going to the board or the wall when they are writing.

On Monday and Tuesday, most of the 30 minutes devoted to working with words is consumed with introducing, adding, and reviewing words on the board and the wall. On the other three days, however, a quick review activity takes only 5–10 minutes; the remaining time is devoted to activities designed to help them see patterns in words. Generally on Wednesday, the teacher does a Making Words activity, on Thursday—an activity designed to teach particular prefixes or suffixes, and on Friday—everyone's favorite—"The Wheel."

9:55–11:00 Unit Time

This time is usually devoted to learning about the topic—expanding both world and word knowledge. Whenever possible, the teacher uses real experiences—experiments and demonstrations during science, simulations, and imagined journeys during social studies. At least one of these days each week includes a guided reading activity and another day includes a focused writing lesson. The students are taught strategies for reading and writing informational text and study strategies, including notetaking and summarizing. Sometimes, the focused writing lesson is a follow-up to the guided reading activity and sometimes the two are topic-related but not related to each other. On Fridays, the class usually brainstorms questions they would still like to know the answers to and goes to the library to find answers to the questions. Students work in pairs to find answers.

This week, the topic being studied is pollution. On Monday, they watch a video that shows some of the most serious sources of pollution and begin to fill in some information on this data chart graphic organizer.

Environmental Pollution			
Where	**Causes**	**Possible Solutions**	**Our Area**
Air			
Water			
Soil			
Land			

The video described some general pollution problems but was not specific to the geographic area in which the school was located. The teacher finishes the lesson by asking students to write down the three pollutants that they thought were most problematic where they lived. For homework they are to interview two adults about pollution in the local area and determine what these adults think the most significant problems are.

Tuesday's lesson begins by having the students share what they found out in their interviews with the two adults. Most had talked with someone about the problem and were surprised to learn how high the level of concern was. The teacher shared some newspaper articles from local sources that she had been saving until this unit. More information—particularly in the last column, "Our Area"—was added to the data chart.

On Wednesday, the teacher leads the students in a guided-reading activity in which they read about what could be accomplished with recycling. She uses a KWL to help them organize and connect what they knew before and after reading. Their homework assignment for Wednesday night is to find out what they could recycle from their homes and where to take the recyclables.

Thursday begins with a discussion of their home recycling efforts. The teacher then describes some recycling efforts that are being made by various businesses. She explains that on her recent plane flight, the flight attendants were collecting cans and other recyclables separately. The school secretary comes in and explains how copying and computer paper are being recycled. Next, the teacher gives out a list of local businesses. Included on the list are the stores and fast-food restaurants that the children go to on a regular basis. She then does a focused writing lesson in which she demonstrates for the children how to write a list of questions they could ask to find out what, if anything, a business is doing about recycling. As the children watch, she writes a list of questions to ask her brother, who works at a car dealership.

After watching her write her questions, she lets each child decide who or what business they would interview and has each child make a list of questions to ask. She helps the children see that some of their questions might be just like hers:

- Do you have a place to collect recyclable aluminum cans?
- Do you have bins in all the offices for recyclable paper?

Other questions were particular to a car dealership:

- What happens to the old oil when you do an oil change?
- What happens to old tires? And worn out car parts?

She gives the children the option of doing the interview by themselves or with a classmate, assuming that the pair could get together over the weekend to do the interview. The children who are going to interview together pair up to make the list of questions. The others do theirs by themselves. The teacher circulates and helps each child make a readable list.

Normally, on Fridays, the class goes to the library to do research designed to answer the unanswered questions they have about a topic. This Friday, however, the teacher decides to have them do some "field research." She gets the class together and asks them to predict what kind of litter and how many pieces of it they would find in the area surrounding the school and where that litter might have come from. Once they have made their predictions, she divides them into teams, arms each team with a trash bag, and gives them 20 minutes to see how much litter they can pick up in the designated area.

Dividing the children into teams is a problem in some classes. The children fuss about who they are with and who gets to do what. In this classroom, however, the teacher has a system for forming teams and distributing responsibilities. She uses this system quite often and it is perceived as fair by all of the students. She uses a deck of playing cards, taking out as many numbers as she has children present today. She has 27 children present and decides to form six groups of four and one group of three. Thus, she takes out all four suits of the cards numbered 1–6 and three of the sevens. The cards are dealt and children form teams based on the number they get! Sometimes, she uses the suits to designate who will do what. Today, she writes these responsibilities on the board:

- *Spade*—Carrier—Carry trash bag.
- *Club*—Leader—Lead the team in whatever direction this person chooses—team must "follow the leader."
- *Diamond*—Tallier—Tally the trash collected into different categories as team counts it.
- *Heart*—Reporter—Report team's results to rest of class.

As she writes these responsibilities, the different class members cheer and grumble as they get responsibilities they like and others they eschew. As in real life, everyone wants to lead and no wants to "carry the load," but the children accept what they get because they have seen the cards shuffled and dealt. They know that it was "the luck of the draw" and not teacher favoritism that determined their "fate." (The team that has only three members is lacking a Tallier and the teacher tells them that the Reporter will have to double up and also be the Tallier for their group.)

The class goes out and collects the litter. As they collect each item, they count and tally their "treasure" and then add up the results for the Reporter to report to the class. As each group reports, the children tally the results reported by the groups. Finally, they compare what they actually found to what they had predicted. They decide that there is much too much litter around and that most of it came from students and that some of it can be recycled. They sort out the recyclables, decide who can take it where, and take the rest out to the big dumpster.

This unit, like some others, extends into the following Monday. The class has done a good job of interviewing local business owners and employees and many children were encouraged by what they had found. Others discovered that there was still much to be done that wasn't being done. After discussing their results on Monday, the teacher leads them in another supported writing activity. This time, they watch as she writes a letter to her interviewee (her brother), thanking him for taking time to be interviewed, praising him for the good things the car dealership is doing, and suggesting that someone needed to find out what was being done with all those old tires that were just being hauled away.

The students then use her model to write their own letters. The teacher uses some of the time (from 12:40–1:45) to help them revise and edit their letters as needed. Then, they copy the letters to make them as "readable" as possible and deliver them to their interviewees (including one to the school principal with suggestions for increasing recycling at the school).

12:25–12:40 Everybody Reads

When the class returns from lunch, everybody settles in to read. They read from any book they choose. Many children have a book at their desk that they are in the middle of reading. Other children choose a book from the trays of books that rotate to different tables each day. Each tray is filled with a wide variety of books, including some high-interest, low-vocabulary books and some informational books with lots of pictures. Children are grouped by days of the week, a fifth of the class for each day. On Monday, the Monday people can read anywhere and anything in the room, including newspapers, magazines, joke books, the newspaper board, etc. On the other days, they stay at their seats and read books. In this way, everyone gets a chance to "spread out" and read anything one day each week but most of the class is seated quietly at their desks reading books.

12:40–1:40 Guided Reading or Writer's Workshop

Each day this time is used for guided reading/thinking activities and for children to write, revise, and edit on topics of their own choosing. It varies according to what they need to do. Most weeks, the teacher does guided-reading lessons on Mondays and Tuesdays and Writer's Workshop on Wednesdays and Thursdays. On Friday, the children often have a choice of whether they want to read or write or do some combination of both during this hour.

The teacher uses a variety of materials and a variety of formats for guiding their reading. The children in this class read on many different levels and the teacher tries to make sure that over the week, children read something at their instructional level or easier during this time. Sometimes, she finds two or three pieces, similar in genre, topic, or theme that different students can read. Whenever possible, she finds something related to the topic being studied, but often, the reading done at this time is unrelated to the topic.

This week, they are going to read two stories. The stories are not about pollution (one is about a current-day family that survives a fire and the other is set in the old west), but the teacher sees possibilities for tying in what they have been learning about pollution to both stories. The story about the family that survives the fire is from a grade-level basal and is too hard for many of the students to read by themselves. The other story is from another series that has stories that are of interest to intermediate-aged children, have more vocabulary control, and are much easier to read.

She decides to have them read the fire story on Monday. Since this story will be difficult for many of her students, she does a listening/reading transfer lesson in which she reads the first three pages of the story to them. Before reading, she begins this character web on the board.

The class has done character webs many times before and knows that they are to decide on a couple of adjectives that best describe the main character in the story. They know that they will fill in details next to the adjectives the teacher has chosen and then try to come up with other adjectives that they think "sum up" the main character.

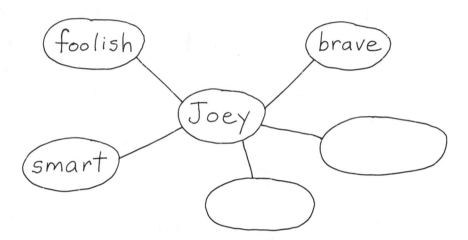

The teacher reads the first three pages of the story and the children listen so that they can tell her what to fill in as evidence that Joey was brave, smart, or foolish. They are also thinking of adjectives they would use to describe Joey.

When the teacher finishes the three pages, the children are eager to offer support for all three adjectives and to suggest others. The teacher writes some of their supporting statements out next to the adjectives and adds the other adjectives that they suggest. She then tells them to finish the story with their partners and to come back ready to add more adjectives and more support for the other adjectives. She reminds them that as they read, they should "think" just as they did when she was reading to them. "Think about Joey and his role in the fire and decide what word you think best sums him up and why you think so."

The children then go to read with their partners. Each struggling reader in the class is paired up with a better reader. The teacher had to change the partnership several times but finally got most of the children paired up with someone they like and who would help them without making it too obvious. Most of the partnerships alternate between periods of oral and silent reading with partners first reading a page to themselves and then alternating the lead role in discussing, summarizing, or asking the other partner questions. They may reread sections aloud to clarify a point or to emphasize a major point. At times, they take turns reading pages to each other. The teacher encourages them to "help with words they don't know" by focusing on the use of appropriate strategies. Generally, better readers do not interrupt to correct or supply a word to their partner. Instead, they respond as their teacher does by saying, "That didn't sound right," or "I didn't get that."

As the partners read, the teacher circulates with her clipboard in hand. She has attached file-folder labels to the clipboard and put the initials of six children whose reading she wants to monitor today. (These six children are six of her average readers. Tomorrow, when they read the selection from the easier basal, she will monitor six of her struggling readers.) She stops and asks each child to read aloud very softly and then asks the child "which adjective they think is best and why." She makes notes on their labels about their reading fluency and their ability to think about characters. She spends about 2 minutes with each child she is monitoring and notes that each child was able to read the story fluently and could think about and justify character traits.

After about 12 minutes, the teacher notices that many of the partners have finished reading the story. She tells them to start a list of adjectives and justifications while the others finish. After another 4 minutes, she signals the class to join her and help complete the web. (One pair has still not finished reading the story; she tells them to continue and join the group as soon as they finish.)

The class joins her and suggests many more adjectives and justifications for each. She adds the adjectives and writes in a few words of justification next to each. She ends the lesson by letting each child vote on the one adjective that they think best describes Joey. She tallies the votes next to each and reminds the class that the story didn't tell us directly what kind of person Joey was. We had to figure out what kind of person he was the same way that we figure it out about a person we meet in real life. Just as we don't always agree about people we meet in real life, we also don't always agree on characters we read about in books. What matters when you read is that you think about the characters and decide what *you* think!

Finally, she tells them, "The story wasn't about pollution, but did it have anything to do with pollution?" The class talks about it and decides that if the newspapers had been recycled and if the old paint had been disposed of, the fire probably wouldn't have happened. They also talk about the air pollution caused by the smoke from the fire.

On Tuesday, they read a story about a family homesteading in Iowa. Before reading, the teacher begins a "Then and Now Chart" and has the children brainstorm some of the differences they thought would exist in their lives if they were transported back to the prairieland of the 1800s. Once again, the partners read the story together. Today, the teacher has put the names of some of the struggling readers on the labels. She makes notes about their reading fluency and their comprehension of this material, which is closer to their instructional level. When the partners finish reading, they reconvene and complete the chart. The teacher then has them vote on whether they would have rather lived "then" or "now." ("Now" won hands down!)

Finally, she asks them if the homesteaders had to worry about pollution. A lively discussion ensues as the children realize for the first time that pollution is a relatively new problem for society to contend with.

On Wednesdays and Thursdays, they use this time for Writer's Workshop. Each day, the teacher models how to think of topics and writes a short piece on the overhead. She tries to write a variety of pieces so the children see that writing can take many forms. She has told the children that she used to write a lot when she was their age—most of her writing was for herself and she didn't let anyone else see it. They know that she used to keep a diary and write in it every night. Sometimes, she writes in her diary the way she did when she was their age. They think it is hilarious when she writes like an intermediate-aged child. She doesn't read aloud what she is writing, except when she is inventing the spelling of a word. Then, she says the word very slowly, exaggerating the sounds. The children are always eager to see "what she will write today."

On Monday, she decides to write an imaginary diary entry. The children always recognize when she is doing this because she writes the date, and then "Dear Diary":

> February 14, 1967
>> Dear Diary,
>> Today was valintin's day. I was so exsited! I sent my best valintin to YOU KNOW WHO! He sent me one too but it wasn't a speshul one he sent a speshul one to ANITA! YUK! I got 23 valentins in all. My Dad bought me some a big box of candy and it was very exspensiv. It cost $1.59!

The children were all reading along as she wrote. They laughed when she sounded out how to spell *valentine, excited, special,* and *expensive.* They couldn't imagine that you could ever buy a big box of valentine's candy for just $1.59. When she finishes writing she says, "Now, I will read it all to make sure it makes sense and that it says what I wanted it to say." She reads it aloud as the children watch. As soon as she finishes, the children's hands are raised, volunteering to be editors.

She reminds the children that a diary entry probably would never be edited because it was personal writing and was certainly not meant to be public. But, in order to provide practice (and since it wasn't a true entry!), she would let them edit it. She then hands a girl a different color marker and the girl goes to the overhead and leads the class in helping the teacher edit her writing. They use a class-created editing checklist that had seven things to check for:

1. There is a title in the middle.
2. Every sentence makes sense.
3. Every sentence begins with a capital and ends with a punctuation mark.
4. People and place names have capital letters.
5. Words that might be misspelled are circled.
6. The writing stays on the topic.
7. Things people say have commas and quotes (She shouted, "Help!").

Each editing convention the children have learned so far is read; the class then checks for these features and volunteers what they think needs fixing. Possible misspelled words are circled, capitals and punctuation marks are added. They decide that a diary entry doesn't need a title but that it does have the things it needs—a date and a "Dear Diary." Some children think that only the first letter of *Anita* should be capitalized, but others argue that it was all in caps for emphasis and that, if it were your diary, you could write it that way!

After this writing minilesson, the teacher takes the children who are publishing a piece this week to the back table with her while the other two-thirds of the class pursue their own writing. Some children begin new pieces. Others continue writing on an already begun piece. Some children look in books to help them get ideas and for words they want to spell. The word wall and Big Word Board are also looked at as children need spelling help. They can be heard saying words very slowly and listening for the sounds they want to represent as they invent-spell some words just like their teacher did.

The third of the class that the teacher takes with her contains a whole range of students. She divides the nine children into three trios and has them read their stories to each other. The children have learned how to help each other revise and edit and know that on the first day they focus only on revising for meaning. When one person reads his or her piece to the other two, the listeners cannot see the writing. They are listening for something they liked about it and for something they can suggest to make the piece more clear or more interesting. It takes about 5 minutes for each member of a trio to read the piece and listen to the praise and suggestions. While they are doing this, the teacher circulates and adds her own praise and suggestions.

Once the children have all read and listened, they return to their seats and make whatever additions or changes they choose to. They do the adding and changing right on the page because they have learned to write all first drafts on every other line in their writing notebooks, leaving space for revisions. The teacher circulates, giving encouragement and suggestions to the revisers and those working on first drafts.

On Thursday, they have their second Writer's Workshop of the week. Once again, the teacher writes, but today she claims to be in a poetry mood so she writes the following cinquain about pollution:

> *Pollution*
> Pollution
> Scary, Disgusting
> Trash, Chemicals, Pesticides.
> They threaten our environment.
> Recycle!

As she writes today, she makes it very obvious that she is getting the spelling of many of the big words from the Big Word Board. After writing, she reads it aloud and then chooses a boy to be the editor. Once again, the editor and the class read through the checklist and help her edit the piece.

The children who are publishing this week bring the piece they revised for meaning yesterday to the back table. The teacher then pairs eight of the children up with partners of similar writing ability. These partners help each other edit using the editing checklist and the procedures used each day when a student edits the teacher's writing. The teacher takes the child who is having the most difficulty communicating through writing as her partner. (When dividing the class into thirds for revising/editing, the teacher made sure to put the three children having the most difficulty writing in three different groups.) This child needs more help from the teacher, but the teacher is able to use the blank line to write in words and to help the child get a piece that he can copy over or type on the computer and can illustrate and be proud of.

As the partners finish helping each other, they bring their piece to the teacher who reads it and helps fill in needed words, punctuation marks, and so on. Misspelled words are corrected and other obvious problems are fixed. Once the piece has been through a "teacher edit," the children publish it in some form, depending on the piece and how it will be displayed/shared. Some children type their piece into the computer and then print it out. Other children copy their piece on some special paper and illustrate it. Still other children make a book from their piece.

On Friday, during this hour, children are engaged in a variety of activities. This Friday, like most Fridays, the children whose week it is to publish are copying, typing, or illustrating their finished pieces. This is also a time during the week when children can do more reading/research on their "expert" topic. Each child has been designated "class expert" on a topic of that child's choice and every three weeks they take a portion of this Friday time to share what new information they have learned about their topic. Today is not an "Expert Share Friday," but children who are not publishing, and who choose to, can spend this time in the room or in the library finding out more about their expert topic. Several children spend this time "just reading"—a Friday afternoon activity that the teacher encourages. Several children who know that next week is their week to revise, edit, and publish a piece are busy finishing up the piece they have decided to work with. The rules for this afternoon time are simple. It is a time for reading and/or writing and children can do whatever they choose to as long as what they are doing involves reading and writing.

2:10–2:25 Teacher Read-Aloud

Every day at 2:10, the teacher reads to the class, choosing books of high-interest to readers at this age but of varying genres so that the children are exposed to a variety of literature. In selecting books, the teacher also incorporates books that depict the multicultural society we have created. This week, she is reading *Get On Out of Here, Philip Hall* (B. Greene, 1981, Dial). When she finishes each book, there are always several children who want to read it for themselves. She has those who want to put their names on little slips of paper. She then pulls one slip (without looking) and hands the book to that lucky child. The other slips are then pulled and used to make a waiting list in the order they were pulled, just like they do at the library. This procedure is perceived as fair by the children and there are always waiting lists for the chapter books that the teacher has read aloud. Even the children who could not read the book for the first time by themselves often can read and enjoy it once they have listened to it read aloud. Whenever possible, the teacher tries to read a book aloud by an author who has written similar books or one that has several books in a series. Children who are on the waiting list for the book are often delighted to get a similar book to read in the meantime. The class doesn't know that the teacher has hidden away a copy of Greene's (1974), *Philip Hall Likes Me, I Reckon Maybe.*

2:25–2:45

The last 20 minutes of any school day are difficult to structure and, in many classrooms, are just "waiting-to-leave" time. When teaching struggling readers, however, we haven't any time to waste. In this classroom, the teacher has a different activity each day. Children look forward to it and it also helps her accomplish some of her weekly goals.

Monday   On Mondays, the children get ready for Tuesday's reading to the kindergarten children. Every Monday after lunch, some kindergartners bring favorite books from the kindergarten. On a sticky note attached to each book is the name of the kindergarten child who would like to have that book read to him or her tomorrow. (The teacher and the kindergarten children have chosen a book for each child.) The books are quickly distributed to the "big buddies" who then practice reading that book in preparation for tomorrow's reading. Some children tape record their reading to check how they sound. The teacher reminds her big kids of the steps they should go through in reading the book to their buddies:

1. Read the book title and author's name and ask your little buddy what she or he thinks the book will be about.
2. Look through the book, talking about the things you see in the pictures before reading.
3. Read the book and help your little buddy talk about it. Ask questions that get your little buddy involved with the book:

   What do you think will happen next?
   Would you like to do that?

4. When you finish reading, ask your little buddy to find his or her favorite page and tell why it was the favorite.
5. Go through the book again and let your little buddy tell you what is happening or help read it to you if some parts are very easy.

The children eagerly read the books, which include such classics as *Robert the Rose Horse, The Little Red Hen,* and *Caps for Sale.* The teacher sits with one boy who is a very hesitant reader and who needs her help in order to read this book successfully tomorrow. She leads him to look through the pictures and to predict what will happen, in the same way she wants him to with his little buddy tomorrow. As they look at the pictures, she supplies words and phrases needed so that he can successfully read the book. She then reads and enjoys it with him. She praises him for his reading and asks him to read it with her once more as soon as he arrives at school tomorrow, so that he will be able to read it with expression and enthusiasm.

Tuesday The kindergartners arrive and the big buddies read to their little buddies. The intermediate-grade teacher and the kindergarten teacher circulate, stopping to listen to children read and helping them engage their young listeners with good "reader involvement" questions. The kindergartners come with all their gear, prepared to go home from here. Many of the big kids walk out with their little buddies in tow.

Wednesday On Wednesdays, the children are divided into groups of four (using the deck of playing cards again) and each child has 3 minutes to read about or to tell about something they have read this week. The cards are passed out and the children get together wherever the teacher has put that number. (The teacher lays big number cards around the room—*1* at the back table, *2* at her desk, *3* in the corner, and so on.) They share in alphabetical order of the suit they got—clubs, diamonds, hearts, spades. The teacher sets her timer for 3 minutes; the children have become good at preparing for this 3 minutes. Most know right where to find the scary, funny, silly, or fascinating part of the book that they want to read. Some children have riddle and joke books with the best riddles and jokes ready to share. The teacher circulates, making notes on her clipboard labels about books children choose and whether the accuracy and fluency exhibited while reading suggest that the book was an appropriate choice. When the timer sounds, she says, "Diamonds" and the second person in each group gets her or his 3 minutes. If a few minutes remain after all four people have had their turns, the teacher asks different children to share something particularly interesting with the whole class.

Thursday On Thursdays, the same procedure is used to have children share writing that was used on Wednesday to share books. Cards are dealt. Children go wherever the teacher has put their number and have 3 minutes to share something they have written or that they are in the process of writing. Usually, but not always, the children who are revising that week share their piece. Other children read a piece they have decided to revise next week. Still other children read a piece they have just begun and tell what else they intend to write. If the child finishes reading before the 3 minutes are up, the reader can call on the listeners to tell "things they liked." The teacher makes notes on her clipboard labels indicating what different children have written about and have chosen to share.

Friday Once again, Friday varies. Usually, the teacher takes a few minutes to have the children, who have just published something, show it to the class. On some Fridays, the whole class has an "Expert Share." On this Friday, the teacher is nearly finished with the chapter book and the children are eager to see how it ends, so the teacher devotes the entire last 35 minutes to finishing reading the book aloud to the class, letting them respond to it and drawing slips to see who gets the book and to form the order of the waiting list.

    Each day, when the children leave, the teacher removes the labels from the clipboard and puts them on the outside of each child's folder. (Inside this folder are samples of writing, reading response, and other work.) As she puts on new labels with new comments, she looks at the previous labels and considers how each child is growing. Sometimes, as she reflects on the different children whose reading and writing she has focused on that day, she will think of other questions she has about that child's literacy development. She then puts this child's initials, tomorrow's date, and a few words to remind her of what to look for on the label and spends some time focusing on the same child again tomorrow. While some children are focused on more often, she tries to focus on each child at least once a week. The combination of weekly anecdotal records and samples of writing and reading responses kept in the folder gives her a basis for deciding how well children are progressing toward becoming more literate as well as information that guides her whole-class, small-group, and individual instruction.

11

BEYOND THE CLASSROOM: THINGS WORTH FIGHTING FOR

This book was written to help classroom teachers provide the highest quality literacy instruction for all children. As much as possible, we have confined ourselves to discussing changes, adaptations, and additions that, as classroom teachers, are within your power. You can decide that real reading and writing will take precedence in your classrooms and then provide the necessary time, materials, models, and motivation. You can decide to involve all children in guided reading and writing activities on a daily or weekly basis. You can decide that all children should learn to automatically read and spell the high-frequency words that are required by all reading and writing and that they should develop strategies that really help them figure out how to read and spell unfamiliar words. You can make sure to include effective science and social studies instruction and expand your children's knowledge.

To some extent, you have control of grouping and scheduling. You can provide large blocks of time by integrating reading and writing with the knowledge subjects. You can help your children learn to work cooperatively with one another and can use a variety of partner, trio, and team groupings. You can pair up with another like-minded teacher and have "big buddy-little buddy" arrangements. You can coordinate with specialists and/or enlist the help of tutors, so that your most needy students receive additional instruction.

The premise of this book is that you, as a classroom teacher who has control of almost 1,000 hours of learning time, can make and carry out decisions that will result in greatly increased literacy levels for your children. Research and experience tells us that what the classroom teacher does, day in and day out, minute-by-minute, has the greatest effect on what children learn. For most children who "beat the odds," it was a teacher who made the difference. Most elementary teachers become teachers because they want to make a difference in the lives of children. The strategies, activities, organizational patterns, etc. contained in this book are a compilation of what the most effective teachers do.

There are other factors that we know will accelerate the achievement of at-risk children, but they are not within the power of classroom teachers. These changes, additions, and adaptations usually require a total school effort, an administrative decision, or some form of community action. Some will require political action in legislative arenas. (For more specifics on these beyond-the-classroom solutions, see *Schools that Work*, Allington & Cunningham, 1996). While the major efforts of a classroom teacher are rightfully expended within one classroom, we feel that you should know which "beyond the classroom" suggestions are worth whatever crusading efforts you are able to make. Here is our list of "things worth fighting for."

BREAKFAST AND LUNCH

Many schools already have breakfast and lunch programs that children from limited-income homes can qualify for. Other school programs have been hurt by budget cuts and concerns for individual responsibility. The budget does need balancing and parents should assume as much responsibility as possible for the care of their children, but hungry children are hard to teach. Children who are sitting in classrooms with empty stomachs cannot devote their full attention to learning and thinking, regardless of how good the instruction is. Our country has the resources to provide two nutritious meals each day for all children who need them. If we are serious about filling their brains with ideas and their hearts with a love of learning, we must get serious about filling their tummies with food! We must schedule, however, so that breakfast time does not come out of allotted instructional time.

SMALLER CLASS SIZE

A smaller class size all by itself does not necessarily make a significant difference in children's learning, but smaller class size combined with the best instruction does. Recently, many large states have moved to reduce class size, particularly in the primary grades, but with increasing school enrollment, class size is creeping back up in many schools. McGill-Franzen and Allington (1991) note that we are now spending substantial sums of money on things that we know do not work—retention in grade and transitional-grade programs—to name but two. If the money allocated to support these practices was redirected, class sizes could be reduced substantially in many schools. If we reorganized many of our special programs and reassigned special teachers to regular classrooms, we could reduce class size. In our experience with several schools that have elected these strategies (reducing or eliminating retention and transitional-grade programs and reorganizing support services), we have seen that class size could be cut as low as 12–15 students in the primary grades.

In many schools, classroom space is a greater barrier to lower class size than money. Some schools have solved this problem by dividing classrooms in half for the language arts/math time and having two teachers each teach a class in one-half of the classroom. For the rest of the day, the two classes make one larger class that the two teachers teach as a team or that one teacher teaches while the other teacher provides individual tutoring for the children who are most at-risk.

Still, another solution to the problem of classroom space and class size is found in schools where the "special teachers" form teams that spend 45–90 minutes in each classroom. During this block of time, the classroom teacher and the special teachers divide the children into three or four groups and provide the reading and writing instruction that they feel requires the most teacher direction and assistance. In most classrooms, the guided reading and writer's workshop portion of the instruction take place in these reduced pupil-teacher ratio settings. Each teacher is totally responsible for this instruction for the same one-third or one-fourth of the class each day. The team of special teachers rotates to another classroom to provide intensive small-group reading and writing instruction. During the rest of the day, the classroom teacher teaches all of the children and the pupil-teacher ratio returns to normal.

Our point about class size is that smaller classes do facilitate better teaching and more personalized instruction. But facilitating is not the same as ensuring. The key to enhancing the quality of instruction lies in increasing the personalized knowledge teachers have about each child and helping teachers act appropriately with that knowledge. With smaller classes, both are easier to accomplish, but neither are ensured.

NONCATEGORICAL SPECIAL HELP

Millions of dollars of federal, state, and local money are spent each year on children who fall in specific "categories." In many cases, the special education programs and remedial programs have simply established scores and levels that determine whether or not a child can receive any special help. Some children qualify for many programs and may be seen by several different special teachers each day. These different specialists rarely coordinate what they do with each other (e.g., speech teacher, reading teacher, counseling psychologist). Some of these children receive minimal classroom instruction because they are seldom in the classroom. In spite of this, their assigned classroom teacher is usually "held accountable" for their progress! Other children "fall through the cracks." Often, these children just miss the cutoff point on whatever test or tests have been selected for determining eligibility. Those who score but a single point above the cutoff often receive no instructional support even though there are no tests that are reliable within a one-point range of error.

We soon hope to see more "responsive" programs and fewer children labeled and categorized. Responsive programs respond to children's needs as soon as they are evident, not when they finally test eligible for some available categorical program. We hope to see interventions that provide children with access to extra-instructional efforts on the day they first need them. For instance, if Maria has missed four days of school because of illness, we would hope to see a school program that provided her with extra assistance the day she returned and until she was caught up with her classmates.

We hope to soon see schools that design intervention programs that provide children with sufficient extra-instruction to return them to the classroom on-level with their peers in a very short time. Too often today, at-risk children receive what is available not what they need. Too often, special help comes a year or more after it becomes apparent that a child is in trouble. A whole year may be spent waiting for the child to become eligible for some categorical program. By not providing immediate extra-instructional support, the problem is intensified and becomes more difficult to resolve.

In addition to the problems of deciding who qualifies for what categories, there are also problems with how schools continue to receive the funding they need from the state and federal sources that support these programs. Too often, good results are rewarded with the loss of funds. Schools that design instructional efforts, which are so effective that many children "test out" of the special programs, often lose the fiscal support for the program that was just beginning to make a difference!

Clearly, there must be some way to determine which schools get what kind of extra funding support, but the present system of categorizing children and specifying what kind of support various children can or must receive is not meeting the needs of most struggling readers. Classroom teachers should work with administrators, parent groups, and others to develop ways of meeting the children's needs that do not require rigid entry standards and inflexible categories. In most schools, there is enough money being spent and enough special personnel available to teach all of the children we have. Classroom teachers should have a say in how the money and personnel can be used most effectively.

EARLY INTERVENTION

A variety of studies have demonstrated the effectiveness of early intervention programs (K–2) compared to interventions begun later (Pikulski, 1995). The best early-intervention programs are targeted to the needs of children (Spear-Swerling & Sternberg, 1996), rather than designed as a "one size fits all" effort. All schools, but especially schools that serve large numbers of children who arrive with few experiences with books, stories, and print, need effective early-intervention programs in place. A successful early-intervention program would likely involve reorganizing classroom instruction to better focus on literacy instructional needs of all children and the development of a support program that provides targeted children with added instruction in the specific areas identified as problems. There are several national early-intervention projects that deserve mention.

Reading Recovery

One special program that we think has earned the support of classroom teachers is Reading Recovery. Reading Recovery was developed by Marie Clay in New Zealand (Clay, 1985; 1991) in the seventies and has been used in the United

States since the mid-eighties. Reading Recovery is a one-to-one tutoring model that provides daily 30-minute sessions for the bottom 20 percent of first graders. Reading Recovery teachers participate in a year-long intensive training program in which they learn to carry out lessons that help the most at-risk readers develop literacy skills. During the training, teachers teach and observe each other teaching. They learn to diagnose what kind of help, support, or information is most needed by a young reader to move that reader forward in the development of a "self-improving system."

No other remedial program has ever come close to achieving the results demonstrated by Reading Recovery. In a school where there were 25 children in a class, Reading Recovery would work with the bottom five children and have four of the five reading on grade level in less than a semester! Reading Recovery has been equally successful in teaching young learning disabled children to read and in returning them to their classrooms.

But, good kindergarten and first grade instruction makes Reading Recovery more successful and reduces the number of children who need to participate. In schools that have high-quality classroom instruction and Reading Recovery, almost all of the children, including the high-risk children, achieve high levels of literacy (Hall, Prevatte, & Cunningham, 1993).

Success for All

Another early intervention that has demonstrated effects on reducing early literacy failure is "Success for All" (Slavin, R. E., Madden, N. A., Dolan, L. J., & Wasik, B. A., 1996), although the impacts have varied from site to site. This is an externally driven schoolwide restructuring effort that involves comprehensive modifications to existing practices and responsibilities. A primary concern is redesigning school support services such that no children fall "through the cracks" but, instead, receive the sorts of instructional interventions needed, including tutoring when necessary.

Learning Network

A different approach to early intervention has been developed and initiated by the Learning Network (Herzog, 1997). This is a long-term, site-based professional initiative that focuses on the development of skillful teachers as the method for enhanced early-literacy achievement. The goal is developing a "self-winding" school where reflective practice and continual improvement become part of the school's daily life. Initially, teachers are trained as teacher leaders and these teacher leaders observe in classrooms as part of their duties and then meet to engage the observed teacher in a conversation about the lesson. These conversations focus on instructional moves made by the teacher and include an action plan that focuses on acquiring the new expertise necessary to teach more responsively.

Community-wide professional conversations are held weekly with all staff and foster discussion of "big ideas" and the small details of daily teaching activities. Over time all teachers are expected to serve as teacher/leaders, with staff switching to fulfill that role for the year and then returning to the class-room. The evaluation studies to date illustrate enormous growth in teacher expertise and improved early-literacy attainment.

BETTER SCHOOL LIBRARIES AND BETTER ACCESS TO BOOKS

Perhaps it is not surprising that schools with large numbers of struggling read-ers often have wholly inadequate school libraries and nonexistent classroom libraries. We must provide all children with access to books. Currently, chil-dren in schools that are located in low-economic neighborhoods have about 50 percent fewer books in their schools than children going to schools located in wealthy communities (Guice, et al., 1996). The schools located in these low-eco-nomic neighborhoods are the schools that serve the very children who are least likely to live in literate-home environments and least likely to have access to public library facilities. They are also the schools that must have the very best school libraries with the largest selection of informational texts, picture books, and multicultural literature. The classroom libraries in these schools need to include several hundred books.

These schools need to have the most liberal library policies for loaning books to students and their families. They need to have the library open before and after school so that children without books at home can have access to the resources here. They need to have a library that invites children to drop in at virtually any time to browse, read, search for, study, and select books. These libraries need multiple subscriptions to magazines so that, they too, can be loaned out. They even need to be open during the summer vaca-tion period.

Upgrading the quality and quantity of library resources in schools with large numbers of disadvantaged children is worth fighting for. Enhancing access to the school library is also important. Expanding classroom library collections is necessary. Having wonderful books is of little use if access is limited!

HELPFUL STANDARDS AND THOUGHTFUL ASSESSMENTS

Across the United States individual states are involved in developing new stan-dards for literacy learning. Much of this activity has been stimulated by federal initiatives intended to raise achievement goals and to make the grade-level com-petencies that are expected of all students clearer (Rothman, 1995). Different states have taken very different approaches to standards development and this seems to be one reason that the nature of the standards varies quite widely from state to state. In some states you will find scores of very specific grade-level standards, while in others there are only a few standards. Those states with many standards typically have statements such as: Students will recognize words containing the *er, ir, ur* letter-sound patterns. In other states there are far fewer standards that are broader, for example: Students will use letter-sound relationships, onset-rime patterns, and the syntax of the sentence to independently arrive at the pronunciation of an unknown word.

Once the standards are developed, states are to develop student assessments that match the assessment plan. Again, different states seem to be taking different paths in developing assessments. Several have adopted an approach that largely assesses attainment of standards with more authentic reading and writing tasks. For example, students are to read an actual book (e.g., an Eyewitness book in a content area), and then respond to some multiple-choice items and some extended-response items (items that involve writing a short or long-response essay). Typically, the extended-response items are weighted at least as heavily as the multiple-choice items. In other states the assessments have taken a different form with word recognition tasks (perhaps even involving nonsense word pronunciation) and more traditional assessments of comprehension using short passages and multiple-choice items predominately.

We can only hope that the new standards and the accompanying assessments do two things: (1) provide teachers with better information on how student literacy is developing, and (2) provide teachers with a clearer understanding of the important elements of a comprehensive, thoughtful literacy program.

Relatedly, we can hope that the work on the standards and the assessments provide both the profession and the public with an improved system for reporting the progress children are making in developing literacy. Currently, there exists an enormous naïveté about what traditional test performances means and this has resulted in a general misunderstanding of reading achievement in the United States. While raising the standards and shifting the assessments can be seen as a worthy goal, schools and state and federal education agencies need to design more reliable ways of reporting student achievement to parents and the public (Afflerbach, 1993; Bracey, 1997).

USEFUL ASSESSMENTS AND BETTER REPORTING

Standardized testing in schools has expanded enormously in the past 25 years. In many schools, we now test all children every year (and in some schools twice a year). Yet the test results seem to have little impact in terms of improving instruction. Rather, no one seems to look at the results or decide to improve the classroom libraries in low-achieving schools. Nor does anyone decide to reduce class size or develop a long-term staff development plan. Rarely does anyone actually follow up on the test results in an attempt to determine why scores are high, low, or average.

Instead, test scores are used primarily to sort students. We can defend the use of some testing to monitor how well the school is doing in its attempts to educate children, but one hardly needs to assess each child every year to accomplish the monitoring function. If we were simply to assess all children after three, four, or five years of school, we would have sufficient evidence from a system-management perspective. If we want to know how well children are doing in first grade and whether some children need extra assistance, we can just ask their teachers. We can watch the children themselves. We can read the anecdotal reports kept on the labels. We can listen to parents. We can collect student work over a week's period and examine the levels of growth. Simply put, current tests rarely *improve* instruction. Tests that do not help us teach better are generally a waste of time and resources.

Report cards tend to be bothersome to teachers and not very informative to parents, especially parents of at-risk children. Parents report that teacher written comments are the most informative section on report cards. We would suggest that schools consider doing away with the current common report card design. In its place we would put a written essay about each child as a learner, reader, writer, and citizen. For this to be considered, however, will require undoing the idea that everyone should get a report card every six or nine weeks, all on the same day.

In our proposed system, a teacher would prepare the first learner report essay after about three weeks of school. Then, every Monday, Wednesday, and Friday, one child would receive his or her essay to take home. In a class of 24 children, each would take home such a report approximately every eight weeks. Teachers would describe the child as a learner and describe the kind of work the child was doing, attaching a sample or two to illustrate comments in the essay. Teachers would use the sticky label notes and other information to inform parents of progress and future goals. This shift provides not only the opportunity to better communicate with parents, but also provides a way for teachers to focus their thinking on individual students. These essay reports, combined with parent conferences and reviews of children's portfolios, produce a much more reliable and powerful evaluation of learners and learning. (See Johnston, *Knowing Literacy* for a detailed discussion of assessment approaches and the value of different options.)

TEACHER INPUT ON THE BUSINESS OF RUNNING SCHOOLS

In many schools today, teacher committees have a say in how the money will be spent, how special subjects will be scheduled, and who their administrators will be. This power has been entrusted to teachers not because of any new high regard for "regular" teachers, but because it is becoming increasingly clear that the "top-down" bureaucratic procedures of the past have not resulted in better schooling. In many schools, classroom teachers have the opportunity to affect changes beyond their classroom; they should "seize the moment." The kind of decisions they make will determine whether or not they continue to have any power.

While individual schools must set their own priorities, some general considerations apply to all schools. Teachers who want children to engage in lots of real reading and writing should see to it that a good chunk of whatever money is available is spent on books and magazines, both for the school library and for classroom libraries. Writing materials are generally not expensive, but a variety should be available. Paper for making books and a book binding machine should be as accessible as ditto paper and the ditto machine. Every classroom should have a few computers, a good printer, and some writing/publishing software.

The schedule is another area that classroom teachers should try to affect. In some schools, special teachers set their own schedules or have them set by a supervisor. Children come and go at all hours and classroom teachers seldom have an uninterrupted hour in which to teach to everyone. In other schools, a certain period of time—between 45 and 90 minutes—is designated for specials for each grade level. In addition to having only one time period each day when the children go somewhere and then come back again, scheduling specials by grade-level blocks provides the teachers with some grade-level planning time each week. Other schools work in the reverse, but still achieve a similar result. These schools have "safe" periods for each classroom every day—periods of 90–120 minutes when no child is to be pulled out for any special service.

Too many children, especially struggling readers, spend their school day moving from pillar to post, from program to program, from teacher to teacher, and subject to subject. Too often, teachers work in schools where their work is constantly interrupted by children leaving for support services (remedial reading, resource room, speech, etc.), children leaving for specials (art, P.E., music, computer, etc.), and loudspeaker announcements from the office. In some schools, classroom teachers rarely have more than 10–15 minutes of uninterrupted time with all of the children in their classroom. No sane human being would design such an organizational plan if teaching and learning were high on the agenda!

It is important that teachers and children have large uninterrupted blocks of time to work together. Two- or three-hour uninterrupted blocks are worth fighting for. We have found that when schools set a goal of providing these blocks, they can almost always be achieved. But first, it must be decided that this goal is important.

Finally, classroom teachers should be involved in the hiring of their administrators. Administrators are supposed to be instructional leaders. Teachers are more apt to follow that leadership if they have some say in who their leader is. We also believe that, as a general policy, elementary administrators must have had several years of successful classroom teaching experience at the *elementary* level.

EXTENDED DAY/YEAR

While we are not in favor of the mandatory, for-everyone, "more is better" time extensions that many reformers are calling for, we would like to see optional extensions "for children who want it or need it most," which provide enrichment for all students as well as remediation for those who need it. We don't have enough hours in the present school day/year to provide struggling readers with all the mind and body enriching experiences that would result in optimal learning. Many "latchkey" children are going home to empty houses and mindless hours in front of the TV. We would like these children to be able to stay at school and participate in the kind of activities that will increase their world knowledge and their motivation to learn.

Many elementary schools could work with extended school days without additional personnel and with no additional funding. For instance, schools could have the special teachers—art, music, guidance, P.E., remedial reading, resource room, and so on—begin their working day at 11:00 and end at 5:30. All their special classes for children would be scheduled between 12:00 and 4:00 and then a variety of optional after-school programs would be available. In addition to providing both intensive and enriching after-school activities, this arrangement would result in all classroom teachers having totally uninterrupted teaching time from 8:30–12:00 each day!

Some schools are coordinating with various community agencies to provide after-school programs. Scouting, Great Books, 4H, Big Brother/Big Sister, and Police Athletic League programs can be carried out right at the school and provide the club and project experiences often denied to at-risk children. Some YMCA/YWCAs and public libraries provide on-site, after-school programs for children.

In schools with high concentrations of poor children, current federal program guidelines allow those schools to use categorical program funds to extend the school year into the summer months. In these cases, the schools operate for an extra five to six weeks each year instead of spending the funds on special teachers during the year. Because too many struggling readers read and write very little during school vacation periods, these children often suffer the greatest "summer reading loss" without any summer school experience. Summer school, like smaller classes, can be operated in a way that will not have much of an impact on children's learning. At the same time, however, well-designed summer programs can be enormously effective in maintaining and accelerating reading development.

Classroom teachers know that there are "not enough hours in the day." Some children will simply need extended-day programs to keep up or catch up with their peers. Too many children live in homes that provide little stimulation and enrichment during the after-school hours and the summer months. Optional extended-day and extended-year programs provide additional time in which we can provide not only better literacy instruction, but the whole range of educational experience as well.

FAMILY AND COMMUNITY INVOLVEMENT

Schools that have unusually high success rates with struggling readers are usually schools with high levels of family and community involvement. These schools make superhuman efforts to reach out to the parents and surrogate parents—aunts, cousins, grandmothers—and involve them in the school. Getting the parents of at-risk children to come to school is often not an easy task. Many of the parents did not succeed in school and their memories of school are not pleasant. Many of the parents have very limited literacy levels and many are not proficient in English.

But all parents want the best for their children and, when they do feel welcome or included, can become a powerful source of support for teachers. Schools that want parental support provide a variety of school-based programs and services. They have monthly parent meetings in which the children "star" in a variety of productions. They send home weekly "parent friendly" newsletters that have lots of pictures and announcements showing their children excelling! Administrators and home/school coordinators visit homes and bring along games, books, tape recorders, computers, and other activities that parents can borrow and use with their children. Parents form advisory councils and are consulted about the day-by-day decisions that must be made. Some parents of struggling readers are not employed and have time to volunteer. When schools set up volunteer programs and work with parents to give them meaningful jobs to do, they can become avid, active workers. Some schools provide space for community services, including parent classes and daycare for younger children.

In addition to family involvement, successful schools foster community involvement. Many businesses today are concerned about the quality of education their future employees are receiving, and many schools are forming partnerships with local businesses. In addition to some nominal financial support, the businesses provide and coordinate a variety of activities and lend moral support to the school and the teachers. Different businesses provide different kinds of support. A school that has a nearby retirement home for a business partner finds that the retirees can make many teaching aids that the teachers need. Many of the residents participate in an "adopt-a-grandchild" program. They are paired with a particularly needy or neglected child and provide some special treats at holidays, write regular letters to their child, and visit with the children at the retirement home each month.

In another neighborhood, a dry cleaning firm provided space for a lending library during the summer months when the school was closed. When some of the books were not returned, the business owner went out and purchased additional books to restock the shelves. His counter staff became familiar with the books and began to offer reviews and advice to children and their parents.

In another community, an immigrant turned entrepreneur began by supplying the city's schools with informational books on his native land. When he came to school to receive a gracious thank you he saw how few informational books were available and donated funds for a set of encyclopedias and several atlases. His partnership with the school continues, as does the flow of maps, globes, and other materials to support his interest of increased global awareness.

The Greensboro, North Carolina Junior League took on one housing project as their own project. They equipped four rooms with computers, printers, encyclopedias, and other reference sources as well as paper and other school supplies. They volunteer some time each week to assist children with their research, homework, and other school-related projects. The homework centers are always filled with children who appreciate having the tools and support that more fortunate children find in their own homes.

Many teachers feel like the "Little Red Hen." They have to do everything for everybody! The efforts invested in developing real parent and community involvement are often paid back by having other people who can help you "plant, weed, reap, and bake." Catherine Snow and her colleagues (1991) found that urban teachers who rated their parents as interested and involved were teachers who made 10–15 teacher-initiated parent contacts for every contact that teachers who reported uninterested parents made. Parents of at-risk children often do not initiate contact with schools and teachers. However, they can be enticed to involve themselves in the school and their child's schooling. But the enticing of the involvement seems critical.

Finally, some parents would like to help, and know they should, but do not know how. Patricia Edwards, from Michigan State University, notes that many low-income parents simply did not know *how to read to* their children, even if they could read (some could not). If parents never experienced lap reading themselves, where would they learn how to do it? The parents that Edwards worked with learned from a series of videos she prepared (available from Children's Press) that showed parents reading to and with their children, and explained what it was that they were doing. These videos can be shown at parent meetings or loaned out to parents to review at home. The point that Edwards makes is that, just telling parents to read to their children or helping them with school work is often insufficient.

This was the same message that researchers delivered at the Center for Disadvantaged Students (at Johns Hopkins University) as a result of their work developing homework packets for parents. They found that low-income parents were very willing to work with their children, but that they often needed more guidance than schools made available. The CDS team worked with teachers to target key skills and strategies that parents could work on with their children, and then organized homework packets with easy-to-follow directions. Not only were they surprised at the overwhelmingly positive response from parents, but also at the increase in student achievement that followed.

HEAD START/EVEN START

Head Start and Even Start are programs for at-risk 4-year-olds. Head Start has been around since the sixties and has a fairly high success rate, particularly because there is some follow-up to the Head Start experiences when the children enter public school. Even Start is a family literacy program that includes preschool children and their parents. Both the children and a parent go to school. Parents work to complete their high school education or receive adult-literacy instruction. The children are provided with an enriched preschool program. Parents also learn more about parenting, including ways to involve their children in reading and writing.

We know that children from high-literacy homes enter school with over 1,000 hours of informal reading and writing encounters, from which they develop an understanding about print that is essential to success in beginning reading. The literate home simulation kindergartens described in this book are designed to make up for some of the experiences many at-risk children have missed out on. Children who spend part of their preschool years in Head Start or Even Start programs can be provided with many of the critical early-literacy experiences, especially if the programs are modeled after the opportunities that are available in the literate home environment. When preschool programs immerse children in a print-rich and story-rich environment, the children acquire the same kind of knowledge about reading and writing as more advantaged children. When these programs also include effective parent training, we can begin to close the gap that now exists between children from different communities. Mothers who learn how to provide early-literacy experiences for their children will send us better prepared children. Preschools that offer children the opportunity to listen to stories, to memorize favorite predictable books, to participate in big book activities, and to drite when they want to, also send us children who have already learned a lot about books and print and about the activities we call reading and writing.

HEALTH/DENTAL CARE

Currently, over 35 million people in this country are without any health insurance. This number includes a large percentage of children and mothers. Pregnant women are carrying their children with no prenatal care and inadequate nutrition. Many children do not get immunizations and there have been outbreaks of both measles and tuberculosis—diseases we thought we had conquered. Among the affluent countries, we rank at the very bottom in the provision of health care to all our children and near the top in the infant mortality rate. Children who are sick and who don't get care miss more school and find it harder to attend when they go back. Teachers who have seen children sitting in their classrooms whose health needs are neglected realize that this inhibits their ability to learn. We each must do whatever we can to provide for the health and dental needs of all children.

FAIRNESS IN FUNDING

Jonathan Kozol, in *Savage Inequalities,* candidly describes the steady movement in this nation toward a two-tiered educational system—one system that serves our suburbs and the other that serves our urban and rural areas. The former is substantially better funded than the latter. Why would we create an educational system in which schools with large numbers of at-risk children routinely receive 50 percent less funding per child than schools with virtually no disadvantaged children? A system in which poor parents pay a substantially larger proportion of their paychecks to support schools but still cannot match the wealth generated in the communities serving wealthier families? Why would we have a system in which New York City schools receive 50 percent less money than those in suburban Scarsdale? Why would we have a system in which New York City receives less education funding than it pays in state taxes? A system whereby some public schools spend three to four times as much per pupil as others in the same state? A system in which some children have carpeting and air conditioning while others have sewage and rats in the hallways?

It costs money to educate children. Some children will inevitably cost more to educate than others. Currently, our system is more likely to provide more funding for schools with few at-risk children than to schools with many. If we are serious about all children learning to read and write, then we must seriously work to alter existing funding patterns and to provide some sort of modicum of fairness in funding. It is not that money will cure everything. But good education does cost more than offering the bare minimum.

WELL-PLANNED PROFESSIONAL DEVELOPMENT

For too long, few states and few school districts developed any sort of comprehensive, professional development initiatives. Instead, "inservice" sessions were scheduled but often offered a generally haphazard and somewhat shallow approach to enhancing teacher expertise. What we know about teacher learning suggests that such approaches have little effect on improving (or changing) instruction. Instead, teachers need to develop their expertise in supportive, long-term professional relationships that focus on developing an understanding of how instruction impacts learning in very specific ways (Duffy, 1997).

Recent ideas such as "Teachers As Readers" conversation groups and online lists serve as professional discussion opportunities when combined with more traditional methods, such as membership in professional associations and attending the associated conferences, invited professional workshop presenters, and professional journal reading, can promote the sort of on-going information needed to trigger reflection on personal practices. But teachers need to discuss their teaching and have professional discussion, not just read or hear about the best practice. They need opportunities to observe others and to be observed in a non-evaluated setting and then to engage in professional conversation about teaching.

None of us is ever finished learning about teaching. Our best efforts can always be improved and it would be useful if schools and education agencies provided stronger leadership and greater funding in this end.

REFERENCES

Afflerbach, P. (1993). Report cards and reading. *Reading Teacher, 46,* 458–465.

Allington, R. L., & Guice, S. (1996). Something to read: Putting books in their desks, backpacks, and bedrooms. In P. H. Dreyer (Eds.) *Visions and realities in literacy (Yearbook of the 60th Claremont Reading Conference)* (pp. 1–16). Claremont, CA: Claremont Graduate School.

Bracey, G. W. (1997). *Setting the record straight: Responses to misconceptions about public education in the United States.* Alexandria, VA: Association for Supervision and Curriculum Development.

Clay, M. M. (1985). *The early detection of reading difficulties, 3rd ed.* Portsmouth, NH: Heinemann.

Clay, M. M. (1991). *Becoming literate: The construction of inner control.* Portsmouth, NH: Heinemann.

Clay, M. M. (1993). *An observation survey of early literacy achievement.* Portsmouth, NH: Heinemann.

Duffy, G. G. (1997). Powerful models or powerful teachers? An argument for teacher-as-entrepreneur. In S. S. &. D. Hayes (Eds.) *Instructional models in reading.* (pp. 351–365). Mahwah, NJ: Lawrence Erlbaum Associates.

Dyer, P. C. (1992). Reading recovery: A cost-effectiveness and educational-outcomes analysis. *ERS Spectrum, 10,* 10–19.

Fountais, I. C., & Pinnell, G. S. (1996). *Guided reading: Good first teaching for all children.* Portsmouth, NH: Heinemann.

Guice, S., Allington, R. L., Johnston, P., Baker, K., & Michelson, N. (1996). Access?: Books, children, and literature-based curriculum in schools. *The New Advocate, 9,* 197–207.

Hall, D., Prevatte, C., & Cunningham, P. (1994). Eliminating ability grouping and failure in the primary grades. In R. L. Allington & S. A. Walmsley (Eds.) *No quick fix: Rethinking literacy programs in America's elementary schools.* Teachers College Press.

Herzog, M. (Ed.) (1997). *Inside Learning Network schools.* Katonah, NY: Richard C. Owen.

Johnston, P. (1997). *Knowing literacy.* York, ME: Stenhouse.

Knapp, M. S. (1995). *Teaching for meaning in high-poverty classrooms.* New York: Teachers College Press.

Kozol, J. (1991). *Savage Inequalities: Children in America's Schools.* NY: Crown.

McGill-Franzen, A., & Allington, R. L. (1991). Every child's right: Literacy. *Reading Teacher, 45,* 86–90.

Pikulski, J. J. (1994). Preventing reading failure: A review of five effective programs. *Reading Teacher, 48,* 30–39.

Pinnell, G. S. (1990). Success for low achievers through Reading Recovery. *Educational Leadership, 48,* 17–21.

Power, B. M. (1996). *Taking note: Improving your observational notetaking.* York, ME: Stenhouse.

Rothman, R. (1995). *Measuring up: Standards, assessment, and school reform.* San Francisco: Jossey-Bass.

Slavin, R. E., Madden, N. A., Dolan, L. J., & Wasik, B. A. (1996). *Every child, every school: Success for all.* Thousand Oaks, CA: Corwin.

Snow, C. E., Barnes, W. S., Chandler, J., Goodman, I., & Hemphill, L. (1991). *Unfulfilled expectations: Home and school influences on literary.* Cambridge, MA: Harvard University Press.

Spear-Swerling, L., & Sternberg, R. J. (1996). *Off track: When poor readers become "learning disabled."* Boulder, CO: Westview Press.

FURTHER READINGS

W hile a complete bibliography of important works on specific topics is beyond the scope of this book, this list includes some of the most seminal, complete, and practical pieces on topics that you may want to research.

The Processes of Reading and Writing and How They Are Learned

Anderson, R. C., Hiebert, E., Scott, J. A., & Wilkinson, I. A. G. (1985). *Becoming a nation of readers.* Washington, DC: National Institute of Education.

Caine, R. N., & Caine, G. (1991). *Teaching and the Human Brain.* Alexandria, VA. Association for Supervision and Curriculum Development.

Clay, M. M. (1991). *Becoming literate: The construction of inner control.* Portsmouth, NH: Heinemann.

Fountais, I. C., & Pinnell, G. S. (1996). *Guided reading: Good first teaching for all children.* Portsmouth, NH: Heinemann.

Johnston, P. (1997). *Knowing literacy.* York, ME: Stenhouse.

Power, B. M. (1996). *Taking note: Improving your observational notetaking.* York, ME: Stenhouse.

Rayner, K., & Pollatsek, A. (1989). *The psychology of reading.* Englewood Cliffs, NJ: Prentice Hall.

Samuels, S. J., & Farstrup, A. E. (Eds.) (1992). *What research has to say about reading instruction.* Newark, DE: International Reading Association.

Comprehension

Beck, I. L., McKeown, M. G., Hamilton, R. L., & Kucan, L. (1997). *Questioning the author.* Newark, DE: International Reading Association.

Brown, R. G. (1991). *Schools of thought: How the politics of literacy shapes thinking in the classroom.* San Francisco: Jossey-Bass.

Dole, J., Duffy, J., Roehler, L., & Pearson, P. D. (1991). Moving from the old to the new: Research on reading comprehension instruction. *Review of Educational Research, 61,* 239–264.

Gambrell, L. B., & Almasi, J. F. (Ed.) (1996). *Lively discussions: Fostering engaged reading.* Newark, DE: International Reading Association.

Knapp, M. S. (1995). *Teaching for meaning in high-poverty classrooms.* New York: Teachers College Press.

Maria, K. (1990). *Reading comprehension instruction: Issues and strategies.* Parkton, MD: York Press.

Pearson, P. D., & Fielding, L. (1991). Comprehension Instruction. In Barr, R., Kamil, M. D., Mosenthal, P. B., & Pearson, P. D. (Eds.) *Handbook of Reading Research* (Vol. II, pp. 815–860). White Plains, NY: Longman.

Writing/Connecting Reading and Writing

Atwell, N. (Ed.). (1990). *Coming to know: Writing to learn in the intermediate grades.* Portsmouth, NH: Heinemann.

Heller, M. F. (1991). *Reading-writing connections: From theory to practice.* NY: Longman.

Irwin, J. W., & Doyle, M. A. (Eds.) (1992). *Reading/writing connections: Learning from research.* Newark, DE: International Reading Association.

Learning Media (1992). *Dancing with a pen: The learner as writer.* Wellington, New Zealand: New Zealand Ministry of Education.

Moline, S. (1995). *I see what you mean: Children at work with visual information.* York, ME: Stenhouse. Gere, Anne Ruggles (Ed.) (1985). *Roots in the sawdust: Writing to learn across the disciplines.* Urbana, IL: National Council of Teachers of English.

Pappas, C. C., Kiefer, B. Z., & Levstik, L. S. (1990). *An integrated language perspective in the elementary school.* New York: Longman.

Routman, R. (1991). *Invitations.* Portsmouth, NH: Heinemann.

Shanahan, T. (1988). The reading-writing relationship: Seven instructional principles. *The Reading Teacher, 41,* 636–647.

Tierney, R. J., & Shanahan, T. (1991). Research on the reading-writing relationship: Interactions, transactions, and outcomes. In Barr, R., Kamil, M., Mosenthal, P., & Pearson, P. D. (Eds.) *Handbook of Reading Research* (Vol. II, pp. 246–280). New York: Longman.

Walmsley, S. A., & Walp, T. (1990). Integrating literature and composing into the language arts curriculum. *Elementary School Journal, 90,* 251–274.

Decoding and Spelling Fluency

Adams, M. J. (1990). *Beginning to read: Thinking and learning about print.* Cambridge, MA: M.I.T. Press.

Bear, D. R., Invernizzi, M., Templeton, S., & Johnston, F. (1996). *Words their way: Word study for phonics, vocabulary, and spelling instruction.* Columbus, OH: Merrill.

Cunningham, P. M. (1995). *Phonics they use: Words for reading and writing.* NY: HarperCollins.

Ehri, L. C. (1991). Development of the ability to read words. In Barr, R., Kamil, M. L., Mosenthal, P. B., & Pearson, P. D. (Eds.) *Handbook of Reading Research* (Vol. II, pp. 383–417). White Plains, NY: Longman.

Gentry, J. R., & Gillet, J. W. (1993). *Teaching kids to spell.* Portsmouth, NH: Heinemann.

Moustafa, M. (1998). *Beyond traditional phonics.* Portsmouth, NH: Heinemann.

Stahl, S. A. (1992). Saying the "P" word: Nine guidelines for exemplary phonics instruction. *Reading Teacher, 45,* 618–625.

Stanovich, K. E. (1991). Word recognition: Changing perspectives. In Barr, R., Kamil, M., Mosenthal, P., & Pearson, P. D. (Eds.) *Handbook of Reading Research* (Vol. II, pp. 418–452). New York: Longman.

Literature/Reading Materials

Danielson, K. E. (1992). Picture books to use with older students. *Journal of Reading, 35,* 652–654.

Duthie, C. (1996). *True stories: Nonfiction in the primary classroom.* York, ME: Stenhouse.

Fielding, L., & Roller, C. (1992). Making difficult books accessible and easy books acceptable. *The Reading Teacher, 45,* 678–685.

Freeman, E. B., & Person, D. G. (Eds.). (1992). *Using nonfiction trade books in the elementary classroom: From ants to zeppelins.* Urbana, IL: National Council of Teachers of English.

Harms, J. M., & Lettow, L. J. (1991). Recent poetry for children. *The Reading Teacher, 45,* 274–279.

Harris, V. J. (Ed.). (1992). *Teaching multicultural literature in grades K-8.* Norwood, MA: Christopher-Gordon.

Hart-Hewins, L., & Wells, J. (1990). *Real books for reading: Learning to read with children's literature.* Portsmouth, NH: Heinemann.

McCracken, R., & McCracken, M. (1988). *Songs, Stories and Poetry to Teach Reading and Writing.* Manitoba, Canada: Penguin.

McGill-Franzen, A. (1993). "I could read the words!": Selecting good books for inexperienced readers. *Reading Teacher, 46,* 424–426.

Pilla, M. L. (1990). *The best high/low books for reluctant readers.* Englewood, CO: Libraries Unlimited.

Tunnell, M. O., & Ammon, R. (1993). *The story of ourselves: Teaching history through children's literature.* Portsmouth, NH: Heinemann.

Walmsley, S. A. (1993). *Children exploring their world: Theme teaching in elementary school.* Portsmouth, NH: Heinemann.

Programs/Schools/Activities for Children with Special Needs

Allington, R. L., & Cunningham, P. M. (1996). *Schools that work: Where all children read and write.* New York: HarperCollins.

Allington, R. L., & Walmsley, S. A. (Ed.) (1995). *No quick fix: Rethinking literacy programs in American elementary schools.* New York: Teachers College Press.

Crandall, J. A. (Ed.) (1987). *ESL through content-area instruction: Mathematics, science, social studies.* Englewood Cliffs, NJ: Prentice-Hall Regents.

DeFord, D. E., Lyons, C. A., & Pinnell, G. S. (1991). *Bridges to literacy: Learning from Reading Recovery.* Portsmouth, NH: Heinemann.

Faltis, J. C. (1993). *Joinfostering: Adapting teaching strategies for the multilingual classroom.* New York: Macmillan.

Fitzgerald, J. (1993). Literacy and students who are learning English as a second language. *The Reading Teacher, 46,* 638–647.

Herzog, M. (Ed.) (1997). *Inside Learning Network Schools.* Katonah, NY: Richard C. Owen.

Honig, B. (1996). *Teaching our children to read: The role of skills in a comprehensive reading program.* Thousands Oaks, CA: Corwin Press.

Kozol, J. (1991). *Savage Inequalities: Children in America's Schools.* NY: Crown.

Rhodes, L. K., & Dudley-Marling, C. (1996). *Readers and writers with a difference: A holistic approach to teaching learning disabled and remedial students.* Portsmouth, NH: Heinemann.

Roller, C. M. (1996). *Variability not disability: Struggling readers in a workshop classroom.* Newark, DE: International Reading Association.

Slavin, R. E., Madden, N. A., Dolan, L. J., & Wasik, B. A. (1996). *Every child, every school: Success for all.* Thousand Oaks, CA: Corwin.

Snow, C. E., Barnes, W. S., Chandler, J., Goodman, I., & Hemphill, L. (1991). *Unfulfilled expectations: Home and school influences on literacy.* Cambridge, MA: Harvard University Press.

Weber, R. (1991). Linguistic diversity and reading in American society. In Barr, R., Kamil, M. L., Mosenthal, P. B., & Pearson, P. D., (Eds.) *Handbook of Reading Research* (Vol. II, pp. 97–119). New York: Longman.

INDEX